Bisexuality and Same-Sex Marriage

In our society, the argument for or against same-sex marriage becomes even more heated when the debate turns to bisexual women and men. *Bisexuality and Same-Sex Marriage* thoughtfully explores this debate from a wide range of interdisciplinary perspectives, presenting respected scholars from fields as diverse as American Studies, Communication, Criminology, Human and Organizational Systems, Law and Social Policy, LGBT Studies, Organizational Behavior, Psychology, Sociology, Women's Studies, and Queer Studies. This clear-viewed volume is organized into three perspectives—theoretical, research, and personal—that frame the debate from a macro to micro level of analysis.

This book goes beyond the intense acrimony and divisiveness to rationally examine the issue from various viewpoints and through the latest research. This informative text presents and analyzes in depth the current findings and the diverse LGBT and straight perspectives on the issue. This insightful resource discusses in detail personal views, the latest theories, and is extensively referenced.

Bisexuality and Same-Sex Marriage is an essential volume for LGBT studies, professionals, psychologists, counselors, educators, students, and interested general public.

This book was published as a special issue of the *Journal of Bisexuality*.

M. Paz Galupo is Professor of Psychology and Director of LGBT Studies at Towson University, in Baltimore, Maryland.

Bisexuality and Same-Sex Marriage

Edited by M. Paz Galupo

Routledge
Taylor & Francis Group

LONDON AND NEW YORK

First published 2009 by Routledge
2 Park Square, Milton Park, Abingdon, Oxon, OX14 4RN

Simultaneously published in the USA and Canada
by Routledge
270 Madison Avenue, New York, NY 10016

Routledge is an imprint of the Taylor & Francis Group, an informa business

© 2009 Edited by M. Paz Galupo

Typeset in Times by Value Chain, India
Printed and bound in the United States of America on acid-free paper by IBT Global.

British Library Cataloguing in Publication Data
A catalogue record for this book is available from the British Library

ISBN 10: 0-415-99632-5 (h/b)
ISBN 10: 1-56023-776-7 (p/b)

ISBN 13: 978-0-415-99632-7 (h/b)
ISBN 13: 978-1-56023-776-1 (p/b)

CONTENTS

Acknowledgment   vii

About the Contributors   viii

1 Introduction   1
    M. Paz Galupo

THEORETICAL PERSPECTIVES: FRAMING BISEXUALITY
   IN THE SAME-SEX DEBATE

2 Supremacy by Law: The One Man One Woman Marriage
    Requirement and Antimiscegenation Law   7
    Jacqueline Battalora

3 The Dyadic Imaginary: Troubling the Perception
    of Love as Dyadic   33
    Danielle Antoinette Hidalgo
    Kristen Barber
    Erica Hunter

4 On the Potential and Perils of Same-Sex Marriage:
    A Perspective from Queer Theory   53
    Ajnesh Prasad

RESEARCH PERSPECTIVES: ATTITUDES TOWARD
   BISEXUALITY AND SAME-SEX MARRIAGE

5 Bias Toward Bisexual Women and Men
    in a Marriage-Matching Task   79
    Angela L. Breno
    M. Paz Galupo

6 "This is Not a Lesbian Wedding": Examining Same-Sex
    Marriage and Bisexual-Lesbian Couples   99
    Pamela J. Lannutti

7 Make Love, Not Law: Perceptions of the Marriage Equality
      Struggle Among Polyamorous Activists   123
      Hadar Aviram

8 Bisexual Attitudes Toward Same-SexMarriage   149
      M. Paz Galupo
      Marcia L. Pearl

   BISEXUAL PERSPECTIVES ON SAME-SEX MARRIAGE

9 Bisexuals are Bad for the Same Sex Marriage Business   165
      Mia Ocean

10 A Bisex-Queer Critique of Same-Sex Marriage Advocacy   175
      Hameed (Herukhuti) S. Williams

11 Dancing with My Grandma: Talking with Robyn Ochs About
      Complex Identities and Simple Messages in the Marriage
      Equality Movement   181
      Laurie J. Kendall

   Index   207

Acknowledgments

I would like to thank Regina Reinhardt for her patience and editorial support. Thanks also to the anonymous reviewers of the articles in this volume. Your thoughtful reviews added to the quality and significance of the contributions.

Thanks to Marcia Pearl for our many conversations about research and same-sex marriage and for help in formatting the contributions. I could not have done this without you.

As a researcher with a professional interest in same-sex marriage and marriage equality, I am grateful for the woman who inspires my personal interest on the topic–my partner and wife, Carin–and for our daughters (Isabel Pilar, Maya Pilar, and Lucia Pilar) who sustain us. Special thoughts to my sister Pilar, who supported me always and even wore purple to my wedding. I miss you everyday.

–M. Paz Galupo

About the Contributors

Hadar Aviram, PhD, is Associate Professor at UC Hastings College of the Law, where she teaches criminal law and socio-legal courses. She holds a PhD in Jurisprudence and Social Policy is from UC Berkeley. Her previous degrees are in law (LL.B., Hebrew University, Jerusalem) and criminology (M.A., Hebrew University, Jerusalem). Prior to her academic career, she worked as a military defense attorney. Her main research interests include sociology of law, criminology and criminal justice, class, gender and inequality, social movements, and queer theory; this paper is part of a larger project looking at legal consciousness and social activism in the polyamorous community.

Kristen Barber, MA, is a Doctoral Student in the department of Sociology at the University of Southern California. There she is beginning dissertation research focusing on performances of masculinity and sexuality by men in a traditionally feminine context, the hair salon. Her research interests include gender, sexuality, embodiment, popular culture, and qualitative methods. She is published in the *Handbook of the New Sexuality Studies*. Prior to continuing her graduate studies at the University of Southern California, Barber earned her Masters degree in Sociology from Tulane University.

Jacqueline Battalora, PhD, is Associate Professor of Sociology at Saint Xavier University, Chicago, Illinois. She is currently completing a book project that explores the intersections of race, gender and sexuality in the training and work of police. With Diana Vallera, she is filming, photographing and interviewing women who worked during and in the decades following WWII with an eye toward the challenges they posed to white male dominated spaces and the transformations they helped to shape. She has published articles on white supremacy and race ideology in the U.S.

Angela L. Breno, BA, received her master's degree in Experimental Psychology from Towson University. She is currently a researcher with the Orphan Foundation of America. Her research interests include experiences and outcomes of the child welfare system, women and lesbian health issues, and queer studies.

Danielle Antoinette Hidalgo, MS, received her Masters degree in Sociology from the London School of Economics and Political Science. She is currently a doctoral student at the University of California, Santa Barbara, where she is completing dissertation research on spatio-temporal relations of gender and sexuality in the context of Bangkok, Thailand. Her areas of interest include gender, sexuality, the sociology of the body, immigration, Asian and Asian American studies, the sociology of development, and Southeast Asia with a particular emphasis in Thailand. She is co-editor, with Carl L. Bankston III, of *Immigration in U.S. History: An Encyclopedia survey of U.S. Immigration* and has authored or co-authored numerous journal articles and book chapters.

Erica Hunter, MA, is a graduate student in Women's Studies and Sociology at the University at Albany. Her research interests focus on the intersection of gender and sexualities in families, marriage as a social institution, heterosexuality, fatherhood, and couple relationships. She is currently working on her dissertation, which examines how heterosexual couples use engagement and marital rituals as a way to symbolically construct their couple status.

Laurie J. Kendall, PhD, is a Visiting Professor in the American Studies department at the University of Maryland, College Park. There, she teaches courses in contemporary American culture, feminist and indigenous theory, ethnographic methods, and lesbian and gay studies. Trained in history and the interdisciplinary programs of American studies, women's studies, and lesbian and gay studies, her areas of interest are broad but her recent work focuses on the ways womyn redefine family, home, and sacred tradition while building a unique culture at the Michigan Womyn's Music Festival.

Pamela J. Lannutti, PhD, is an Interpersonal and Health Communication scholar. She is currently an Associate Professor in the Department of Communication at Boston College. She received her Ph.D. from the Department of Speech Communication at the University of Georgia.

Mia Ocean, LCSW, LMT, is the Executive Director of The Minody Institute where she oversees the administration of the Institute and also works directly with clients living with trauma, mental, physical, emotional, and spiritual distress, and those looking for personal growth opportunities. She provides psychotherapy, bodywork, educational opportunities, and conducts research with non-attachment for the benefit of the public and professional communities. Additionally, Mia is an out and proud bisexual/multisexual wommin who works to empower other bisexual individuals, educate others about bisexuality, and advocate for the rights of all oppressed groups.

Marcia L. Pearl, MS, is a full-time evaluator of HIV prevention programs and teaches LGBT Studies at Towson University. Her research focuses on the development of the Attitudes Toward Same-Sex Marriage Scale (ATSM). Her previous work can be found in the *Journal of Homosexuality* and the *Journal of Bisexuality.*

Ajnesh Prasad, MA, holds a master's degree in political studies from Queen's University, and is currently a Ph.D. candidate in the Department of Organizational Behavior and Industrial Relations at York University's Schulich School of Business in Toronto. His research focuses on theories of sexual difference, a topic he explored in a recent article published in the journal, *Canadian Woman Studies.* He has presented his work at numerous academic conferences, including a paper on postcolonial heteronormativity at the 85th Annual Southwestern Social Science Association conference in New Orleans (March, 2005), where he was awarded the Prize for Outstanding Student Paper.

Hameed (Herukhuti) S. Williams, PhD, MEd, is a clinical sociologist, sex educator, and cultural theorist. He is the founding director of *Black Funk,* a sexual-cultural center for people of color. His column, *From the Cave,* appears on the center's web site http://www. blackfunk.org. Dr. Williams is author of the book *Conjuring Black Funk: Notes on Culture, Sexuality, and Spirituality, Volume I.*

Introduction

M. Paz Galupo

In all of the public and academic debate about same-sex marriage and marriage equality, bisexuality has been invisible or marginalized at best, and demonized at worst. This volume was conceptualized as a way to allow for thoughtful and deliberate discourse on bisexuality and bisexual experience as it informs, and is informed by, the same-sex marriage debate. The resulting interdisciplinary volume includes scholars from diverse fields representing American Studies, Communication, Criminology, Human and Organizational Systems, Law and Social Policy, LGBT Studies, Organizational Behavior, Psychology, Sociology, Women's Studies, and Queer Studies. Contributing authors approach the topic of bisexuality and same-sex marriage from three distinct perspectives (theoretical perspectives, research perspectives, and personal perspectives). This volume, then, is organized into three corresponding sections that frame the debate from a macro to micro level of analysis.

THEORETICAL PERSPECTIVES: FRAMING BISEXUALITY IN THE SAME-SEX DEBATE

Although different in scope, the three articles that comprise this section frame bisexuality in the same-sex marriage debate within a given theoretical context. Taken together these works reveal the ways in which existing frameworks are constrained by dichotomized notions of sex, gender, and sexual orientation and how the discourse and language shift within the same-sex marriage debate when bisexual existence and experience is acknowledged.

In "Supremacy by Law: The One Man One Woman Marriage Requirement and Antimiscengenation Law," Jacqueline Batterlora analyzes the legal arguments against same-sex marriage (Defense of Marriage Act and Federal Marriage Amendment) in the context of antimiscengenation law. Interestingly, Battalora considers the ways in which the conceptualization of bisexuality parallels multiracial (part-White) identities in legal definitions and restrictions of marriage.

Danielle Antoinette Hidalgo, Kristen Barber, and Erica Hunter in "The Dyadic Imaginary: Troubling the Perception of Love as Dyadic," deconstruct the dyadic assumptions used in social science research regarding definitions of love, intimacy, sexuality and kinship. Their analysis reveals the ways in the same-sex marriage debate fails these dyadic assumptions and continues to reinforce dichotomized notions of sex, gender, and sexual orientation.

Ajnesh Prasad in "On the Potential and Perils of Same-Sex Marriage: A Perspective from Queer Theory," considers arguments for and against same-sex marriage. Central to Prasad's consideration of same-sex marriage is the analysis of sexuality as it is understood from a queer theory perspective. Prasad offers a discussion of the ways in which queer marriage and same-sex marriage intersect and how bisexuality is situated within these frameworks.

RESEARCH PERSPECTIVES: ATTITUDES TOWARD BISEXUALITY AND SAME-SEX MARRIAGE

Four research articles are included in this section. Representing both qualitative and quantitative research approaches, these articles further investigate attitudes regarding bisexuality and same-sex marriage. These contributions offer (1) insight into the unique experiences of bisexual women and men in the context of same-sex marriage; (2) an understanding of the ways in which bisexual individuals are connected, or not connected, to the marriage equality movement; (3) an understanding of the implications for broadening the same-sex marriage debate to include bisexual experiences; and (4) suggestions for directions of future research on the topic.

Often attitudes about bisexuality are explicitly measured or displayed. In our article "Bias Toward Bisexual Women and Men in a Marriage-Matching Task," Angela L. Breno and I present a study that allows for a more subtle measure of attitudes toward bisexual women and men with regard to same-sex marriage. In a marriage-matching task, participants were presented with a profile of a fictitious individual (formatted similarly to a personal advertisement) and were asked to create an ideal marriage match for the profile. When making marriage matches there was a clear perception that bisexual partners were best suited to other bisexual individuals. These findings represent a bias in perception towards bisexual individuals in that they are not seen as viable matches for cross-orientation marriages (with either lesbians and gay men or with heterosexual women and men).

Pamela J. Lannutti in "'This is Not a Lesbian Wedding': Examining Same-Sex Marriage and Bisexual-Lesbian Couples," describes a study in which she interviewed bisexual-lesbian couples in Massachusetts who were either married or engaged to be married. Her participants discuss the ways in which bisexual identity is negotiated in the context of same-sex marriage and highlight the unique experiences of cross-orientation couples in same-sex marriage.

When bisexuality *has been* visible in the same sex marriage debate, it has been in ways that often lead to questions of *"what next?"* That is, same-sex marriage for (presumably) lesbians and gay men establishes a "slippery slope" from which bisexuals might want to seek public recognition for polyamorous relationships and family. Hadar Aviram in "Make Love, Not Law: Perceptions of the Marriage Equality Struggle Among Polyamorous Activists," describes the findings of her work with the Bay Area polyamorous community. Based on in-depth interviews, Aviram's research allows an understanding of the ways in which these polyamorous activists view the relation between the marriage equality movement, their personal relationships, and their political strategies.

Marcia L. Pearl and I, in the final contribution to this section, "Bisexual Attitudes Toward Same-Sex Marriage" extend the usage of the Attitudes Toward Same-Sex Marriage Scale (ATSM) to a sexual minority population. Data suggest that ATSM scores for bisexual individuals do not differ from those of lesbians and gay men. However, demographic and relationship factors did impact attitudes toward same-sex marriage for bisexual women and men. Among bisexual participants ATSM scores were higher for women, non-parents, and individuals who were partnered or divorced (versus married). These findings emphasize that there is not a homogenous bisexual viewpoint regarding same-sex marriage.

BISEXUAL PERSPECTIVES ON SAME-SEX MARRIAGE

Three contributions included in this section offer personal perspectives on same-sex marriage and the marriage equality movement. Although informed by the academic literature, these works are compelling because they are rooted in personal experience and elucidate the complex reality for individuals in the context of a very public debate. Each work offers a unique perspective on same-sex marriage reflected through the way in which the issue is resolved at a personal level. Collectively these personal perspectives serve as a reminder that the experiences of bisexual women and men are diverse.

Mia Ocean, in her essay "Bisexuals are Bad for the Same-Sex Marriage Business," provides a personal and political analysis that nicely reflects the tension that bisexual individuals face in advocating for an institution in which bisexuality is invisible. Despite the tension and the knowledge she is not welcome on either side of the debate, Ocean ultimately weighs in on the side for same-sex marriage advocacy.

Hameed (Herukhuti) S. Williams in "A Bisex-Queer Critique of Same-Sex Marriage Advocacy," reaches a different conclusion. Williams uses both personal examples and queer theory analysis to suggest that a more radical argument for marriage equality is necessary in order to support queer forms of relationship structure.

Laurie J. Kendall, in her work entitled "Dancing with My Grandma: Talking with Robyn Ochs About Complex Identities and Simple Messages in the Marriage Equality Movement" provides an excellent interview with Robyn Ochs, a long time bi-activist. Ochs describes the ways in which her bisexuality informs her personal and political experiences within the marriage equality movement.

DEFINING SEXUALITY, DEFINING MARRIAGE

While this volume is organized into three sections, two themes consistently emerge across the contributions: (1) The ways in which bisexuality challenges or fails to challenge dichotomous notions of sex, gender, and sexual orientation and how that shifts the same-sex marriage debate; and (2) the way in which marriage has traditionally reinforced and relied upon sexist, heterosexist, and coupled notions of relationships, and how same-sex marriage simultaneously challenges and fails to challenge these notions.

Both of these themes ultimately center on current definitions of sexuality and marriage. As is evident in the contributions, these definitions differ across personal, legal, cultural, and religious arenas. It is also important to note that within the academic literature definitions differ across theoretical and research contexts and that future academic writing needs to address the disconnect between the two. Collectively these contributions provide a sense of how definitions of sexuality and marriage impact social organization and individual experience. By centering the discourse on bisexual experience, this volume provides unique perspectives from which to consider issues of sexuality and marriage and ultimately allows for a distinct sense of bisexual visibility and vision within the context of same-sex marriage.

THEORETICAL PERSPECTIVES: FRAMING BISEXUALITY IN THE SAME-SEX DEBATE

Supremacy by Law: The One Man One Woman Marriage Requirement and Antimiscegenation Law

Jacqueline Battalora

During a panel discussion on queer social movements at an academic conference, participants inquired as to why transgender, transsexual and bisexual persons were turning to established gay and lesbian organizations for advocacy when it seems clear that social experience, political agendas, and concerns can be quite different. Is there something that unites gay, lesbian, transgender, transsexual, and bisexual persons (GLBTs) even when there might exist conflicting conceptions of gender and sexuality and competing political agendas? It was my sense that, at a minimum, these groups confront a common challenge, that of the dominant cultural assertion of heterosexuality as a singular norm in the realm of sexuality and, it's counterpart, the enforcement of traditional gender roles linked with one's sex classification at birth. In this article, I turn to the current federal ban on same-sex marriage and to race-based restrictions on marriage in the past with an eye toward how, if at all, they might shed light on same-sex marriage bans and unite sexual outsiders.

I begin by discussing the analytical tools that inform the analysis herein. I then discuss concerns over the use of the analogy between same-sex and race-based restrictions on marriage and work to locate them within the larger historical context within which they emerged and were fiercely asserted. Support for same-sex marriage bans is examined. Focus is placed on the voices of support for the Defense of Marriage Act in Congress and the broader culture. The distinctions made between race-based and sex-based marriage bans by supporters of the latter are then considered with attention drawn to the fact claims upon which they rely. These are considered in relation to fact claims deployed in the legal decisions of appellate court judges addressing race-based marriage bans and the history of the law's demise. Because articulations of support for same-sex and race-based racial bans share striking similarities, they are quoted when possible rather than summarized in order to let the words highlight parallels and expose underlying assumptions. Finally, the assumptions that structure the fact claims are excavated for evidence of a thread that might link GLBTs in the context of same-sex marriage bans and challenges thereto.

SEEING FACTS, MAKING DIFFERENCE

This article most generally is directed to an examination of the ways in which law works to define and regulate bodies through facts and the construction of difference. I do not propose a legal framework to challenge same-sex marriage bans but rather, focus upon epistemological concerns. The relationship between marriage restrictions in the United States and ideas or fact claims about nature, God, family, and certain bodies take center stage. Ultimately, I am interested in considering such fact claims in light of the larger context within which they were organized and derive from them their underlying structure. By *structure*, I mean an organizing principal upon which a set of social relations are systematically patterned.

I examine the legal and cultural resources used by supporters of the Defense of Marriage Act (DOMA) and juxtapose them with those utilized in appellate court cases that justified racial restrictions on marriage. There is not data available to tell us why each legislator who supported DOMA voted for the law nor why each appellate judge who upheld a conviction under laws restricting who a person could marry on the basis of race did so. However, those legal actors who directly express their concerns about marriage in the context of the bans and who explain their support for the laws help to shed light on rationale for the laws. In addition, I locate support for the laws within the larger social context. There are common themes in the articulation of support for DOMA just as there are in appellate court decisions upholding and enforcing race-based marriage restrictions.

The deployment of certain ideas about God and nature take center stage as "fact" in the legal battle over marriage. Descriptions of fact have been a well established site of contestation necessitating analysis (Matsuda, 1993; Williams, 1988, 1991). Furthermore, it has been shown that fact description is patterned (Scheppele, 1988). "Pattern" is helpful in that it captures the idea that something, in this case fact claims, are not simply arbitrary but are organized such that a definite design emerges upon examination. One of my objectives is to show that descriptions of fact, in the case of the marriage restrictions examined, are informed by a common structure. In other words, I focus upon fact descriptions with an eye toward the patterns they shape and the structural support without which they would collapse. Another objective is to show how dualistic constructions of difference work to erase, by necessity, those excluded by it.

It is noteworthy that the role of "difference" in these laws functions in distinct ways. Race difference functioned to exclude certain couples from marriage because Whites were understood to be different, in fact "pure" compared to racial "others" whereas sex difference in the case of DOMA justifies only opposite sex couples inclusion in marriage. Where difference worked to exclude in the case of racial marriage bans, it works to restrict inclusion in the case of same-sex marriage bans. Where difference was prohibited in the prior it is required in the latter. Because gender difference functions as the critical component for inclusion within the institution of marriage for the purpose of current federal law, I refer to such male and female marital couplings as "different-sex" marriage.

A number of scholars have challenged the appropriateness of a legal analogy between the history of race-based marriage restrictions and current sex-based marriage restrictions primarily because the prior was part and parcel of a much larger system of legal segregation (Gerstmann, 2004; Sunstein, 1994). There is no perfect analogy because historical contexts change and any attempt to equate the pervasive limitations and degradations imposed upon Black people in particular, first under slavery and then under a Jim Crow regime, with the harms experienced as a result of gender discrimination today, is without compelling historical support. This does not mean, however, that women are not harmed because of gender inequalities and that these harms are not significant. Race-based marriage bans were a pillar of systemic racial segregation while sex-based marriage bans are not. This does not mean however, that same-sex marriage bans are not part of the systemic exclusion and suppression of GLBTs. What it does mean is that any attempt to draw from the history of racial exclusions in marriage must be contextualized in order to fairly evaluate its relevance to a very different context.

There are many differences between racial restrictions on marriage, called "antimiscegenation"[1] law and DOMA. While the prior restricted access to marriage on the basis of race, the latter restricts access to marriage on the basis of sex. Antimiscegnation law made illegal the marriage of a White person to an opposite-sex partner who was not White. Antimiscegenation law will be expounded upon later in this article. DOMA has two facets: (1) it defines "marriage" and "spouse" as involving one man and one woman; and (2) it provides that no state is required to honor a same-sex marriage contracted in another state (1 U.S.C.A. §7 and 28 U.S.C.A. §1738C).[2] While antimiscegenation laws were exclusively a matter of state law, DOMA is federal legislation with many states having largely duplicated it by passing DOMA legislation at the state level and/or amending the state constitution.

The lived experience of those most restricted and harmed by antimiscegenation law and those by DOMA cannot be easily equated. Unlike DOMA, Antimiscegnation law was a criminal statute with the imposition of prison sentences often ranging from two to seven years. Challenging antimiscegenation law was not a priority of Black rights organizations though it was the *most* important issue for Whites (Myrdal, 1944). The dismantling of antimiscegenation was not a priority of The National Association of Colored Persons (NAACP) in its infancy (1910s) nor during the Civil Rights Movement in the 1960s. Rather, priorities for the NAACP included challenging discrimination in employment, education, exercise of the vote, and basic mobility without threat of violence. Furthermore, challenging racial marriage bans was not a priority because most black people could marry the person they loved. This, of course, is not the case for a gay or lesbian person nor a bisexual, transsexual or transgender individual whose partner is the same sex.

The historical context that gave rise to the laws was certainly distinct. Enactments of the Colonial Assemblies of Maryland and Virginia, which served as the precursors to the first antimiscegenation law, reveal that the law was not an effort to express a government (colony) based fundamentally in White supremacy. Rather, the enactments suggest that the law initially was intended to enforce the largely taken for granted practice of marrying within the tribe, here the tribe being British, that was threatened within the context of Colonial North America. In Colonial Maryland, the first enactment that placed a racial restriction on marriage applied only to British women (Fowler, 1963). Later enactments imposed racial restrictions on British men and British women as well as other Whites (Hening, 1809-1823).

This suggests that the forces and pressures of the Colonial context demanded that the borders of the tribe expand from its former homeland parameters. It also suggests that whiteness, in the United States, was built upon the idea of Englishness as White. That "white" became the new tribal border is not surprising in light of the constructs of black and white that dominated England well before such colonial enactments. According to Winthrop Jordan, the British "found blackness in human beings a peculiar and important point of difference. The Negro's color set him radically *apart* from Englishmen" (1968: 20) As rationalizations and justifications for slavery, the slave trade, and the expropriation of lands from native populations expanded, race-based marriage restrictions were one logical means of (re)creating and enforcing the racial hierarchy upon which they depended. In Colonial North America, those who wielded the most power were increasingly invested in slavery (Jordon, 1968; Saxton, 1990).

While invented by North American Colonists, antimiscegenation laws were asserted with vengeance after the Civil War when Whites confronted the potential of social equality with former slaves. It was at this historical juncture when antimiscegenation law can be identified as a cornerstone of White supremacy, as a critical component of the effort to express a state based fundamentally in White supremacy.

In contrast, DOMA was a response to the recommendation made in the December 1995, report by Hawaii's *Commission on Sexual Orientation and the Law* stating that same-sex marriage be recognized in the state by finding that denying same-sex partnerships is discriminatory under Hawaii's Equal Rights Amendment in the absence of a compelling state interest (Goldberg-Hiller, 2002). It is also noteworthy that during the years preceding the report, sexual matters were at the forefront of the national stage. These include: the 1991 Christian Coalition vocal critique of the National Endowment for the Arts funding of Robert Maplethorpe among other artists whose work had sexual content labeled obscene by some; the "Tailhook" scandal that involved the physical and sexual assault of female Navy cadets by male cadets; and the televised hearings of then U.S. Supreme Court nominee Clarence Thomas accused of sexual harassment. Sexually charged matters frequented the public arena and fueled an evangelical Christian political movement that claimed a foundation within Christian morality that regularly deployed the idea of the "traditional family" to unite people otherwise often sharply divided (D'Emilio & Freedman, 1988).

Anxiety about gay marriage and public discourse concerning sexual matters sheds light on only part of the context out of which DOMA emerged and the Federal Marriage Amendment (FMA) was proposed. The FMA to date has not been adopted. It provides that marriage shall only consist of the union between a man and a woman and that neither the federal nor any state constitution shall require that marriage be conferred upon any union other than one between a man and woman. (Calendar No. 620, 108th Congress, 2nd Session, S. J. Res. 40). Changes in Congressional understanding of the proper relationship between federal law and the institution of marriage also played a role. For decades preceding the mid 1990s, Congress approached the institution of marriage as a private contractual relationship that was best undisturbed by federal policy (Cott, 2000). However, in the mid 1990s same-sex marriage, welfare reform, and the promotion of responsible fatherhood were concerns expressed in Congress that translated into a Congressional willingness to address marriage at the federal level (Ooms, 2001). Finally, DOMA reflects challenges to the exclusivity of different-sex marriage. The laws are a response to challenges made possible by changing conceptions of marriage in the larger society, most specifically an understanding of marriage as not principally about creating powerful dynasties nor about money nor reproduction as in the past, but rather, about love for a chosen partner (Graff, 1999).

The context that gave rise to DOMA and that out of which antimiscegenation laws emerged and were asserted was certain to shape important differences. While the laws share some significant commonalities in that they function to name, to construct reality, knowledge and power, to distribute and deny resources, a simple equation is unwarranted.

SUPPORT FOR THE ONE MAN AND ONE WOMAN MARRIAGE REQUIREMENT

While differences between these laws and differences between the lived experiences of those most intimately subjected to them cannot and should not be taken lightly, there is instruction that can be derived from a consideration of the two. The patterned descriptions of fact and the assumptions supporting them reveal striking similarities. Both laws pre sume a human difference that reflects God's intent. Both declare that reproduction establishes a consistency with nature. Finally, they both claim that the civility of the nation/state demands the law.

The arguments advanced for DOMA in the House of Representatives, Committee of the Whole, those of legal scholars, and those of public advocates for DOMA are excavated for the fact claims relied upon, the patterns they shape, and the assumptions upon which they depend. Fact claims about God and nature, the true family, and reproduction are prominent in the claims of those who oppose same-sex marriage.

Supporters of DOMA argue that the fundamental distinction between different-sex couples and same-sex couples is rooted in nature specifically, the possibility for "natural" procreation on the part of different sex couples, presumed to be heterosexual. In contrast, same sex couples presumed to be homosexual are described as properly excluded from the institution of marriage because they are incapable of "natural" procreation. This distinction is made by Allan C. Carlson, of the Family Research Council:

Heterosexual unions can create a child at any moment, so the public has a deep interest in the stabilization from the very beginning. In contrast, same-sex unions are "absolutely infertile;" a public interest in their stabilization would come only at the time of adoption, not at the beginning of such a relationship (2005: 5).

Along similar lines but formally distinct are the arguments rooted in natural law. From a historical perspective, natural law is derived from God rather than humanity, thereby demanding obedience, and yet is located within the "confines of human nature" (Morant, 1998: 76). These laws "occur 'naturally,' making them an inexorable part of the world in which we live. Because humanity's existence is rooted in God, the Supreme Being, natural law becomes that which is a preservative of human nature itself" (Ibid.). Contemporary lawyers who have rooted their opposition to same-sex marriage firmly within natural law claim that different-sex marriage is intrinsically good for humanity because it reflects a union that a same-sex couple cannot achieve (Finnis, 1994; George & Bradley, 1995). Again, we see the presumption of homosexuality in reference same-sex marriage and heterosexuality with regard to different-sex marriage.

Where fact claims about nature are prominent among legal scholars who support DOMA, fact claims about God and Christianity are prominent among the vocal members of the House of Representatives, Committee of the Whole (1996). Representative Canady (R-FL) addressing DOMA before the committee states:

What is at stake in this controversy? Nothing less than our collective moral understanding as expressed in the law of the essential nature of the family the fundamental building block of society . . ., I believe that the traditional family structure centered on a lawful union between one man and one woman comports with nature and with our Judeo-Christian moral tradition (Ibid. at lines 138-142 & 147-150).

The claim that same-sex marriage threatens the very essence or "nature" of marriage is reinforced by Representative Hutchinson (R-Ak) who draws upon a 1970 decision of the Supreme Court of Minnesota wherein that court stated: "the institution of marriage as a union of man and woman uniquely involving the procreating and rearing of children within the family is as old as the Book of Genesis" (Ibid. lines 229-232). Hutchinson and Largent go on to claim that marriage is a covenant created by God for one man and one woman to unite for the purpose of producing and maintaining a family (Ibid.).

Arguments in Congress in support of the law reveal an understanding of difference articulated through a construction of family that is timeless, natural, and essentially heterosexual. This procreative possibility, which is neither a possibility for all different-sex marriages nor a legal requirement for access to the institution of marriage, translates into the obligation and responsibility to perpetuate the species. Here, reproduction and "the family" function as rationale for the law working to plant DOMA firmly within nature and God's intent. The biological impossibility of a same-sex couple together producing children functions to establish such couplings as defective and, therefore, a violation of nature. Through such logic, Congressional lawmakers and legal and political advocates of DOMA disregard and erase GLBT families as "family" both definitionally and as a matter of God's intent.

Supporters of DOMA assert a dualistic construction of sexuality. There is appropriate sexuality (heterosexual), on the one hand, and defective sexuality (homosexuality), on the other. The dualism is relied upon to support and bolster the claim of true difference. This dualistic assertion of sexuality not only functions to justify exclusion and inclusion by law but furthermore functions to erase those whose bodies pose a threat to the dualism, bisexuals. A bisexual person can marry a different-sex partner and while this would be permitted under DOMA it would not reflect a "heterosexual" marriage. Similarly, a bisexual person married to a person of the same-sex would not reflect a "homosexual" marriage. Recognition of bisexuality would change the discourse of the same-sex marriage debate. It is significant however, that bisexuality is absent. DOMA supporters reveal and impose a sexual dualism in dominant U.S. culture that works to make difference and to erase those who may fracture the dividing line.

According to DOMA supporters, nature informs the requirement that marriage is between a man and a woman. According to Representatives Largent and Hutchinson, not only nature but God demand that marriage law be structured in accordance with DOMA. Through these knowledge claims, supporters work to make DOMA a law of God and nature's design. Support for DOMA relies upon the belief that different-sex couples bear both the burden and responsibility of protecting God's intent, the laws of nature, family itself, and nothing less than the survival of society. According to Hutchinson, "our country can survive many things, but one thing it cannot survive is the destruction of the family unit which forms the foundation of our society. Those among us who truly desire a strong and thriving America for our children and grandchildren will defend traditional heterosexual marriage . . ."(Ibid. at lines 266-272). He is joined by Representatives Canaday and Largent who link the one man and one woman marriage requirement with the nation's well being, if not survival, and its status as civilized and moral (Ibid.)

Claims that DOMA promotes a healthy society are not unique. Maggie Gallagher, president of the Institute for Marriage and Public Policy, claims that society is best served by different-sex marriage arguing that same-sex marriage should be opposed because it would function to dilute this ideal. The social scientific material relied upon in the text she co-authored with Linda J. Waite, *The Case for Marriage,* a text that argues the virtues of marriage, is for Gallagher and others, the "science" supporting DOMA. The co-author of the text however does not interpret the material in the same way. Rather, Waite supports same-sex marriage (Waite & Gallagher, 2000: 200).

DOMA supporters presume that only a different-sex couple can constitute a pure or true family, reflective of nature or God's intent, and only a different-sex couple can create a social structure for a healthy society. The patterns these "facts" shape reveal essentialist beliefs about sexuality that become more prominent as DOMA supporters work to distinguish their stance vis-à-vis same-sex marriage from that of racial restrictions on marriage.

DESCRIPTIONS AND DISTINCTIONS

Legal actors sought to challenge the belief that DOMA is discriminatory or violates equal rights. Similarly, it is not uncommon for advocates of DOMA to distinguish support for these laws from support for race-based marriage bans. Supporters of DOMA distinguish restrictions on interracial marriage from DOMA in one of two ways. First, by arguing or presuming that difference claimed on the basis of race is not real while difference on the basis of both gender and sexuality is real. Second, by making distinctions about how race-based marriage bans, on the one hand, and DOMA, on the other, impacts marriage.

The deployment of "civil rights" by same-sex marriage advocates to describe the fight for inclusion within the institution of marriage has been rejected by the most vocal DOMA supporters on Capital Hill. According to Largent, ". . . this [DOMA] is not about equal rights. We have equal rights. Homosexuals have the same rights I do. They have the ability to marry right now, today. However, when they get married they must marry a person of the opposite sex, the same as me" (H.R. Committee of the Whole 1996, at lines 421-428). Senator Michael Enzi (R-WY) advocating support for a constitutional amendment to define marriage as between one man and one woman states, "[m]arriage is a union of a man and a woman in a partnership aimed at producing children and nurturing their growth and developments. It is not about social acceptance, or about economic benefits, or an exercise in civil rights, as some would try to lead us to believe." (150 Cong. Rec., 2004 at S8081)

Still others argue that the power of the words "civil rights" within a U.S. context is derived from a specific historical experience that must be honored (Steele, 2004).[3] The root of this claim is not only grounded within a specific historical moment but in the belief that same-sex marriage is not a civil rights issue because unlike racial variety, "homosexuality and heterosexuality reflect genuine difference" (Ibid.). Steele argues that racism projects a false difference in order to exploit while homophobia is a reactive prejudice against a true difference that already exists and he claims that while homosexuals focus upon marriage, an institution appropriate only for heterosexuals, they will keep from developing institutions and practices that reflect their true nature (2004). Here, *real* difference functions as the distinction that separates support for DOMA from race-based marriage restrictions. Un-real difference incorrectly alleged as "real" and enforced in law then, is what roots a claim within the civil rights tradition.

The historical memory within which some DOMA supporters root their rejection and critique of the deployment of the "civil rights" label vanishes when they address "real" difference with regard to sexuality. Here the non-reality of race as a human difference is treated as if the innocuousness of racial difference was *always* a given, as if convincing courts and communities that race is socially constructed and merely a trivial difference was not one of the ultimate victories of the civil rights movement (Lawrence, 1993). Still others argue that race-based marriage restrictions served to preserve a social system of racial segregation but were, "utterly irrelevant to the fundamental nature of marriage" (Sprigg, 2005: 5). Supporters of DOMA who argue that these laws concern the fundamental nature of marriage and claim that antimiscegenation law did not, have similarly suffered historical amnesia.

The historical memory that alludes the supporters of DOMA is this: just as firmly and genuinely as they and others find different-sex couples and same-sex couples to be separate and distinct by nature and God, those who wielded authority in this country's courtrooms and within communities across this country, firmly and genuinely believed White and Black people were just as separate and distinct. Furthermore, they too claimed that the survival of "the family," the very civility of the nation/state and the fundamental nature of marriage depended upon maintaining the separation of Whites from racial "others" via marriage. From few sources can historic memory of essentialist beliefs about race and the link between race and marriage be recalled and refreshed more poignantly than in court cases addressing marriage or fornication between a White and nonwhite person when race-based marriage restrictions were the rule of the day.

UPHOLDING ANTIMISCEGENATION LAW

Antimiscegenation laws functioned to control the legitimate expression of sexuality by those racialized White. These laws prohibited those understood to be White from either marrying or having consensual sex with an individual of the opposite sex understood as racially not White by criminalizing such acts. Taking the constructions of racial categories on their face, every antimiscegenation law prohibited a White person from marrying a Black person and some also prohibited a White person from marrying such racial "others" as an Indian, Mulatto, Mestizo, Half-breed, Mongolian, or Malay.[4] While these state laws are frequently referred to as preventing "interracial marriage," suggesting a restriction shared equally by all racial groups, such a claim is not supported by the statutes. No antimiscegenation law prohibited a marriage between two individuals of the opposite sex understood to be of different races *except* where one was White.

The emphasis on controlling Whites' expression of legitimate sexuality is rooted in the combination of meanings assigned to both Whites and nonwhites especially, Blacks. Whiteness as the British ideal was already centuries old by the late Sixteenth Century and was understood in complete contrast to those seen as nonwhite especially, Black such that white and black "connoted purity and filthiness, virginity and sin, virtue and baseness, beauty and ugliness, beneficence and evil, God and the devil" (Jordan, 1968: 7). The Seventeenth Century colonial laws that were the genesis of antimiscegenation law reveal that whiteness signified freedom, assumed certain citizenship rights and privileges while nonwhiteness, on the other hand, became increasingly associated with servitude and bestiality. (Fredrickson, 1981; Harris, 1993; Lopez, 1996). Whiteness was viewed as possessing valuable qualities that were perceived to be at risk by the marriage of a White woman, in particular, to a Black man, in particular (Getman, 1984; Gilmore, 1996; Hodes, 1991, 1993). Within the midst of a racial hierarchy upon which slavery became more and more dependent, marriage as a legitimizing institution creating rights and responsibilities in law, made the physical presence of such a marital couple intolerable (Bardaglio 1995; Bynum, 1992). White women were the bearers of racial purity. Therefore, the gendered meanings assigned to Whiteness were at stake.

Antimiscegenation law reflects the work of "moral entrepreneurs"[6] (Becker, 1963) invested in asserting and preserving a sense of tribe among the British in the context of colonial North America. Almost all laws adopted by assemblies within colonial North America were derived from the common law of England. However, like the legal rule that made a child's status dependent upon the condition of the child's mother, antimiscegenation laws were an invention of North American colonists (Fowler, 1963; Martyn, 1979; Sickels, 1972). The crime of miscegenation was a reflection of the political, economic, ethical and psychological needs of first, the British ruling elite as they interacted with and responded to the free White people of the North American colonies and later, the political elite who exerted power and influence within state governments of the United States (Battalora, 1999).

Antimiscegenation laws and the racial belief system that supported them were pervasive and so deeply culturally embedded as to endure for three hundred years in the land now the United States. First developed in the Seventeenth Century, these laws survived the ratification of the U.S. Constitution and the Bill of Rights, the Civil War, Congressional Reconstruction, the Fourteenth Amendment and civil rights legislation. After the Civil War, facing the prospect of racial equality, Whites asserted antimiscegenation law as a cornerstone of a state based fundamentally in White supremacy. Antimiscegenation law worked with Jim Crow laws to keep not only Blacks and Whites separate but to deny basic rights and freedoms to Blacks. At the turn of the Twentieth Century, twenty states and territories restricted by statute whom a White person could marry on racial grounds while an additional six states also did so by state constitution. In 1967, in the aptly captioned case, *Loving v. Virginia,* the Supreme Court of the United States ruled that Virginia's antimiscegenation law violated Mildred and Richard Loving's liberty without due process and found that the law's restriction of the freedom to marry solely because of racial classifications is in violation of the Equal Protection Clause (388 U.S. 1, 3 (1967)). It is noteworthy that numerous state courts previously found that the antimiscegenation law violated the Fourteenth Amendment of their states' constitution with California leading the way in 1948 (*Perez v. Sharp*, 32 Cal.2d 711, 198 P2d 17 (*sub. nom. Perez v. Lippord*) (1948)).

Support for antimiscegenation law can be found in appellate court rulings. For example, in affirming the conviction of a White woman who married a Black man, the Alabama Appellate Court stressed the social necessity of the law by claiming, ". . . it is for the peace and happiness of the black race, as well as of the white, that such laws should exist" (*Green v. The State*, 58 Ala. 190, 195 (1877)). The court explained, "there cannot be any tyranny or injustice in requiring both alike, to form this union with those of their own race only, whom God hath joined together by indelible peculiarities and which declare that He has made the two races distinct" (Id.). The Virginia Appellate Court affirmed the conviction of a Black man for violating Virginia's antimiscenegnation law and in doing so stated:

The purity of public morals, the moral and physical development of both races, and the highest advancement of our cherished southern civilization, under which two distinct races are to work out and accomplish the destiny to which the Almighty has assigned them on this continent–all require that they should be kept distinct and separate, and that connections and alliances so unnatural that God and nature seem to forbid them, should be prohibited by positive law . . . (*Kinney v. The Commonwealth*, 30 Gratt. 858, 869 (1878)).

The belief that White and Black people are separate and distinct by nature and God was not unique to the South. According to the Indiana Appellate Court, the people of Indiana declared that they oppose racial mixing and all amalgamation (*The State v. Gibson,* 36 Ind. 389 (1871)). Then in support of this stance, the court cites at length from the Pennsylvania Supreme Court ruling in *The Philadelphia and West Chester R.R. Co. v. Miles*, wherein that court upheld the railroad company policy of requiring Whites and Blacks to have separate seating on the carrier. The Pennsylvania Supreme Court stated in part:

> . . . the question remaining to be considered is whether there is such a difference between white and black races within this state, resulting from nature, law, and custom, as makes it a reasonable ground of separation. The question is one of difference, not of superiority or inferiority. Why the Creator made one black and the other white, we do not know, but the fact is apparent, and the races are distinct, each producing its own kind, and following the peculiar law of its constitution. Conceding equality, with natures as perfect, and rights as sacred, yet God has made them dissimilar . . . The natural law which forbids their intermarriage and that social amalgamation which leads to a corruption of races, is clearly divine as that which imparted to them different natures . . . the fact of a distribution of men by race and color is as visible in the providential arrangement of the earth as that of heat and cold. The natural separation of the races is therefore an undeniable fact . . . (2 Am. Law Rev. 358, 404-405 (1867)).

The racial ideology[6] supporting these court decisions was not unique to the Post Civil War era. While the cases above are from the period following the Civil War when the Fourteenth Amendment and Civil Rights Act briefly placed into question the constitutionality of the law, the assumption of essential human difference because of race constructs threads back to North American colonial assembly enactments through legal decisions of the 1950s. Before being overturned by the U.S. Supreme Court in 1967, the Virginia Circuit Court in 1959, claimed:

> Almighty God created the races white, black, yellow, malay and red, and he placed them on separate continents. And but for the interference with his arrangements there would be no cause for such marriages. The fact that he separated the races shows that he did not intend for the races to mix. (*Loving v. Virginia*, 388 U.S. 1, 3

(1967), quoting trial court judge of the Circuit Court of Caroline County Virginia. See also, *Griffin v. State*, 50 So.2d 797 (1951)).

Essentialist notions of race were buttressed by claims that the children of a White and Black couple were viewed as defective and therefore proof that the coupling is unnatural. These claims were often portrayed as scientific support. The Supreme Court of Mississippi in 1883 claimed that if the child of a Black man and a White woman, and the child of a White man and a Black woman intermarry such a coupling is incapable of reproducing and such a fact sufficiently justifies antimiscegenation law (*State v. Jackson*, 80 Ms, 175, 179 (1883)). Alabama's antimiscegenation statute imposed a more severe punishment for consensual sexual relations outside of marriage when it involved a Black and a White person. In affirming the conviction of Tony Pace for living in adultery, the Alabama Appellate Court justified the disparity in punishment claiming "fornication between persons of different races is the amalgamation of the two races, producing a mongrel population and a degraded civilization." (*Pace & Cox v. The State*, 69 Ala. 231, 232 (1881). *Affirmed, Pace v. Alabama*, 106 U.S. 583, 1 Sup. Ct. 637, 27 L. Ed. 207 (1882)). Not only were the children of White and nonwhite racial mixing analogized to mules and described as mongrels but they were constructed as physically defective and the product of evil.

The Georgia Appellate Court, in affirming the conviction of Charlotte Scott who was tried and convicted for violating Georgia's antimiscegenation law, praised the law as enlightened and rooted in common sense, stating:

The amalgamation of the races is not only unnatural, but is always productive of deplorable results. Our observations show us, that the offspring of these unnatural connections are generally sickly and effeminate, and that they are inferior in physical development and strength, than the full-blood of either race. They are the product of evil, and evil only, without any corresponding good. The Legislature had as much right to regulate marriage between persons of different races as to prohibit it between the Levitical degrees, or between idiots . . . Social equality between the races does not in fact exist, and never can. The God of nature made it otherwise, and no human law can produce it, and no human tribunal can enforce it (*Scott v. The State of Georgia*, 39 Ga. 321, 323-26 (1869)).

In a case involving the estate of a deceased wife whose husband made claim to her estate, the lower court denied the husband's claim finding that their marriage was invalid because it violated the state antimiscegenation law *(Eggers v. Olson,* 231 p. 483 (1924)). The Oklahoma Appellate Court affirmed the lower court ruling and described the state's antimiscegenation law as enlightened policy, sustained by sound reason and common sense stating:

> The amalgamation of the races is not only unnatural, but is always productive of deplorable results. The purity of the public morals, the moral and physical development of both races, and the highest advancement of civilizations, under which the two races must work out and accomplish their destiny, all require that they should be kept distinctly separate, and that connections and alliances so unnatural should be prohibited by positive law and subject to no evasion (Id.).

Today there is little debate that these judicial constructs of mixed-race children, are grounded not in science but in a racial ideology that assumes Whites are superior and that this meaning of whiteness is threatened by racial "others" who, through marriage and offspring, "pollute" whiteness. The frame organizing such "fact" claims in antimiscegenation law is a supremacist structure. By *supremacist structure,* I mean an organizing principle that constructs a group status as more valuable and ultimately superior to a different group status, often formed in opposition here, White and nonwhite, upon which a set of social relations are systematically patterned. In the case of antimiscegenation law, the supremacist structure is White supremacy. These Appellate Court decisions show that claims about nature and defective procreation have a long history of constructing "real" human difference, the nature of marriage, and the civility, purity and morality of a nation.

Only whiteness, in antimiscegenation law demanded protection. For example an Indian could marry a Chinese person despite these bodies being understood as racially distinct. Despite the claims of appellate court judges that the law is for the protection of the races, children, and society itself, these have been exposed as fiction rather than fact. The court decisions reveal an understanding of Whites "intermixing" with nonwhites as constituting a violation of the divine order. Through claims of knowledge about God's intent, the crafters and enforcers of the law made antimiscegenation a law of God's design. As such, God's "order of creation" is seen as a hierarchy of being wherein God created humankind to live in relationships of inequality determined by certain particularities (Ruether,1992). Within this hierarchy of racialized bodies, White people are made the purest reflection of God and through such fact finding, God is race-ed white.

Antimiscegenation cases expose the contention that racial difference between Whites and nonwhites especially, Blacks is innocuous or that it does not reflect a "real" difference between humans as having a relatively recent genesis in U.S. law and culture. Similarly, the claim that racial segregation was irrelevant to the fundamental nature of marriage is not substantiated by a review of antimiscegenation cases. Rather, court decisions and findings of fact reveal that marriage–in its purest form, uniting White with White, was necessary as a protection of God's order and as such a protection of a fundamental nature of marriage.

THE STRUCTURE AND DISCOURSE OF SUPREMACY

Antimiscegenation law was one component of a larger social program of segregation and eugenics (Destro, 1998). As a critical tool of such social programs, antimiscegenation law and expressions of support for them serve as important flags. They signal an effort to assert social control through the making of an "other" constructed as essentially different and the assertion of it's opposite as superior.

Claims of reproductive defectiveness that worked to justify antimiscegenation law are similarly deployed by those supporting DOMA. The biological impossibility of a same-sex couple themselves producing children through sexual intercourse functions to establish such couplings as defective and a violation of nature. In this way, arguments in support of DOMA treat different-sex marriage as a false homogeneity. Different-sex marriage, presented as exclusively and essentially heterosexual, is deployed in such a way that submerges the reality that not all different-sex couples are capable or desirous of having children. In addition, access to marriage for such couples imposes no requirement of reproduction. For supporters of Antimiscegenation law, defective progeny was the "science" to support a claim of improper coupling. For DOMA supporters, the incapability of a same-sex coupling to biologically produce a child together, functions as the "science" that proves the coupling defective.

The arguments of those supporting DOMA erase by definition the families of GLTBs that include biological children, for at least one parent, adopted children, and no children. The tautology of this rationale translates as follows: a different-sex couple equals heterosexual, equals access to marriage, equals family, equals God's (nature's) intent, and then back to the top of the circle. As such, an opposite-sex couple becomes the essence of marriage ("the nature of marriage") while sharing in a life commitment "until death do you part" and even parenting children is ultimately rendered unimportant. Through this tautology, the structural support for the fact claims alleged by DOMA supporters, becomes apparent. Ultimately, the fact claims fail to justify the law. Furthermore, the logic of the claims is fundamentally dependent upon the presumption of different-sex coupling as reflective of heterosexuality and upon a hierarchy of bodies wherein heterosexuals are made the purest reflection of nature and God's intent.

It is noteworthy that bisexual, transgender, and transsexual men and women simply do not exist in the eyes of DOMA supporters or are thought not relevant to the debate. Because the issue is framed in dualistic and oppositional terms, with heterosexuality on one side and homosexuality on the other, bisexual, transgender, and transsexual individuals in a same-sex relationship are either "really" heterosexuals and require discouragement from deviant sexual exploration or they are "really" homosexual and therefore properly excluded from the rights and responsibilities of marriage. The recognition of bisexuality in particular, would muddy DOMA waters by challenging this dichotomous construction of sexuality and demand a reframing that is porous. Acknowledgement of bisexuality, as neither heterosexual nor homosexual threatens a critical component of the formula used to exclude. It is not surprising that the language utilized by supporters of DOMA treats different-sex couplings and heterosexual as synonymous. Their language of sexuality and marriage erases bisexuality, by necessity.

In much the same way, multiracial bodies that included "White blood" posed a threat to the racial ideology that provided the logic for a structure of White supremacy. Here, the dualism is racial. White reflects purity and being more God-like while a nonwhite racial status reflects impurity and a step further away from God's image. Like the sexual dualism relied upon by DOMA supporters, this racial dualism supported and bolstered the claim of true human difference that worked to justify exclusion in law. Recognition of multiracial persons, particularly where whiteness was included, as anything other than defective would, like bisexuality, pose a threat to the difference making potential of the dualistic construct. Supporters of DOMA and judicial opinions upholding antimiscegenation law reveal a reliance upon a dualistic construct of sexuality on the one hand and race on the other that works to make difference. In the case of DOMA those who threaten the dualism are simply unspoken and rendered invisible. The only possibilities are those reflected in the dualism, heterosexual and homosexual. In the case of antimiscegenation law those who threaten the racial dualism are not erased but rather are constructed as a new entity separate from the racial dualism and inferior to each.

Antimiscegenation law is shown to share its structural underpinnings with arguments in support of DOMA. Antimiscegenation laws and the court cases that challenged them constitute a 300 year history imbedded in the idea and genuinely held belief that White people and non-white people are essentially separate and distinct by nature and God. The children of such "mixtures" or the procreative product served as the evidence of its violation of nature, described by courts as "an abomination," "corrupt," "effeminate," "mongrel," the product of evil, and analogized to a mule. Here, fact descriptions organize around reproduction, purity, and essentialist notions of human difference. These descriptions of "fact" are shown to only be possible within a structure of White supremacy.[7]

Antimiscegenation law and DOMA tend to be understood as reflecting racial bias and gender bias respectively (Koppelmann, 1994). The role of difference, to exclude in the case of antimiscegenation law, as a requirement for admission in the case of DOMA, is key and helps to explain why DOMA is not a reflection of gender discrimination as a matter of law. In order for a claim of gender discrimination, one gender has to be harmed in relation to the other. This is not the case with DOMA. Both women and men who seek to marry a partner of the same sex are equally blocked by DOMA. Therefore, it is not gender per se but sexuality that is the location of discrimination and it is this location that helps us to identify what truly underlies the law.

Efforts by those who make and seek to influence policy today, to separate themselves from support for racial restrictions on marriage in the past, are significant. These efforts are a testament to a hard won recognition in law that race cannot function as a means to exclude without a showing that no less restrictive means are available to accomplish a legitimate state interest. These efforts are also revealing in that they attest to the erasure of the history of antimiscegenation law, as a cornerstone of systemic racial segregation, from cultural memory. Rather than allow for a distancing from antimiscegenation law via claims of "real" difference and the fundamental "nature" of marriage, antimiscegenation case law exposes the law as: a race-based restriction upon marriage rooted in essentialist beliefs about Whiteness on the one hand and non-whiteness on the other; and as a law that served to protect the fundamental nature of marriage, in its purest form, uniting white with white, a protection dictated by God's order. Strategies deployed to distinguish support for DOMA from antimiscegenation law, ultimately fail when the history of antimiscegenation law is surfaced.

The claims of lawmakers and other legal actors who supported antimiscegenation law make sense only within the framework of a racial logic that held those understood as White to be superior to racial "others". This detailed examination of fact description drawn upon to support both antimiscegentation law and DOMA expose a common underlying structure. Like white supremacy, heterosexual supremacy is a hierarchy of beings that awards and denies symbolic and material resources based upon a logic that presumes the superiority of heterosexuality. It is the assertion of heterosexual supremacy in DOMA that presents a core of unity for GLBTs since ultimately, all are constructed through direct claims and/or through erasure as sexual outsiders. As such GLBTs are made essentially different from that which is a reflection of God and nature's intent as well as the fundamental nature of marriage–heterosexuality.

Like the fact claims that served as cultural resources held together by a structure of White supremacy reflected in support for antimiscegenation law, those deployed in support of DOMA reveal an architecture of exclusion from civil marriage in U.S. law built upon supremacy. The structure of supremacy revealed in these laws is important not merely to ground challenges to the validity of DOMA but because it suggests a structured means of exclusion that warrants attention. The patterned description of facts and their structural support takes on more significance than Whites and nonwhites gaining access to marry one another or same-sex couples gaining access to marriage. This analysis of support for DOMA and court decisions upholding antimiscegenation law, reveals that essentialist claims combine with supremacy to create a successful formula for exclusion in law. The history of antimiscegenation law remains relevant knowledge. It suggests a gauge for evaluating fact claims and suggests that a formula of essential difference combined with an organizing structure of supremacy, may well signal a legal sanctioning of supremacy.

NOTES

1. I am grateful to Mindie Lazarus Black for her comments on an earlier draft. I would also like to thank Rosemary Radford Ruether, Josef Barton, and Bernard Beck who offered comments and advice which have contributed to the development of this essay. Diana Vallera and Elizabeth Reid have provided careful editorial assistance and Diana especially helped to clarify and sharpen the ideas presented here.

2. The first statutes in which North American Colonists recognized slavery for black people also addressed intimate sexual relations between White and Black people and the offspring resulting from such unions. "Mixing" between a White and nonwhite person would eventually be called "miscegenation" and the laws that prohibited such relations would be referred to as "antimiscegenation" laws. The word "miscegenation" was coined by David Goodman Croly in an anonymous pamphlet published in New York by H. Dexter, Hamilton, and Co., 1863. The pamphlet was an attempt by Democrats David Croly and George Wakeman to attribute favorable views on "racial mixing" to Republicans thereby promoting support for the Democratic candidate for president. (Sickels 1972).

3. Defense of Marriage Act, Pub. L. No. 104-199, 100 Stat. 2419 (codified at U.S.C.A. § 7 and 28 U.S.C.A. § 1738C).

4. Shelby Steele's essay published in the Wall Street Journal is drawn upon here not because his argument in support of DOMA is unique, but rather, because it is representative of the descriptions, patterns and framework of so many commentaries and editorials promulgated in support of the law *and* because his argument seeks to de-legitimize links made between struggles for civil rights on the part of Blacks in the U.S. and that of Gay, Lesbian, Bisexual and Transgendered people (GLBTs) seeking access to the institution of marriage.

5. South Carolina antimiscegenation law prohibited a white person from marrying someone who was Indian, negro, mulatto, mestizo, or half-breed. Laws of S.C., 1864-5, p. 271. California's antimiscegenation law prohibited white persons from marrying Negroes, Mongolians, Mulattoes, or Malays. Civil Code, 1906, sec. 60.

6. The phrase is Howard Becker's (1963: 149).

7. By *ideology*, I mean a system of beliefs about reality.

8. White supremacy can best be understood as a "racial logic" that affords psychological benefits and organizes social systems in such a way that awards more advantageous economic, political, cultural, and social benefits to those understood as White over those understood as not white (Bonilla-Silva 2001).

REFERENCES

Bardaglio, P. W. (1995). *Reconstructing the Household: Family's, Sex, & the Nineteenth-Century South.* Chapel Hill: University of North Carolina Press.

Battalora, J. (1999). Toward a critical white racial ethics: Constructions of whiteness in antimiscegenation law. Ph.D. dissertation, Northwestern University.

Becker, H. S. (1963). *Outsiders: Studies in the Sociology of Deviance.* New York: Free Press.

Bonilla-Silva, E. (2001). *White Supremacy & Racism in the Post-Civil Rights Era.* Boulder, CO: Lynne Reinner Publishers.

Bynum, V. E. (1992). *Unruly Women.* Chapel Hill: University of North Carolina Press.

Carlson, A. C. (2005). *Marriage on Trial: Why we Must Privilege and Burden the Traditional Marriage Bond.* Washington, DC: Family Research Council.

Cott, N. F. (2000). *Public vows: A History of Marriage and the Nation.* Cambridge, MA: Harvard University Press.

D'Emilio, J. & Freedman, E. B. (1988). *Intimate Matters: A History of Sexuality in America*. (2nd ed.) New York: Harper & Row.

Destro, R. A. (1998). Law and politics of marriage: *Loving v. Virginia* after thirty years introduction. *The Catholic University Law Review* 47, 1207-1230.

Finnis, J. M. (1994). Law, morality, and "sexual orientation." *Notre Dame Law Review,* 69, 1049-1076.

Fowler, D. H. (1963). Northern attitudes towards interracial marriage: A study of legislation and public opinion in the Middle Atlantic and the states of the Old Northwest. *Ph.D. Dissertation*, Yale University.

Fredrickson, G. M. (1981). *White Supremacy*. New York: Oxford University Press.

George, R. P. & Bradley, G.V. (1995, Dec.). Marriage in the liberal imagination. *Georgetown Law Journal*, 84, 319-328.

Gerstmann, E. (2002). *Same-Sex Marriage and the Constitution*. Cambridge, UK: Cambridge University Press.

Gilmore, G. E. (1996). *Gender & Jim Crow: Women and the Politics of White Supremacy in North Carolina, 1896-1920*. Chapel Hill: University of North Carolina.

Goldberg-Hiller, J. (2002). *The Limits to Union: Same-Sex Marriage and the Politics of Civil Rights*. Ann Arbor: The University of Michigan.

Graff, E. J. (1999). *What is Marriage For?* Boston, MA: Beacon Press.

Hodes, M. (1991). Sex across the color line: White women and Black men in the nineteenth-century south. *Ph.D. Dissertation*, Princeton University.

Hodes, M. (1993, Jan). The sexualization of Reconstruction politics: White women and Black men in the south after the Civil War. *Journal of the History of Sexuality*, 3, 402-17.

Jordan, W. D. (1968). *White Over Black*. Chapel Hill: University of North Carolina.

Koppelman, A. (1994). Why discrimination against lesbians and gay men is sex discrimination. *New York University Law Review*, May, 69, 197-287.

Lawrence, III, C. R. (1993). If he hollers let him go. In M. J. Matsuda, C. R. Lawrence, III, L. R. Delgado, & K. Williams. (eds.), *Words that Wound,* (53-88), Boulder, CO: Westview Press.

Lopez, H. (1996). *White by Law: The Social Construction of Race*. New York: New York University Press.

Martyn, B. C. (1979). Racism in the United States: A History of the anti-miscegenation legislation and litigation. *Ph.D. Dissertation*, University of Southern California.

Matsuda, M. J. (1993). Public response to racist speech. In M. J. Matsuda, C. R., Lawrence, III, L. R. Delgado, & K. Williams. (eds.), *Words that Wound,* (pp. 17-51), Boulder, CO: Westview Press.

Morant, B. D. (fall 1998). The teachings of Martin Luther King, Jr. and contract theory: An intriguing comparison. *Alabama Law Review,* 50, 64-113.

Myrdal, G. (1944). *An American Dilemma: The Negro Problem and Modern Democracy*. New York: Harper & Brothers.

Ooms, T. (2001). The role of the federal government in strengthening marriage. *Virginia Journal of Social Policy & the Law,* 116 (9:1), 163-191.

Ruether, R. R. (1992). *Gaia & God: An Ecofeminist Theology of Earth Healing*. San Francisco: Harper.

Saxton, A. (1990). *The Rise and Fall of the White Republic: Class Politics and Mass Culture in Nineteenth-Century America.* London: Verso.

Scheppele, K. L. (1988). *Legal Secrets: Equality and Efficiency in the Common Law.* Chicago: University of Chicago Press.

Sickels, R. J. (1972). *Race, Marriage, and the Law.* Albuquerque: University of New Mexico.

Sprigg, D. (2005). Questions and answers: What's wrong with letting same sex couples "marry?" *Family Research Council,* 256.

Steele, S. (2004, March 18) Selma to San Francisco? *Wall Street Journal,* p. A16.

Sunstein, C. R. (1994). Homosexuality and the constitution. *Indiana Law Journal,* 70, 1-28.

Waite, L. J. & Gallagher, M. (2000). *The Case for Marriage: Why Married People are Happier, Healthier, and Better Off Financially.* New York: Doubleday.

Williams, P. J. (1988). On being the object of property. 14 Signs 000, 5-24.

Williams, P. J. (1991) *The Alchemy of Race and Rights.* Cambridge: Harvard University Press.

STATUTES & CONGRESSIONAL HEARINGS

CA Civil Code, 1906, sec. 60.

Defense of Marriage Act, Pub. L. No. 104-199, 100 Stat. 2419 (codified at U.S.C.A. § 7 and 28 U.S.C.A. § 1738C).

Hearings on the Marriage Amendment Act, 150 Cong. Rec. 2004.

Hening, W.W. (1809-1823) *The statutes at large: Being a collection of all the laws of Virginia (1619-1792).* (13 vols.) Richmond: Published by Act of the General Assembly of Virginia and printed by and for Samuel Pleasants Jr., printer to the commonwealth.

House of Representatives, Committee of the Whole, July 11, 1996.

Laws of S.C., 1864-5.

Marriage Amendment Act, Calendar No. 620, 108th Congress, 2nd Session, S. J. Res. 40.

CASES

Eggers v. Olson, 231 P. 483 (1924)

Green v. The State, 58 Ala. 190 (1877).

Griffin v. State, 50 So.2d 797 (1951).

Kinney v. The Commonwealth, 30 Gratt. 858 (1878).

Loving v. Virginia, 388 U.S. 1, 12 (1967).

Pace v. Alabama, 69 Ala. 231 (1881). *Affirmed, Pace v. Alabama,* 106 U.S. 583, 1 Sup. Ct. 637, 27 L. Ed. 207 (1882).

Perez v. Sharp, 32 Cal.2d 711, 198 P2d 17 (*sub. nom. Perez v. Lippord*) (1948).

The Philadelphia and West Chester R.R. Co. v. Miles, 2 Am. Law Rev. 358 (1867).

Scott v. The State of Georgia, 39 Ga. 321, 323-26 (1896).

State v. Jackson, 80 Ms, 175, 179 (1883).

State v. Gibson, 36 Ind. 389 (1871).

The Dyadic Imaginary: Troubling the Perception of Love as Dyadic

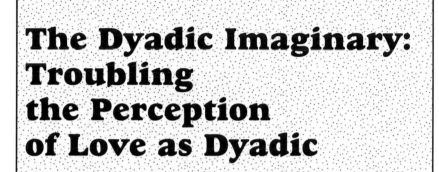

Danielle Antoinette Hidalgo
Kristen Barber
Erica Hunter

When love and intimacy are considered across disciplines, the dyad or couple remains a definitional or assumed feature of intimate and sexual relationships. The dyad serves as an institution that "constitutes the standard for legitimate and prescriptive sociosexual arrangements" (Ingraham, 1994, p. 204). Euro-American literature on love, romance, intimacy, and kinship is largely based on notions of dyadic relationships, to the point that theory and research "circulate [the dyad] as a taken-for-granted, naturally occurring, and unquestioned" social phenomenon (p. 204). As a result, love, as it is conceptualized across fields, assumes the following conceptual apparatuses: in dyadic intimate and sexual relationships, love is conceptualized as legitimate regardless of gender and sexual identities, in non-dyadic intimate and sexual relationships, however, love is conceptualized as illegitimate. Using the conceptual framework of Ingraham's (1994) *heterosexual imaginary*, we propose that sociological, anthropological, psychological and historical literature is not only replete with 'a heterosexual imaginary,' but also imbued with a *dyadic imaginary*. We define the dyadic imaginary as an ideology or hegemonic concept that renders non-dyadic intimate and sexual relationship forms invisible and unnatural.

This conceptualization of love and intimacy through the dyadic imaginary influences academic literature in two distinct ways: theory and methodology (Rose, 2000). Theories fail to address how those in multiple relationships might "do love" and romance. Methodologically, when love and intimacy are considered, couples and/or dyads are overwhelmingly chosen as research subjects.

In this initial paper, we seek to explore how the "ruling ideas" of the dyadic imaginary are produced. The dyadic imaginary has an exclusionary characteristic and thus silences other relationship forms; these dyadic knowledges and practices have real social consequences for issues related to both other-sex and same-sex marriage, sexuality, families, parenting, and love. We aim to illustrate how social dynamics such as family networks, sexual practices, gendered practices, childcare, and household maintenance must be rethought and re-conceptualized outside of a dyadic framework.

Sexual and gender practices that necessarily challenge the gender binary, for example, similarly challenge assumed notions and practices pertaining to dyadic love. As a result, the dyadic imaginary forces us to ask the following questions: What would love look like when coupling is disrupted? How do those who engage in multiple relationships do love and intimacy? If queerness, as it has been discussed as a state of fluidity that transcends both sexual and gender binaries, necessarily opens up space for problematizing the relationship between heterosexuality and homosexuality, what does/would queer love look like? Does a disruption of binaries (male/female, feminine/masculine, heterosexual/homosexual) necessarily upset a coupled notion of doing intimacy? How is this disruption played out in the current debates on same-sex marriage as well as bisexual and queer identity? What different sociological methods would we have to use to study non-dyadic relationship forms? While we do not address all of these questions in this paper, we hope to provide a conceptual framework-*the dyadic imaginary*-that will begin to bring these issues to the forefront of feminist and queer literature. While some of these topics have begun to emerge through various works on polyamory (Rust, 1996; Sheff, 2006), marriage (Shanley, Cohen, & Chasman, 2004), kinship (Weston, 1997), and other topics, we have seen neither a critical analysis of the existing literature on love and intimacy nor suggestions for necessary revisions and reconsiderations.

LOVE AND INTIMACY AS SOCIAL PHENOMENA

Romantic passion is a complex multifaceted emotional phenomenon that is a byproduct of an interplay between biology, self, and society. (Jankowiak 1995: 4)

Love is a highly contested and thus far unresolved social science phenomenon (Felmlee & Sprecher, 2000; Jankowiak, 1995; Johnson, 2004; McCullough & Hall, 2003; Robinson, 1997; Rose, 2000; Seidman,

1991). Many scholars have offered theories about love, but few have ventured outside of a Western definition of the "normal" relationship or dyadic framework when conducting thorough, cross-cultural investigations of sociological patterns of love (Fisher, 1995; Jankowiak, 1995). In *Love and Intimate Relationships: Journeys of the Heart*, Brown and Amatea (2000) write that "the concepts of bisexuality are so fluid that they challenge social norms and mainstream thinking about sexuality and identity" (p. 263). Although they recognize the fluidity of sexuality and gender, they fail to redefine love and intimacy as it relates to these more fluid identities. Research on polymorphous perversities, varied sexualities, and the like further illustrate our impoverished understanding of love and intimacy in relationships as social processes (Herdt, 1996; Jankowiak, 1995). There are few systematic and sociologically rigorous discussions on *how* relationships that fall outside of the dyadic norm are intimately negotiated (Rust, 1996). Research on polyamory (defined as the love of many), for example, is in its beginning stages.

In terms of research on monogamy (Robinson, 1997), non-monogamy (a contested term that has been criticized for reproducing the ideal norm, monogamy),[1] polyfidelity, polyamory (Lano & Parry, 1995), and open relationships,[2] we know far more about dyadic romantic love than we do about romantic love in triads and other multiple relationships (Felmlee & Sprecher, 2000; Hall & Pramaggiore, 1996). As Munson and Stelboum (1999) show, multiple relationships can take many forms, such as the following: group marriage, primary and secondary relationships, and casual sexual involvement with two or more people, just to name a few. This research, which defines love as necessarily dyadic, also often fails to complicate the ways in which love changes throughout the life course and across different levels of social analysis such as race, class, gender, and sexuality for those in relationships beyond the dyad. Thus, in order to gain a better understanding of the social process of love, we suggest two modifications: (1) The definition of love must be expanded to account for relations both in a dyad and beyond the dyad; and (2) Analyses of love must be historically and culturally specific; ahistorical and ethnocentric accounts will necessarily impoverish future social investigations of love and relationships.

Jankowiak and Fischer's (1992) definition of romantic or *passionate love* captures the general way in which it is understood and discussed in the literature, both in anthropological accounts and across other social science disciplines:

Romantic love is "any intense attraction that involves the idealization of *the other*, within an erotic context, with the expectation of
enduring some time into the future." (p. 150; adopted from
Lindholm's (1988) definition, emphasis added)

Jankowiak and Fischer's interest lies in this earlier stage of love between two people where there is both a specific erotic context and an expectation that this love relationship will endure into the future. The
latter attachment phase of a relationship, however, is understood as consisting of duration, less emotional intensity, and a more friend-
ship-based relationship. Throughout this paper, we remain committed
to investigating the "erotic" phase of love.

While there is a dearth of literature on different emotional experiences (for example, love and intimacy) in most social science research,
anthropologists are the ones who have conducted studies that challenge
western preconceived notions of kinship, monogamy, and sexual practices (see especially Hua's 2001 study of the Na of China). In addition,
Jankowiak, Sudakov, and Wilreker (2005) recently conducted a study
of co-wife conflict and cooperation in multiple marriages, Goldstein
(1987) studies Tibetan fraternal polyandry, Weston (1997) discusses
new kinship patterns among gays and lesbians in the U.S., Dunne
(2000) re-conceptualizes gay fatherhood, and Strassberg (2003) com-
pares Mormon Fundamentalist Polygamy with "New Age" Polyamory.
All of these studies challenge Western fundamental constructions of
kinship, dyads, and heterosexuality while highlighting how some new
family forms, while not monogamous dyads, can still be very gendered
(Strassberg, 2003).

THE DYADIC IMAGINARY

Unlike many anthropologists researching relationships in "non-
Western" contexts, academics trained in the West continue to construct
gender and sexuality within narrowly defined binaries and thus render
relations outside monogamy, marriage, and kinship based on heterosexuality unreal or illegitimate (Rubin, 1984). Butler (2004) considers the
"ideology" of the dyad, suggesting that the "dyad is an achievement, not
a presupposition" (p. 146). Just as she argues regarding gender, any relationship (between two, three, or four people) is not a "natural" occur-
rence but, rather, an achievement and social process that shifts and
contorts, both spatially and temporally. For instance, instead of concep-

tualizing intimacy as static, we could think about it as a kind of "doing." Just as we "do" gender (West & Zimmerman, 1987) in our everyday interactions, intimacy and love changes over time, space, location, and as our bodies change.

In other work, Butler refers to these new possibilities of embodied interaction as a "materializing of possibilities" (Butler, 1990, p. 272). Butler (1990) adds that our understanding and experience of the dyad is deeply wedded to a fantasy notion of our "one true love"; however, those in dyads are actually, in reality, faced with their lover's past relationships, feelings, and desires that are not entirely related to the current dyad:

> But if we accept the desire for the Other might be desire for the Other's desire, and accept as well the myriad equivocal formulations of that position, then it seems to me that recognizing the Other requires assuming that the dyad is rarely, if ever, what it seems. (p. 146)

Further, this "idea" of loving another, one other person, also necessarily requires an acceptance of your lover's love of others, both real and imagined, past and present. Following this imagined formation of the dyad, while we imagine romantic love as necessarily related to love between two people, the real unintended consequence of this imagining is actually not truly dyadic. As Butler (1990) shows, our love of another is actually the love of many others: "when one recognizes that one is not at the center of the Other's history, one is recognizing difference" (p. 146).

Butler is not the first theorist to challenge the dyad. In 1973, John Alan Lee wrote: "pluralism has yet to become fully incorporated into our vocabulary of intimacy" (p. 6). The lack of pluralism in theoretical and empirical scholarship on love and intimacy is still felt today. Following Jankowiak and others' definitions of love as necessarily dyadic and anthropological constructions of kinship as heterosexual (Weston, 1997), relationships outside of the dyad are consistently rendered invisible. Mainstream theoretical frameworks do not inclusively account for non-dyadic relations as they relate to love, thus definitions and research on love do not fully address the nuances of personal relationships that do not fit a dyadic framework. In the next section, an historical review of the institution of marriage and coupling further illustrates the power and assumed legitimacy of the dyadic imaginary.

COUPLING HISTORIES:
MARRIAGE AND THE CONSTRUCTION
OF DYADIC LOVE

Consistent with the problematic status of the dyad and love as noted earlier, marriage and families are not terms easily conceptualized within a binary. A majority of the scholarship on marriage, couple relationships, and families historically and currently remain structured within a framework of "one true love," emotional intimacy, and heterosexuality. The couple relationship is traditionally central to our understanding of love and intimacy in families. Also, current accounts of historical constructions of families and love are often filtered though a modern lens of love- and intimacy-based relationships. Even with historical accounts of families consisting of more than just a couple and their children (i.e. grandparents, boarders, others' kin in the household), the language used to describe these families persistently constructs the couple as central to the family and renders other members as 'outsiders within' the family.

HISTORICAL ACCOUNT OF MARRIAGE/COUPLING:
PROBLEMS OF GENDER AND SEXUALITY

It is important to understand and view marriage as an historically changing institution. The problem with the current debate in the United States regarding the state of marriage is that it fails to account for the dramatic changes that occurred already in not only who marries, but also the shape marital unions take and the meanings they have for their members. Not only has the place of marriage in an individual's life changed over time, but changing gender roles and the creation of sexual identities have also revolutionized the way people view themselves within relationships. In order to better frame the need to recognize the dyadic imaginary to expand our notions of love, we will provide a brief historical overview of the three major periods of marriage in the United States: colonial/preindustrial, the Industrial revolution, and contemporary culture. As we note the historical trends in marriage, we will also discuss the changes in gender and sexuality that helped co-create marriage as both dyadic and heterosexual at various points in time.

Marriages in early American history centered on family-based production and economic survival; they were essentially economic arrangements (Coontz, 2005; D'Emilio & Freedman, 1988). Partner selection was based on finding an other-sexed partner who could help provide what was needed to maintain a family-based production system. Men sought women who were capable of having children and assisting around the home. Women wanted to marry men who were able to provide for a wife and children, either through a small business or farm. The combination of marriage being both a gendered institution and one rooted in reproduction provided an early basis for marriage being seen as a heterosexual institution. Both high infant mortality rates and the need for help around the farm necessitated large families. In addition, the family was not seen as a private unit. Often families had boarders and other extended family members living with them because society lacked the resources at this time to support individuals who were not based within a family. Men and women's relationships were primarily economically-based; strong family units were central to survival, thus marriage choices and childrearing were rooted in economic and practical choices, not those of love and romance.

One of the first major shifts in how marriage and love were understood occurred during the Industrial Revolution and shift to Victorian ideologies of love (Seidman, 1991). The relationships between individuals and their families were restructured in dramatic ways; individuals could now choose to leave their families of origin and support themselves in the new wage-based economy. In addition to supporting themselves, individuals were able to purchase many of the goods they had once relied on their families for, such as clothing, food, and shelter. This resulted in a shift in how individuals viewed their own family choices. Women were no longer tied to finding a husband who had assets and men did not have to wait to inherit land before marrying and starting a family; individuals had more control over leaving or staying in their families than ever before. The market economy allowed both men and women to leave their families of origin and determine for themselves how they wanted to live their lives (Giddens, 1992).

This change affected the way people sought marriage partners. Victorian ideologies of spiritual or romantic love started to appear, with good marital relationships being based in companionship (Seidman, 1991). Couples were seen as spiritually connected to one another, supporting ideologies of the time that understood pure partnerships as ones not based on sexual attraction. Rather, love was desexualized and seen as separate from sexuality; while sex was conceived of as a central and healthy part of a marriage, it was also seen as a force that could threaten marriage (Seidman, 1991). Although the concept of how people couple began to change, sexuality at this time was still primarily based on notions of reproduction and heterosexuality. While there is mixed evidence as to the norms surrounding proper sexuality within and outside marriage (see D'Emilio & Freedman, 1988; Seidman, 1991), heterosexuality remained the socially proper way of doing sexuality.

With this dramatic shift in how families were created as a result of industrialization, gender expectations for men and women started to shift (Coontz, 2005; D'Emilio & Freedman, 1988). The ideology of the separate spheres became more prominent among the wealthier white classes, with men and women each taking on specialized roles within the family. Men were members of the public sphere: they negotiated family matters that were located outside the home, such as paid work. Women, on the other hand, were constructed as being nurturers of the family whose sphere was within the home. With this, femininity was seen as pure and noble; in terms of female sexuality, women were seen as not interested in the purely sexual pleasures of sex. With this co-construction of gender and sexuality, women found it their job to make sure that their husbands maintained themselves as good sexual citizens (Seidman, 1991).

Contemporary expressions of marriage and love take their influence from earlier times. Yet, like the shift that occurred during the Victorian era, today we understand marriage and love as personal and individual. No longer are individuals tied to either their birth or marital families, resulting in many changes over the past sixty years that have greatly restructured the way we view intimacy and marriage. Individualism and ideologies of self-fulfillment manifest themselves in many ways and often compete with marriage. For example, nonmarital cohabitation, delay of first marriage, and high divorce rates have lead some sociologists to argue that marriage is becoming deinstitutionalized, or that the norms and purposes that marriage held are loosing their "power" and meaning (Cherlin, 2004). However, marriage continues to maintain and promote heterosexuality and dyadic love as normative (Ingraham, 1999). Although the overall percentage of women who ever marry has declined in recent decades, there remains a great desire to marry: approximately three quarters of American men and women have married by age 34 (Fields, 2004).

Love today is constructed around personal self-fulfillment and has become re-sexualized. Unlike the Victorian love that was seen as creating a complementary spiritual relationship, today's love is centered on personal fulfillment and enjoyment (Cherlin, 2004; Giddens, 1992; Seidman, 1991). When a relationship is no longer working, it is acceptable to end it and move on to a new love relationship. The idea of finding one true love remains prevalent today, despite the actualities of how individuals couple and uncouple. However, this "serial mo-

nogamy" is socially normalized and enforced; sex with multiple partners is not seen as a negative thing as long as it is done within dyads,
i.e., one coupled relationship at a time. The re-sexualization of love is
highlighted in the ways we discuss sexuality today. For example,
many now understand sex as a way of expressing love. This can most
clearly be seen in the fact that sexual intercourse is often referred to as
"love-making." This re-conceptualization also makes it possible to see
same-sex intimacies as legitimate. While sex and love are now connected, love and sex between two same-sex individuals is not seen as
completely illegitim famate (as long as it is dyadic). However, these
relationships are still held inferior to heterosexual unions in terms of
civil rights and marriage law.

Gender roles have also started to shift, both within and outside of
marriage. Individualism leads men and women to take on tasks that
have historically been designated for the other sex. Most notable is the
change in the ways women experience the world. Many women today
enter into the paid labor force and maintain employment even after marriage and childbirth (U.S Bureau of Labor Statistics, 2005). While the
roles women play in families have opened up new possibilities of creating new identities for women, male gender expectations in marriage and
love are still based in more traditional ideologies. Hochschild (1989) refers to the delay of men taking on more responsibilities in the home as
women spend more time in the paid labor market as the *stalled revolution*; while definitions of what is appropriate for women become more
fluid, masculinity is still constructed as dichotomous to femininity. The
issue of power in families remains consistent; men have the social and
political power to structure the family around their interests and needs.
When all is said and done, at the end of the day it remains the women's
responsibility to cook, clean, and raise children, regardless of any other
statuses she may hold.

Early family accounts are often structured on heteronormative models, even though these constructions of gender and sexuality were not
created until more recently. The assumption that the heterosexual nature
of these relationships equaled heterosexual identities and that love and
intimacy were the foundation of these relationships is problematic because these couple arrangements were not as much based in mutual love
and affection but instead reflected the social and economic situations of
the time. It was not until production was removed from the family that
the emergence of an ideology of love-based couple relationships
emerged. At this time we also start to see arguments for interracial and

same-sex partnerships; the ideology of "loving" another was thought to be strong enough to transcend old-fashioned social markers for who made an appropriate couple. However, consistent across the history of marriage and love, the idealization of the couple remains strong. Even today, when having multiple partners over the course of one's life is not considered out of the ordinary, the foundational ideal is that of a dyadic union.

While this overview highlights how marriage and love have been historically constructed as dyadic, there is one illustration that supports our larger argument: an example of non-dyadic love during the Victorian era. Many changes to how couples viewed marriage occurred during this time, which may have made possible one of the first times that non-dyadic love was an accepted practice. Romantic friendships allowed a woman to be married to a man yet have romantic friendships with other women (Faderman, 1992; Seidman, 1991). While there is some debate as to the romantic/sexual nature of these relationships, this example supports the notion that moving beyond erotic love as dyadic is crucial to fully understand it. For example, the debate with romantic friendships is centered on whether or not the women were in what modern terminology characterizes as "lesbian relationships." While we do see some evidence of non-dyadic love, previous scholars have maintained the dyadic conceptualization of love. The question asked regarding the nature of the women's relationships with one another-i.e., a woman loves either her husband or her female friend/lover-remains dyadic. The possibility for the women to love both is silenced under the current hegemonic conceptualization of love relationships as dyadic.

The dyadic imaginary has important implications for marriage and, in particular, the current same-sex marriage debate. The same-sex marriage debates today maintain notions of marriage being a heterosexual union because, critics argue, the history of marriage is based on heterosexuality and childrearing. However, with the changes to how love and intimacy are viewed and practiced, it is possible to explode the myth of marriage as an inherently heterosexual and dyadic institution. Thus, heterosexuality as an identity did not exist when marriage became the norm for couples to startiies. With the variety of options individuals have today in terms of how they want to live their lives, we cannot maintain that dyadic unions own marriage.

THEORETICAL APPLICATION OF THE DYADIC IMAGINARY TO ISSUES ON SEXUALITY AND MARRIAGE

Next we apply the dyadic imaginary to issues of same-sex marriage for those who identify as bisexual and/or queer. We do so in order to illustrate how the dyadic imaginary exposes the assumed dyadism surrounding and reinforced through contemporary discussions of marriage and intimate/erotic sexual relationships. The concept of the dyadic imaginary forces us to move beyond taken-for-granted notions of erotic relationships as existing solely within couples, unveiling the difference between ideology, i.e. dyadic relationships as sole legitimate (happy) relationships, and reality, i.e. the existence and experience of innumerable forms of desires, relationships, and familial units.

Debates concerning monogamy, non-monogamy, and other relationship forms are slowly becoming a part of discourse concerning sexuality, gender, and marriage. For example, in "Queer Parenting in the New Millennium," Nancy A. Naples (2004) notes:

> In the gay marriage debates, many scholars, students and activists have become 'quite impatient [with gay marriage discourse], stressing that this normalizing goal would lead inevitably to assimilation into a heterosexual regime, undermine radical queer organizing, and further marginalize those who did not fit into a monogamous dyad. (p. 680)

That is, as current debates concerning love, relationships, and marriage include and highlight same-sex unions, heterosexuality is made salient through the perpetuation of the heterosexual/homosexual binary. Also, while the same-sex marriage debate *appears* hyper-progressive, it continues to marginalize all other forms of relationships people construct and experience.

Using Demetriou's (2001) theory of the hybridization of *the hegemonic masculine bloc,* we can understand the same-sex marriage debate as a response to critiques on, for our purposes, hegemonic notions of love and relationships. Demetriou's theory of the hybridization of the hegemonic masculine bloc explains that hegemonic masculinities pick up and adopt attributes of gay masculinity that appear useful and do so in a manner that ultimately maintains hegemony. That is, the hegemonic bloc only shifts as much as is required to appear progressive, veiling the continuation of hegemony. The gay revolution of the 1960s and 1970s brought practices of hegemonic society under scrutiny and dubbed them homophobic and exclusionary. In response to this criticism, the same-sex dyad is picked up and adopted into contemporary marriage debates in a way that makes it appear as if hegemony is disintegrating. However, as Naples suggests, making the marriage debate the same-sex marriage debate continues to render invisible and illegitimate all other forms of relationships, including those that are typified by non-monogamous dyadic erotic love. Thus, hegemony is shifting, but only insofar as it is able to maintain dyadic gender and sexual binaries. It leaves intact both the heterosexual/homosexual binary and the dyadic imaginary. The question then becomes, does same-sex marriage challenge hegemonic notions of relationships? We suggest not.

This argument is in no way meant to marginalize the strides gays and lesbians have made within a society that institutionalizes heterosexuality in many ways, shapes, and forms (Ingraham, 1999). It is also not meant to suggest that marriage is in no way being deinstitutionalized and that this deinstitutionalization is not progressive. Rather, taking into consideration the dyadic imaginary, we believe it is important to look critically at the consequences of the same-sex marriage debate and highlight the ways it veils the exclusion of all other forms of love and relationships, including non-dyadic.

BISEXUALITY AND THE MARRIAGE DEBATE

Bringing bisexuality into contemporary debates on sexuality and marriage may superficially appear to complicate the relationship between sexuality, marriage, and the dyad. However, a closer analysis reveals that both bisexuality and marriage are problematic concepts. This is because shifts in personal meanings and experiences of love, desire, family, sexuality, and gender over time reflect social hegemonic ideologies that require people fit into narrowly defined gender and sexual binaries in order to participate in public, state-defined marriage ceremonies.

It may be tempting to argue that because the marriage debate is constructed along the lines of gay/straight, those who identify as bisexual are necessarily left out. But are they? If bisexuality is understood as one's coupling with either a same-sex or other-sex partner, and whose partners are divided by time, does bisexuality challenge/queer the contemporary marriage debate or does it fit right in? It is important to note that gender identities and experiences do not always reflect the woman/man binary. However, for the purposes of this paper and for discussion of the contemporary marriage debate as it relates to sexuality, we problematize same-sex and other-sex couplings because they reinforce an inaccurate gender binary.

Even if we intellectually understand non-dyadic love to include those whose partners are separated only by time (Anapol, 1997), perhaps even lengths of time, such non-dyadic love does nothing to challenge the current marriage debate. This is because state defined marriage and the marriage debate has not yet discussed gender and sexuality in a manner that focuses on embodiment and not identity. The state bases the right to marry on the outward appearance of gender and sexuality, therefore a person who identifies as bisexual can indeed marry as long as it is with someone who embodies the other-sex, or, in Massachusetts, also the same-sex. The only stipulation then becomes that of a dyad. Bisexuality perpetuates dyadic notions of coupledom and love, leaving unchallenged female/male, femininity/masculinity, and heterosexual/homosexual binaries.

Ultimately, bisexuality perpetuates the dyadic notion of coupledom. For example, a bisexual woman couples with and/or marries a man. Though she may have love for multiple people of multiple genders, despite the complex reality of her desires, she forms a supposed dyad, thus not posing a challenge to the current marriage debates. This is because she fulfills the requirements, posed by most states, to marry: one woman marrying one man. Taking into consideration our new concept of the dyadic imaginary, we must ask, if bisexuality and/or queerness is invoked as an identity that fits with practices of "loving" multiple genders (i.e., those who identify as a woman, man, transgender, genderqueer), how does one continue practicing bisexuality when in a "monogamous" marriage and/or dyad? Is it practiced at all? Do desires queer the relationship and thus the marriage? Or does the outward appearance and practice of the dyad sustain the dyadic imaginary? Is dyadism inherently problematic for those who "desire" multiple genders? How does one continue to practice queerness and/or bisexuality if they are fully embedded in a monogamous dyad? These are important empirical questions that explore the complex reality of erotic desires, love, and relationships and may only begin to be explored by taking the dyadic imaginary into consideration.

Bisexuality is technically invisible, but as long as it is understood and exercised along the lines of the dyad, those who identify as bisexual are indeed inadvertently included in the current marriage debate, as the debate now includes both other-sex and same-sex couples. Thus, using the dyadic imaginary as a theoretical framework, the incorporation of bisexuality into marriage debates does nothing to complicate the notion of "one true love."

Bisexuality does contradict the notion of "straight" marriage, but no more than does homosexuality. Thus, we suggest that the overt incorporation of bisexuality into the marriage debate would not challenge or queer it. We argue that it is not homosexuality and/or bisexuality in which the marriage debate should be solely embedded. Rather, by offering the theoretical framework of the dyadic imaginary, we encourage scholars and activists to also think critically about the notion of the dyad or the couple in order to further problematize marriage as an institution. Contemporary marriage is really an optimistic ideology that does not reflect people's real gender and sexual identities and practices. Marriage is therefore an institution that only guarantees state benefits and protection to very few.

The current marriage debate leaves much unsaid, concealing the variety of people's real life experiences and thus marginalizing non-dyadic relationships and families. As the institution of marriage stands today, even taking into consideration the same-sex marriage debate, many families are left without the ability to legally call one another family. This inability leaves people without rights to visit partners and children in hospitals and without the ability to share health insurance and social security with loved ones who support one another financially and emotionally. Ultimately, the current benefits of marriage, such as legal recognition of the relationship, tax breaks, and other forms of legal assistance, are regulated to heterosexual dyads, with the exception of Massachusetts that recognizes same-sex dyadic unions through marriage.

IMPLICATIONS OF THE DYADIC IMAGINARY FOR GENDER, SEXUALITY, AND MARRIAGE

Compulsory heterosexuality is to mainstream gender theories (Ingraham, 1994) as "the dyad" is to Euro-American theories concerning love, intimacy, sexuality, and kinship. Taking into consideration the dyadic imaginary, we agree with work that suggests marriage is a problematic institution. However, for the purpose of this paper, we are not simply interested in sexuality along the lines of gender, but rather pluralism and non-monogamy. If both the same-sex marriage debate and bisexuality reinforce hegemonic and dichotomous notions of legitimate love and relationships, we posit: What sort of non-dyadic love and relationships would challenge or queer the marriage debate? Would non-dyadic love where partners are not separated by time *or* dyadic and non-dyadic relationships that are not rooted in erotic sexual love, but still intimacy and dependency, challenge the marriage debate? For example, we plan in a later paper to expand the definition of love as erotic to include those relationships that are not sexual but are still rooted in dependency.[3] We will discuss these relationships as they are associated with both the dyadic imaginary and the contemporary marriage debate.

This paper is the first in what we anticipate to be a series of papers examining the dyadic imaginary as it relates to notions of love, gender/sexuality, families, and marriage. Given that little scholarship has examined non-dyadic love, we hope that this initial paper provides an invitation to other scholars to reexamine how we currently investigate queer and non-dyadic love, especially in how it is practiced in everyday life.

We are not interested in resolving the debate on marriage and sexuality within the confines of this paper. Rather, our goal for this paper is to apply our new theoretical framework in order to demonstrate the insufficiency and inaccuracy of both contemporary literature and debates concerning love, relationships, and marriage. We aim to spark debate regarding sexuality, marriage, non-monogamy, and the dyad. The dyadic imaginary helps us more fully understand what is left unsaid in the contemporary same-sex marriage debate and queer literature. Leaving the reality of non-dyadic love and relationships veiled by perpetually evoking the taken-for-granted dyadic imaginary, the current debates continue to exclude people and experiences from both the *theories* and *methodologies* used to study intimacy.

NOTES

1. To further complicate matters, Deporah Anapol (1997) argues that serial monogamy is, in fact, closer to polyamory than we would assume. She claims that those who engage in serial monogamy (different partners over time), in reality, have multiple mates that are only divided by time.

2. Terms and sexual practices have been contested: "it is a point of contention in the poly community whether "swinging" can be regarded as responsible non-monogamy" (Lano, et al. (eds.) 1995: vi).

3. We thank Steven Seidman for his suggestions regarding the definitions and terms we are using throughout this paper. In future work, we will expand these definitions and address deeper questions concerning how the dyadic assumption has remained pervasive in research and writing on romantic love/intimacy.

REFERENCES

Anapol, D. M. (1997). *Polyamory: The new love without limits.* San Rafael, CA: IntiNet Resource Center.

Brown, N. M., & Amatea, E. S. (2000). *Love and intimate relationships: Journeys of the heart.* Philadelphia, Pennsylvania: Brunner/Mazel.

Butler, J. (1990). Performative acts and gender constitution: An essay in phenomenology and feminist theory. In Sue-Ellen Case (Ed.), *Performing feminisms: Feminist critical theory and theatre* (pp. 270-282). Baltimore, MD: Johns Hopkins University Press.

Butler, J. (2004). *Undoing gender.* New York: Routledge.

Cherlin, A. (2004). The deinstitutionalization of American marriage. *Journal of Marriage and Family* 66:848-861.

Coontz, S. (2005). *Marriage, a history: From obedience to intimacy or how love conquered marriage.* New York: Viking Group.

Demetriou, D. Z. (2001). Connell's concept of hegemonic masculinity: A critique. *Theory and Society* 30:337-361.

D'Emilio, J., & Freedman, E. B. (1988). *Intimate matters: A history of sexuality in America.* New York: Harper and Row.

Dunne, G. (2000, January). *The different dimensions of gay fatherhood: Exploding the myths.* LSE Gender Institute Discussion Paper 8.

Faderman, L. (1992). *Odd girls and twilight lovers: A history of lesbian life in twentieth century America.* New York: Penguin Books.

Felmlee, D., & Sprecher, S. (2000). Close relationships and social psychology: Intersections and future paths. *Social Psychological Quarterly* 63:365-76.

Fields, J. (2004). American's family and living arrangements: 2003. *Current Population Reports,* 20-553. Washington, DC: U.S. Census Bureau.

Fisher, H. (1995). The nature and evolution of romantic love. In W. Jankowiak (Ed.), *Romantic passion: A universal experience?* New York: Columbia University Press.

Giddens, A. (1992). *The Transformation of intimacy: Sexuality, love and eroticism in modern societies.* California: Stanford University Press.

Goldstein, M. (1987). When brothers share a wife. In *Annual Editions: Anthropology.* Guilford, CT: McGraw-Hill/Dushkin.

Hall, D. E., & Pramaggiore, M. (Eds.). (1996). *RePresenting bisexualities: Subjects and cultures of fluid desire.* New York: New York University Press.

Herdt, G. (Ed.). (1994). *Third sex, third gender: Beyond sexual dimorphism in culture and history.* New York: Zone Books.

Hochschild, A. (1989). *The second shift.* New York: Avon.

Hua, C. (2001). *A society without fathers and husbands: The Na of China* (A. Hustvedt, Trans.). New York: Zone Books.

Ingraham, C. (1994). The heterosexual imaginary: Feminist sociology and theories of gender. *Sociological Theory* 12:203-19.

Ingraham, C. (1999). *White weddings: Romancing heterosexuality in popular culture.* New York: Routledge.

Jankowiak, W. (1995). Introduction. In W. Jankowiak (Ed.), *Romantic passion: A universal experience?* New York: Columbia University Press.

Jankowiak, W., & Fischer, E. F. (1992). A cross-cultural perspective on romantic love. *Ethnology* 31:149-155.

Jankowiak, W., Sudakov, M., & Wilreker, B.C. (2005). Co-wife conflict and cooperation. *Ethnology 44*(1), 81-98.

Johnson, P. (2004). Haunting heterosexuality: The homo/het binary and intimate love. *Sexualities* 7(2):31-53.

Lano, K., & Parry, C. (Eds.). (1995). *Breaking the barriers to desire: Polyamory, polyfidelity and non-monogamy–New approaches to multiple relationships.* Nottingham: Five Leaves Publications.

Lee, J. A. (1973). *Colours of love: An exploration of the ways of loving.* Toronto: New Press.

McCullough, D., & Hall D. S. (2003). Polyamory: What it is and what it isn't. *Electronic Journal of Human Sexuality* 6. Retrieved August 12, 2006, from www. ejhs.org.

Munson, M., & Stelboum J. P. (Eds.). (1999). *The lesbian polyamory reader: Open relationships, non-monogamy, and casual sex.* New York: The Haworth Press, Inc.

Naples, N. (2004). Queer parenting in the new millennium. *Gender & Society* 18:679-684.

Robinson, V. (1997). My baby just cares for me: Feminism, heterosexuality, and non-monogamy. *Journal of Gender Studies* 6(2):143-57.

Rose, S. (2000). Heterosexism and the study of women's romantic and friend relationships. *Journal of Social Issues* 56(2):315-328.

Rubin, G. S. (1984). Thinking sex: Notes for a radical theory of the politics of sexuality. In Kauffman (Ed.), *America Feminist Thought at Century's End: A Reader.* Cambridge, MA: Blackwell.

Rust, P. C. (1996). Monogamy and polyamory: Relationship issues for bisexuals. In B. A. Firestein (Ed.), *Bisexuality: the psychology and politics of an invisible Minority.* London: SAGE Publications.

Seidman, S. (1991). *Romantic longings: Love in America, 1830-1980.* New York: Routledge.

Shanley, M., Cohen, J., & Chasman, D. (2004). *Just marriage.* Oxford: Oxford University Press.

Sheff, E. (2006, March). *Destabilizing the dyad: Polyamorists queering non-traditional families.* Paper presented at the Southern Sociological Society Annual Conference, New Orleans, LA.

Strassberg, M. (2003, April). *Comparing Mormon fundamentalist polygamy with "new age" polyamory.* Paper presented at the *Feminisms and Fundamentalisms Conference* at Cornell Law School: Feminism and Legal Theory Program, Ithaca, NY.

U.S Bureau of Labor Statistics. (2005, May). *Women in the labor force: A workbook.* Retrieved August 2006 from: http://www.bls.gov/cps/wlf-databook2005.htm.

West, C., & Zimmerman, D. H. (1987). Doing gender. *Gender and Society* 1(2): 125-151.

Weston, K. (1997). *Families we choose: Lesbians, gays, kinship.* New York: Columbia University Press.

On the Potential and Perils of Same-Sex Marriage: A Perspective from Queer Theory

Ajnesh Prasad

What we need now is quiet discussion of the difficulties that hold back our understanding of same-sex behavior and suggestions about how to get beyond them. (Kutsche, 1997, p. 495)

We have not tended to look at the social forms particular to heterosexuality, or to consider the effects that heterosexuality has on a person, except for the limited times and occasions when *they* impinge enough on our consciousness to provide a momentary contrasting backdrop. (Hunter, 1991, p. 368)

Just as the heart of male privilege lies in the 'right' of access to women, so the heart of heterosexual privilege lies in the 'heart' of access to sexual-romantic-marital-familial relationships. (Calhoun, 1994, p. 581)

At the World Congress of Families (WCF) held in Mexico City in March 2004, delegates from around the globe and from a mosaic of religions gathered under a conservative mandate to affirm the orthodox family. Amongst those who convened was Ellen Sauerbrey, the United States representative to the United Nations Commission on the Status of Women, a position so appointed by the Bush administration, who passionately declared: "As one of the pillars of civilization, families must remain strong and we must defend them during a time of great change" (cited in Kane, 2004, p. 57). The "great change" which Sauerbrey decries, encapsulates what she and other social conservatives deem to be the *unnatural* diversification of the traditional family, of which the most pronounced and visible challenge is posited in form of same-sex unions. It is not surprising, then, that the possibility of such unions manifesting in formal marriage, an exclusionary institution hitherto reserved for 'heterosexuals,' has tenaciously put the family values movement on the offensive (Cahill, 2005, p. 170). The WCF is but one forum through which this movement coordinates internal commonalities and collectively unleashes a vehement assault against those individuals that are seen to subvert the conventional family through engaging in and demanding recognition for their seemingly heterodox lifestyles.

There is an urgent need, I would argue, for progressive thinkers and social justice activists to advocate for the cause of same-sex marriage. At the very least, the debate over same-sex marriage provides the litmus test for assessing the cultural limitations on equality. Indeed, for its ability to ascertain provocative, zealous, and often ideologically polarized positions, same-sex marriage may emerge, if it has not done so already, as the vanguard issue for early twenty-first century's rights discourse.

In this paper, I offer exploratory analysis on same-sex marriage as a concern for public policy and critical theory. To this end, this paper is divided into three interdependent sections. First, I explain how the orthodox marriage has been conceptualized thus far. I focus primarily on how traditional marriage's socially constructed derivation undergirds an overarching assumption of ontological sexual difference. Here I am indebted to the ideas of Myra Hird developed in two graduate courses at Queen's University. I also delve into the dominant critiques that have been cast against marriage by scholars from within and outside the feminist community. Second, I illustrate how queer theorists appreciate sexuality, and how this appreciation fundamentally repudiates the premise upon which marriage pivots: heteronormativity. Again, many of these ideas were developed by Hird in the graduate courses. In the final section, I elucidate how queer theorists might respond to same-sex marriage, accentuating both its potential and perils. In short, I make a case for same-sex marriage, albeit, not without some reservations.

Whilst I contend that marriage ought to be an institution available to same-sex couples, my support remains tenuous insofar as I forward this argument strictly on grounds of symmetrical equality; that I deem it to be unjust for heterosexuals to exclusively benefit from certain legal and political rights on the one hand and a brand of cultural recognition on the other.

Within this purview equality should be contextualized critically and not reduced to rights discourse alone, however. As such, I do not accept the
flawed argument, promoted by the reigning Conservative Party of Canada
among others, that intimate relationships between members of the
same-sex should be classified under the category of *civil unions*, in which
homosexuals would be permitted to enjoy the same rights as heterosexuals
yet without the designation of marriage. As the dean of Osgoode Hall Law
School, Patrick Monahan (2005) asserts:

> [S]eperate is not equal . . . Denying gays and lesbians the right to
> marry (while permitting them to enter into relationships that bear
> all the legal attributes of marriage) can only be based on the dis-
> criminatory assumption that gays and lesbians are unworthy to
> participate in the legal and social institution of marriage. (p. A15)

In this regard, the conventional marriage shows itself to be the institutional
front of heterosexism-an establishment from which non-heterosexuals are
barred. Reasoning from this observation, I continue to be opposed to marriage's prejudicial effects, which include among other things, the fortifica-
tion of inequality through the reification of patriarchy and heterosexism,
and the unnecessary regulation of human sexual expression.

This paper is indebted to Adrienne Rich's (1980, p. 659) remark on
marriage made more than a quarter of a century ago: "We have been
stalled in a maze of false dichotomies which prevents our apprehending
the institution as a whole: 'good' versus 'bad' marriages; 'marriage for
love' versus arranged marriage." In attempting to transcend this maze, I
hope this paper assists in achieving what Paulo Freire refers to as
"conscientization," a critical awareness and engagement that would encourage self and collective realization (cited in hooks, 1994, p. 14).
With the ongoing acrimonious debate over same-sex marriage manifesting in political and popular forums across the United States, Canada,
and elsewhere, there is an imminent need to develop diverse perspectives through conscientization, so to fully appreciate the ramifications
imparted by this divisive issue.

I-MARRIAGE:
RELIGION, POLITICS, ECONOMICS, AND CULTURE

The orthodox conception of marriage, ensconced in the assumption
that it is the purveyor of kinship relations, has long been an institution

through which to reify social inequalities and sustain political hierarchies. In this section, I underscore the socially constructed origins of marriage by engaging with a plethora of theoretical schools, and subsequently explicate how marriage is customarily premised on the essentialist foundation of ontological sexual difference. Any discussion on marriage should, however, commence with consideration of the realm in which the institution is most commonly situated, that is, of course, religion. For reasons of brevity and contextual relevance the discussion of religion here is intentionally focused on Christianity.

The Christian right makes reference of the Bible to purport marriage to be a natural event, part of the human experience from which few-mainly members of the clergy-ought to be exempt. In their claims for maintaining marriage as a strictly heterosexual institution which unifies one man and one woman through what they delineate to be most sacrosanct of bonds, marriage and God's law are habitually conflated;[1] thereby, situating the institution almost wholly within the realm of religion, and either entirely precluding or relegating as incidental, other ideological variables that have motivated its endurance. Indeed, as Andrew Lister (2004, p. 50) notes, it is commonly believed that "the institution of marriage was structured according to God's will," and equally, "it was God who empowered husbands to rule." It may be expected, then, for the social and the legal meaning of marriage to remain grounded in the allocution of the divine. Take, for instance, how marriage was understood in the classic 1866 case over polygamy, *Hyde v. Hyde*. The presiding judge concludes: "I conceive that marriage, as understood in Christendom, may for this purpose be defined as the voluntary union for life of one man and one woman, to the exclusion of all others" (*Hyde v. Hyde*, 1866, p. 133). The Supreme Court of Canada has astutely observed that this interpretation of marriage rendered, "a society of shared values where marriage and religion were thought to be inseparable" (*Reference re Same-Sex Marriage*, 2004, p. 22). In other words, the religious-or more accurately here, the Judeo-Christian-definition of marriage permeates jurisprudence and becomes a constituent of the Western legal canon.

Moreover, because the moral family is validated by the level of their adherence to God's image and regulated by the divine tenets so proscribed by God, the Christian right has few complications in extending their theological position unto other social realities, such as the rearing of children and the maintenance of positive cultural values. This is evident in the remarks made by born again Christian George W. Bush (2006) in a recent presidential radio address: "Ages of experience have taught us that the commitment of a husband and a wife to love and to serve one another promotes the welfare of children and the stability of society" (also see Schowengerdt, 2002, pp. 506-509). Evangelicalist James Dobson (2004) has even gone so far as to predict that the blasphemous legalization and cultural acceptance of same-sex marriage will unthread the very fabric of Western civilization. Whereas Christians are not homogenous in their denunciation of same-sex marriage (Adam, 2004, pp. 273-274), orthodox followers have largely, and at times credulously, declared their abhorrence for the possibility of lesbian and gay couples being afforded access to this institution.[2]

Notwithstanding the integral contributions imparted by Judeo-Christian arguments into this debate, for it to move forward it is crucial to envision marriage in relation to how it engenders material consequences and how it has evolved. Even a cursory analysis of marriage across cultures and times-and in contexts precluding religion-divulges a disturbing, if not, an entirely contemptuous genealogy. During the ancient period, Hebrew law for example, dictated that should a woman become widowed then her deceased husband's brother ought to take her as his wife. In ensuring the prevalence of certain bloodlines and the patriarchal consolidation of private property, the purpose of this practice was far from benevolent. Up until the eighteenth-century, marriage was the primary method of transferring property, occupational status, personal contacts, money, tools, livestock and women across generations and kin groups (Hunt as cited in Coontz, 2004, p. 977). More recently, the prohibition of interracial marriage, often codified in law, was part of a broader project guaranteeing racial segregation and white hegemony. Indeed, it was not until the 1967 landmark decision in *Loving v. Virginia* did the American Supreme Court finally declare miscegenation laws to be unconstitutional (Stacey, 1996, p. 121). In an endeavor to meet ideological ends, each of these examples posits marriage in the context of the socio-political and the political economy rather than preserving it exclusively within religious conviction (for an excellent discussion on the evolution of marriage, see Coontz, 2005). As such, it is imperative that when conceptualizing marriage that it be assessed holistically and not reduced to theology alone.

At minimum, marriage should be contextualized first as an institution governing cultural bodies, and second in terms of how it traverses with other social systems that construct our heterogeneous realities. Several erudite writers, from a plethora of disciplines and political commitments, have engaged with the lofty assignment of comprehensively appraising marriage as a socio-political institution.

In his book *The Origin of the Family, Private Property and the State* (1986/1884), Friedrich Engels presents a superb critique of marriage through a class-based analysis. He depicts the derivation of the monogamous patriarchal marriage as being engendered by the socio-economic subjugation of one sex (read: female) by the other (read: male). Engels conjectures that the dynamics of marriage, and particularly the division of labor within it, render men and women in the roles of the bourgeois and the proletariat, respectively. These socio-economic positions become congealed by the public/private dichotomy, which obligates the man to sell his labor on the public market and economically sustain *his* family. By being the one responsible for his family's solvency, Engels hypothesizes that this ensures his paternalistic supremacy over his wife and children who are relegated to the private domain. Thus, according to Engels, women's liberation is diametrically contingent upon their ability to enter and adapt to the public labor market and successfully abolish the patriarchal marriage which is presently the quintessential source for their marginalization.

Extending from Engel's critique, many feminists observe marriage to fabricate a seemingly judicious and unproblematic relationship between women and men, whereby the former's oppression is systematized into the natural, or is otherwise rationalized away. Carole Pateman (1988) contends that marriage guarantees the sexual contract which affords husbands citizenship while, in tandem, conceiving of the wife as the subordinate Other. Because of the disadvantageous social positioning of women, almost universally, it is certainly not exceptional for the patriarchal marriage to be represented as being beneficial for women. Patricia Mann (1994) provides an excellent analysis on this standpoint:

> [P]atriarchal marriage, as an institutionalized structure of kinship placing social boundaries on the physical vulnerability of women, offered obvious advantages for a woman. By accepting the sexual and social demands of one man, by agreeing to provide him with heirs and to serve him, a woman could secure his protection from the sexual threats of other men. (p. 69)

Within this framework, the marital relationship between women and men is a corollary not of love or even non-coercive decision-making, but instead, it is a contract resultant from gendered lived realities. Sex and reproductive faculties become commodities for exchange through which women acquire physical security from the male sexual gaze. Baumeister and Vohs (2004) concur inasmuch as they render intimate heterosexual relationships to be rooted in one sex providing gender-specific services to the other, for what is assumed to be, mutual gain.[3]

Other scholars, particularly political economists, have also conceptualized marriage as a contractual arrangement. In 1973-74 Gary Becker, a Nobel laureate of economics, published two articles in the *Journal of Political Economy* in which he encouraged for postulating a theory of marriage on market dynamics. He elaborates that because women and men compete for partners, and whose selections are restricted by a range of variables including race, education, and financial endowments, it can be logically inferred that there already exists a market in marriages (Becker, 1973, p. 814; also see Becker, 1974). Becker conjectures his theory on two basic assumptions: (1) that each individual seeks to find a partner who will maximize her/his utility, and, (2) that equilibrium governs the marriage market so to ensure that no person could readily change partners and benefit erroneously. What ought to be ascertained foremost from Becker's study is his recourse to "complimentarity." For Becker, sex complimentarity between women and men manifests in love and children, which ultimately "determines the gain from marriage" (Becker, 1973, p. 819). Joyce Jacobsen (1994, pp. 76-77), has extended the political economy perspective by amplifying the profit of marriage and the family unit in terms of what she calls "complementary production processes"-a system which maximizes time efficiency for the individual members of the household.

The notion of sex complimentarity is integral to the functioning of the heterosexual, patriarchal marriage and is, indeed, the cornerstone of how the institution has often been conceptualized thus far. Sex complimentarity operates from the assumption of ontological sexual difference, which affirms the claim that females and males are inherently different.[4] Through the reproduction of sex differences, supposedly codified by ontology, women and men undertake distinct yet complimentary roles which, through their repeated practice come to be understood as natural (Hird, 2004a, pp. 20-24). The forum in which these gendered roles are most unproblematically exhibited is the patriarchal, heterosexual marriage-an institution that demands for a "stable relationship to male authority" (Stacey, 1996, p. 69). As Jean Elshtain (2003, p. 40) points out, sex complimentarity "affords a sense of partnership, of what it means to be in community and in communion." In so doing, it ensures that the inequalities apparent in the relationship between the husband and the wife are interpreted not only as just but also natural. When the heterosexual marriage becomes conflated with the *natural* it conversely catalyzes the establishment of heteronormativity, or what is the "normative idealization of heterosexuality" (Hird, 2004a, p. 27).

It need also be mentioned that by pivoting on heterosexual complimentarity, the orthodox conception of marriage precludes not only same-sex couples from participating in the institution of marriage but it equally constrains partner choice among bisexuals. Namely, it restricts a bisexual individual's right to marry to those instances when s/he is engaged in a relationship with a member of the opposite-sex. Further, because marriage is posited on the fixed reference point of heterosexuality which is naturally contrasted with homosexuality, as will be discussed in the following section, sexual identities that fall in between are rendered invisible in the discourse of marriage.

As alluded in Cheshire Calhoun's quote at the introduction of this paper, heterosexual privilege is manifest, at least in part, of the marital relationship. At the broader conceptual level, this privilege is sustained from the redundant processes that affirm heteronormativity, with the institution of marriage serving as its most potent agent. By undermining heteronormativity, queer theory offers invaluable critique of traditional marriage. Queer theory is able to illuminate the intricate nuances of human sexuality which have been systematically made invisible in the debate over same-sex marriage; such as by identifying 'bisexual' tendencies in individuals who express sexual attraction toward both women and men. In the following section, I survey the ethos of queer theory in an attempt to ascertain an innovative perspective that presents a timely contribution to the debate over same-sex marriage.

THE EFFICACY OF QUEER THEORY

Queer theory has humble beginnings insofar as it is a hybrid manifestation of critical bodies of thought that precede it. It materialized from renewed interest in sexuality studies exhibited within feminist and postmodernist discourses of the late 1980s. While it was initially a term-coined by Teresa de Lauretis in 1990-to revitalize the complacency of lesbian and gay studies, it quickly gained currency as being suggestive of "*new* repertories of political mobilization" (Epstein, 1994, p. 118; *emphasis mine*).

At the crux of queer theory's political project is the underlying objective to disarticulate heteronormativity from the alchemy of social power upon which it is currently grounded. In so doing, it extends from earlier constructionist works to show sexuality to be a phenomenological corollary (Rich, 1980; Weeks, 1986). Heteronormativity is the pivotal element in fabricating and sustaining the ethos governing contemporary sexual regimes. According to the constitutive laws of heteronormativity:

A man has:	desire-to-be M	desire-for F
A woman has:	desire-to-be F	desire-for M
		(Sinfield, 2002, p. 126)

Within this framework, genital determinism is rendered to be a categorical truth and gender socialization is equally considered part of the ontological reality. Consequently, deviations from these laws-which include non-heterosexual subjectivities and possession of indefinite sex morphologies such as individuals born with the intersex condition-are labeled as aberrations, and are often persecuted (Hird, 2000). In addition, through the fabrication of normalized heterosexuality and its juxtaposed inferior difference, fixed sexual object choice is ensured; which aids in the reification of the ideographic heterosexual/homosexual dichotomy (Grindstaff, 2003, pp. 264-265). Derrida's (1976) poststructuralist critique suggests that this dichotomy is essential to the preservation of heterosexuality as a privileged site of sexual practice; it is by way of the censured homosexual that the heterosexual is accorded an inert and unproblematic sexual identity.

Queer theory's mandate becomes especially salient in light of recent attempts to undermine the fluidity in human sexuality. For example, in a 2005 article published in the *New York Times* entitled "Straight, Gay or Lying: Bisexuality Revisited," Benedict Carey questions the normative existence of bisexuality in males. Citing initial studies undertaken by psychologists at Northwestern University, the author suggests that males who assume the label of bisexuality are not usually bisexual insofar as they are unlikely to be equally attracted to males and females. Rather Carey indicates that most males who claim bisexuality are either wholly or predominately homosexual. The questions that we should be asking remain out of the scope of such studies which are problematically entangled with covert heterosexist biases. Why, for example, is our culture so resolved on invalidating the experiences of bisexual men? Tangentially related, why is bisexuality in women seemingly marginalized in this inquiry? The very rationale for this study-and subsequently the conclusions drawn from it-serve two purposes that should be mentioned here: (1) it informs and reinforces the conventional appreciation of sexual identity and sexual practice that pivots on the homosexual/heterosexual continuum, and, (2) it displays a cultural discomfort with males who discredit the enabling hegemonic edifices of heterosexuality and masculinity.

In response, queer theory attempts to illustrate the innate fallaciousness of heteronormativity and likewise restrictive sexual categories, by presenting them to be part of a cultural ideology resultant of social discourses. That is, queer theory seeks to "denaturalize and resignify bodily categories" in an effort to reveal the disjunctive incoherencies in the seemingly natural, and biologically situated, association between sex, gender, and sexual desire (Butler, 1990, p. xii).[5] That mainstream appreciation of human sexuality, especially since the decline in influence of Freudian psychoanalysis, has been informed by biology-and cognately, evolutionary psychology (Hird, 2006)-makes queer theory to be a vital analytical model for sexual inquiry.

Queer theorists have been highly suspect of biology for essentializing tractable narratives regarding sex, sexual difference, and sexuality (Connell, 1987). Two such narratives are pertinent to this analysis: First, that there are only two sexes, and they are genetically differentiated and verified by chromosomes, and second, that there are *a priori* sexual orientations, or that which "[defines] homosexual, heterosexual, and bisexual partner choice in human beings" (Ehrhardt, 1979, pp. 150-151). These two narratives are certainly interrelated as the latter is directly contingent upon the saliency of the former.

Queer theorists disclaim the pervasive assumption that there exists only two sexes-males and females-and that these two sexes are inherently different, thus, producing the sex dichotomy (Hird, 2004a). This dichotomy has shown to be laden in a stringent power hierarchy in which "[m]en become the norm, women the problem to be explained" (Moi, 2004, p. 844). Queer theorists qualify their repudiation of the two-sex model from the works of numerous scholars, across a range of disciplines, who have chronicled how-as well as why-we understand sex and sex differences. For example, historians Londa Schiebinger (1989) and Thomas Laqueur (1990) each provide a genealogy of the social construction of sex in the past few centuries. Biologists Anne Fausto-Sterling (2000) and Evelyn Fox Keller (1985) demonstrate how the essentialist appreciation of sexual difference is propagated by the androcentric predilection in the *natural* sciences. Anthropologist Emily Martin (1991) examines the reification of orthodox gender roles in research concerning the sperm and the egg, and sociologist Alan Petersen (1998) cites how sex differences are perpetuated in a seminal anatomy text. Amplified by each of these scholars is the idea that the conventional understanding of sex differences is a corollary, not of the Archimedean model of disembodied knowledge, but rather of specific cultural manifestations (Prasad, 2005, p. 81). As such, there is judicious evidence to reason that akin to gender "[w]e are all doing sex" (Hird, 2002, p. 363)-which is to deduce, in contrast to popular conception, that sex is largely morphology rather than ontology (for a more comprehensive discussion of these issues, see Hird, 2004a, pp. 29-49).

Sexual difference is the fundamental building block for heterosexuality (Hird, 2004a, p. 27). Queer theorists underscore that without stable definitions of male and female, and the bifurcated gender identities it subsequently produces, heterosexuality would not only be unattainable but it would also be nonsensical (Hird, 2004a, pp. 26-28). In fact, constructionist scholars have noted that heterosexuality as a concept was conceived only in 1892 through its contrast with homosexuality (Halperin, 1990, p. 17), and homosexuality itself was an invention of the ideological currents of the late nineteenth-century; of which its paramount objective was the establishment of heteronormativity (see Katz, 1995). Elucidated in this process, is the notion that "gender informs sexuality; sexuality confirms gender" (Fracher & Kimmel, 1995, p. 367). In depicting gender and sexuality to be an interlocking social phenomenon, wherein one verifies the other, queer theory explicates how sexuality neither subscribes to biological derivation nor metaphysical ontology. As such, bodies should not be considered to be static slaves to their biology (Fausto-Sterling, 2004, p. 31).

Furthermore, for queer theorists, categories of heterosexuality, homosexuality, and bisexuality are inherently erroneous as they are affixed to the idea that sexuality is indifferent to time, space, and thus, experience. In contrast, queer theory amplifies how sexuality is in an unremitting process, continually tentative on the interplay and praxis between external sociological forces and internal psychology. The assertion that sexuality-as well as gender-is fluid vexes its inert definition promoted by essentialists. Unlike the biological determinist school of thought, queer theory's interpretation of sexuality is consistent with the rich diversity of human sexual practices exhibited, to varied degrees of prevalence, throughout history. Even the renowned sex researcher, Alfred Kinsey (1948, 1953), indicated that it was impossible to ascertain, in both women and men, the precise number of persons who are heterosexual or homosexual. According to Kinsey's extensive research, it is only possible to determine sexual behavior at any given time. Herein, Kinsey's observation parallels a principle of queer theory-that temporal variables play an imperative role in cultivating sexuality.

A cursory reading of queer theory may lead to the mistaken notion that it asserts, or advocates for, universal bisexuality. This is a misconception inasmuch as bisexuality remains fixed on biological sex, which queer theory attempts to eschew. That is, the traditional definition of bisexuality suggests that a subject has sexual desire for members of both *sexes*; thereby, validating the primacy of genital morphology and sex dimorphism (Hird, 2004a). Instead, queer theory emphasizes (discursive) identity, and particularly the great potential of agency within identity; therein capturing the liminal transgressions that are endemic to human sexuality. For instance, how should we understand the body politic of male lesbians (Prasad, 2006; Zita, 1994a), which entails an *opposite-sex* couple in which the male identifies as a woman? Does this couple still remain within the conventions of heterosexuality or are its constituents more accurately lesbians? Moreover, in moving the query from identity politics to phenomenology, what would it mean if this same couple engaged in sexual practices in which the male performed in the passive role while the female performed in the active role? Bisexual perspectives that are predicated on genital determinism lack the necessary mechanisms to respond to these questions while holistically appreciating the idiosyncrasies of human sexuality.

Similarly, the aforementioned questions are mute when they are contextualized in the current same-sex marriage debate. Indeed, ongoing same-sex marriage discourse has yet to transcend the overly reduced assumption that sexuality subscribes to a static corporeal ontology. Queer theory recognizes that for it to be possible for a male or female to embody, appropriate, and ultimately stage a role that is incongruent with their biological sex, then the naturalized systems of gender upon which heteronormativity is assembled is also revealed to be manifest of a series of redundant performances.

It is important to note that in being a corollary of feminism and postmodernism, queer theory is able to avoid hazardous trajectories apparent within each project when embarked upon separately. As Nancy Fraser and Linda Nicholson (1997) explain, feminist theories reliance on essentialism is dangerous and laden with ambiguities, whereas postmodernist criticism against normative theorizing-or, what are grand analyses of social macrostructures-is counterintuitive. Postmodernist-feminist theory, alternatively, is "explicitly historical, attuned to the cultural specificity of different societies and periods and . . . inflected by temporality, with historically specific institutional categories" (Fraser & Nicholson, 1997, pp. 143-144). In positing queer theory within feminist-postmodernist thought, sexuality is conjectured to be in constant flux; in a state of Deleuzian "becoming" from the symbiosis between subject and society (see Deleuze & Guattari, 1987). In this way, whilst queer theory is often considered a strand of inquiry that came into existence in the 1990s, its substantive hypotheses can logically be traced to, at the very latest, Foucault's (1990 [1978]) work on the history of sexuality.

This section set out to provide an overview of how queer theory comprehends human sexuality. If queer theorists are correct in suggesting that sexuality is an unremitting process, then, it will certainly have profound impacts on a range of applicable public policy concerns. Next I turn to explore how queer theorists may approach the polemical question of same-sex marriage.

QUEER THEORY AND SAME-SEX MARRIAGE: STRANGE BEDFELLOWS?

Numerous scholars, the seeming majority of whom belong to the family values campaign, have detailed the fruitfulness of marriage without seriously considering its innate dilemmas (for example, see Waite & Gallagher, 2000). As I illustrated in the first section, marriage is not an institution without its many faults. I am suspect of marriage on several fronts: As a feminist, I understand marriage to channel women's oppression into a socially acceptable institution; as a queer theorist, I view marriage to register sexuality into overly reduced categories; and, as an activist for social justice, I consider marriage to be the vanguard for heterosexism par excellence. It is certainly not unexpected for scholars who are sensitive to these concerns to entirely deprecate marriage for being a systematized organization that impedes the egalitarian project for collective liberation (Card, 1996).

Progressive thinkers who have concluded marriage to be a delimiting and a discriminatory institution should not dismiss it posthaste, however. It remains the case that marriage, notwithstanding its virtues beyond religion, or the lack thereof, is amongst the most influential institutions bearing upon people's lives. As a critical school of thought which as mentioned already borrows strengths from both feminism and postmodernism, queer theory has the prerogative to engage in liminal discourse whereby it may ascertain innovative solutions to complex questions. Hence, I believe the rupture between the constantly fluid sexuality and an essence-based institution such as marriage may be tentatively negotiated in the context of queer theory. As Susan Burgess

(2005, p. 126) reminds us, "[q]ueer theory does more than simply unveil the messiness of the supposed purity of the . . . heterosexual/homosexual [binary]." Indeed, it suggests that there may be "no tidy resolution" for the inquiries it makes; therein prompting us to identify provisional solutions to contemporary problems of inequality, less than perfect though the temporary results may be.

It should be clarified here that I concur with feminist philosopher Claudia Card (1996) in conceiving of marriage as an encumbering establishment, overtly intrusive to free sexual as well as emotional expression. Conceding that it will remain a strong institution, not to be eradicated in the near future at least, the pragmatic short-term objective should be, in my opinion, the dislodging of marriage from its fixed reference points of heterosexuality and patriarchy. In exhibiting the social construction of sexual difference-which is a prerequisite for patriarchy-and in repudiating ontological sexuality-which is pertinent to heterosexuality's existence-queer theory obfuscates traditional marriage. It queers marriage.

It needs to also be noted that the queer marriage does differ from same-sex marriage insofar as a same-sex relationship is not a necessary precursor for the queer marriage. A trans performance exhibited by one partner or both in a marriage that is socially understood to be heterosexual-namely, the relationship consists of a biologically-read female and a biologically-read male-can legitimately constitute an example of the queer marriage (Hird, 2004b).[6] The queer marriage is not so much concerned about the anatomy of those engaged in marriage as it is preoccupied with destabilizing the normalization of heterosexual patriarchy. In sum, the queer marriage seeks to defy the dichotomy of good (read: heterosexual, male-headed) versus bad (read: homosexual, female-headed) households (Fraser, 2000, p. 114); it makes marriage more ameliorable by not excluding the already disenfranchised from having full standing in the institution.[7]

The legalization of same-sex marriage would effectively subvert marriage from being an institution that oscillates around heterosexuality; therein, challenging the "mundane" heterosexism that functions as a normative segment of social life (Peel, 2001, p. 541). Borrowing from Fraser's (1995, p. 77) analysis, by imparting same-sex couples with the right to marriage, they would be obtaining an integral form of cultural recognition that would undermine first, "the authoritative constructions of norms that privilege heterosexuality" and second, "the cultural devaluation of homosexuality." That is to say, the cultural persecution encountered by individuals engaged in same-sex relationships may be remedied by affording them equal legal rights and recognitions (Fraser, 1995, p. 77). This necessarily translates to full legal marriage, completely equivalent to those of opposite-sex-or more accurately, *different-sexed*-couples.

It should be underscored that civil unions in which same-sex couples are granted the identical benefits of marriage enjoyed by opposite-sex couples, yet without the formal designation of marriage, is not entirely comparable (Monahan, 2005). This has however been a popular cure invoked by activist courts in both Canada and the United States. In the 1999 case *Baker v. Vermont*, heard in the state's Supreme Court, a unanimous decision rendered that same-sex couples are entitled to the equivalent treatment as opposite-sex couples, as anything otherwise would infringe upon Vermont's constitution. As a remedy, the Court recommended that the state legislature either legalize same-sex marriage or invent another structure through which same-sex couples may utilize rights stemming from marriage. In 2000, the legislature elected for the latter option and instituted a programme for civil unions. Similarly the Supreme Court of Canada's ruling in *M. v. H.* (1999) declared that Ontario's Family Law Act's restrictive definition of spouse to opposite-sex couples violated section 15(1) of the constitutionally entrenched Charter of Rights and Freedoms-the portion devoted to addressing equality rights. As redress, the Court concluded that cohabiting same-sex couples should have all the legal benefits accorded to opposite-sex couples, though again without extending the title of marriage.

Civil unions are lacking insofar as they fail to meet the substantive principle of Fraser's cultural recognition.[8] Whilst same-sex couples come into possession of material rights affixed to the heterosexual marriage, they continue to be deprived of the social acceptance that renders their relationships to be as worthy as those of their opposite-sex counterparts. In short, for marriage to be redeemed from the heteronormativity it customarily entails, it is necessary that same-sex couples have access to the institution, and not have another category designed specifically for them through which they are further distinguished as being contrary to the norm. From the queer perspective, same-sex couples should be allowed to attain complete and full marriage status, whereby they can transform the very norm that previously excluded them.

The queer marriage similarly functions to emasculate patriarchy, "the autonomous system of women's subordination in society" (Yuval-Davis, 1997, p. 6). The auspices of patriarchy govern kinship relations by usurping women's (read: wives and daughters) (re)productive faculties and submitting them to the authority of men (read: husbands and fathers). For this to occur, however, acquiescence to sexual difference must provide as a necessary precursor. Namely, it is integral to the operation of patriarchy for there to be inert but complimentary definitions of woman and man, which are neatly organized around a socially ratified institution such as marriage (Hird, 2004a). Without such definitions, it is unreasonable to make sense of patriarchy as there no longer exists two distinct body politics, bifurcated by sex and gender regimes, which authorizes one's subjugation by the other. Same-sex marriage poses a clear threat to the patriarchal code. By obfuscating the sexed rule that husbands are to dominate over their wives, same-sex marriage posits the institution of marriage in a state of transgression from orthodoxy.

Some critics may question queer marriage's aptitude to substantively subvert patriarchy. They may allege that allocating agency to intimate relationships exclusively for its same-sex status is to undertake a shallow and exaggerated reading of the potential of such relationships–that even the subjects of same-sex marriages would be organized around the dominate/submissive dichotomy analogous to the heterosexual patriarchal marriage. There is already much evidence from the lesbian and gay communities to indicate that many of their intimate relationships revolve around polarized dynamics of butch/femme and top/bottom (Ardill & O'Sullivan, 1990). Same-sex relationships and (would be) same-sex marriage should not, however, be relegated to the overly simplistic idea that it mirrors or reproduces the patriarchal model of the heterosexual marriage (Rubin, 1992). Through same-sex bonding, two women "challenge [Man's] prerogative" to their bodies and "assert the primacy of her own needs" (Radicalesbians, 1973, pp. 241-242); and, equally, two men refuse to engage in a particular form of paternalistic subjugation of women. In this way, if same-sex marriage was legal both instances would come to defy normalized patriarchy as embodied by the heterosexist marriage.

Same-sex marriage certainly has promise in presenting an incisive threat to the codependent edifices of heterosexuality and patriarchy. Much good may manifest from this project. However, it is injudicious, as a queer theorist, to be entirely content with the legalization of same-sex marriage as an end result. The scrutiny must continue. At its crux should rest the question, what meaning does even inclusive marriage have in society? If it is determined that marriage persists in constraining human realization, sexual or otherwise-as I believe it will continue to do-then, the faulty institution should be dismantled. In this purview, the demand for same-sex marriage becomes a tentative matter for symmetrical equality and not a substantively liberating endeavor to alleviate ourselves from the shackles of socially prescribed regulatory systems that encroach upon our consciousness.

CONCLUSION

The ideologically motivated preoccupation with same-sex marriage in Canada and the United States has made it amongst the most imminent and contentious questions posited at the crux of contemporary public policy discourse. Inasmuch as this discourse is able to unveil the problematic cultural limitations of equality and social justice, same-sex marriage rightfully belongs as part of a crucial fray from where to (re)conceptualize the impediments thwarting the project for sexual egalitarianism. There is still, a risk that surfaces when engaging with the cause for same-sex marriage far too hastily-that is, one may impetuously concede to an essentialist dogma of sexuality and, in extension, neglect to consider the nuances, complexities, and indeed, the awesome diversity available to human sexual phenomenology. Of equal importance, there is the coupled danger that in our concerted effort to expand marriage's legal definition, grassroots activism for radical sexual liberation will be co-opted and marriage will come to be conflated with being an institution that is good and just. Thus, marriage as a technology for social surveillance and corporeal regulation may (continue to) be invisible to critique.

Notwithstanding the faults endemic to marriage, it remains to be an influential component of one's lived reality, including for those who do not succumb to the institution directly. Marriage signifies, although perhaps shallowly, social covets of love, commitment, and legitimate procreation. At the very least, then, if equality is the objective marriage must be severed from the heterosexism it has heretofore espoused. In this way, marriage ought to be an institution offered to both opposite–and same-sex couples as anything to the contrary equates to discrimination.

In this paper, I have attempted to illustrate marriage as being a corollary of an intricate set of social constructions. Indeed, there is nothing authentic about marriage; akin to all other norms, conventions and institutions, marriage is contrived within culture to meet various ideological ends. Because this institution affirms ontological sexual difference and heteronormativity, it is not surprising that the challenge posed by same-sex marriage is organized around the fallacious assumption of *a priori* sexuality (Hird, 2004b). Accordingly, I have used queer theory here to explore sexuality as an unremitting process and to, thereby, encourage for a reframing of the same-sex marriage debate-one in which, dichotomized categories of heterosexuality and homosexuality are destabilized. In this effort, I hope that this piece of scholarship assists in bridging the metaphysical gap between theory and practice, and comes to contribute to the growing literature that critiques the perilous nexus between essentialism and the current flavor of social conservatism.

NOTES

1. There are a plethora of Biblical references which explain the existence of the patriarchal, heterosexual marriage, many of which are used in neo-conservative diatribes against making the institution available to same-sex couples. As a spiritual rationale, it states that, "a man will leave his father and mother and be joined to his wife, and the two will become one flesh" (*Ephesians*, 5: 31). As for procreation, it advices married couples to, "be fruitful, multiply, and fill the earth" (*Genesis*, 1: 28). As a sexual outlet, marriage is to ensure monogamy, "For fear of fornication, let every man have his own wife, and let every woman have her own husband" (*Corinthians*, 7: 2). As a method through which to consolidate patriarchy, it describes the proper roles of the husband in relation to the wife: "I want you to understand that Christ is the head of every man, and the man is the head of a woman" (*Corinthians*, 11: 3). Specific to wives, it instructs, "get married, bear children, keep house" (*Timothy*, 5: 14).

2. In this section, I am purposefully focusing the discussion of same-sex marriage to lesbians and gay men. While historical analysis clearly shows that there is a great diversity in sexual identities and sexual practices that transcend well beyond the homosexual/heterosexual binary, I am mainly focusing on the "same-sex" issue to remain consistent with the vernacular of the current debate.

3. Baumeister and Vohs provide an analysis of the causes and consequences of women and men conceiving of and using sex differently. They develop and elaborate the economic analysis of sex from an exchange perspective to show how women negotiate their position in social relations and acquire material goods by using sex as a bargaining chip (Baumeister and Vohs, 2004, p. 340). There conclusion is at least partly informed by an earlier article, in which they along with another scholar attempt to measure sexual drive. They found that men tend to have a quantitatively and qualitatively higher sex drive than do women, and they explain further that credible evidence does not exist to contradict this claim (see Baumeister et. al., 2001).

4. Ontological sexual difference pivots on the rules of gender, so abridged by Harold Garfinkel (1967). These laws conclude that there are two genders, and everyone has one; gender is lifelong, invariant, and unchangeable; exceptions to two genders are jokes and abnormalities; genital (penis, vagina), are the essential sign of gender, and; the categories

of gender are created by nature, and membership in a gender category is assigned by nature. These laws become codified in the mundane through such things as dress and behavior. For a critique of the sex/gender distinction see Hird (2004a: pp. 24-26).

5. Numerous scholars have employed the analytical objective central to queer theory-namely, the undoing of the hegemonic nexus between sex, gender, and sexual desire-yet, without assuming the role of a queer theorist. For example, feminist philosopher Jacquelyn Zita (1994a, p. 121), in her excellent discussion of male lesbians criticizes the perspective in which, "'maleness' implies 'masculinity' implies 'female' as object choice, implies 'heterosexual'-reflecting a seeming logical and maturational order to the body's identities." While challenging heteronormativity here, Zita has elsewhere provided an explanation of the shortcomings of queer theory, an indication of why she remains within the specialty of lesbian feminism and is hesitant to identify as a queer theorist. Interestingly, it seems as though her concern with queer theory is not necessarily the principles it embodies, but instead how it has been mobilized by male theorists to assert that discrimination against sexuality-that is, homophobia-is the primary form of oppression; thus, negating other trajectories of marginalization based on gender, race, class, ability, and age (Zita, 1994b, pp. 259-260).

6. My interest in the queer marriage was catalyzed by a letter written by Myra Hird (2004b) to John Williams, a Member of Parliament from the Conservative Party of Canada. In it, Hird describes same-sex marriage as a "human right" that should be available to those individuals who choose to engage in the practice. Elsewhere, she has raised the fundamental dilemma of ontological sexual difference (see Hird, 2004a). Extending from Hird's work, in this paper I attempt to underscore the inherent problem of anchoring a particular public policy issue on the assumption of ontological sexual difference.

7. Interestingly, the queer marriage is consistent with some arguments that aver the right for bisexuals to marry. The heterosexist institution of marriage only affords bisexuals access to marriage in those instances when they are engaged in opposite-sex relationships. It fails to account for the essence of bisexuality, that is, the sexual predilection for members of both sexes. In being sympathetic to the idiosyncrasies of sexuality, the queer marriage is able to accommodate bisexuals insofar as either opposite–or same-sex relationships is permitted to manifest in marriage.

8. The historic ruling in *Brown v. Board of Education of Topeka* (1954) provides important evidence on the effectiveness of the "separate by equal" doctrine. This case which responded to the merits of racially segregated yet supposedly equal public schools that had operated heretofore under the pretense of fairness demonstrates how having separate but equal policies is unable to rectify social stratification. Funneling two entities that are demarcated by physical indicators such as race or sex into separate but equal categories merely makes the inequality more clandestine. It is not a substantive move towards equality or the eradication of social injustices.

REFERENCES

Adam, B. D. (2003). The Defense of Marriage Act and American Exceptionalism: The 'Gay Marriage' Panic in the United States. *Journal of the History of Sexuality*, 12(2): 259-276.

Ardill, S., & O'Sullivan, S. (1990). Butch/Femme Obsessions. *Feminist Review*, 34: 79-85.

Baumeister, R. F., Catanese, K. R., & Vohs, K. D. (2001). Is There a Gender Difference in Strength of Sex Drive? Theoretical Views, Conceptual Distinctions, and a Review of Relevant Evidence. *Personality and Social Psychology Review*, 5(3): 242-273.

Baumeister, R. F., & Vohs, K. D. (2004). Sexual Economics: Sex as Female Resource for Social Exchange in Heterosexual Interactions. *Personality and Social Psychology Review*, 8(4): 339-363.

Becker, G. S. (1973). A Theory of Marriage: Part I. *Journal of Political Economy*, 81(4): 813-846.

Becker, G. S. (1974). A Theory of Marriage: Part II. *Journal of Political Economy*, 82(2): S11-S26.

Burgess, S. (2005). Did the Supreme Court Come Out in *Bush v. Gore*: Queer Theory on the Performance of the Politics of Shame. *differences: A Journal of Feminist Cultural Studies*, 16(1): 126-146.

Bush, G. W. (2006). President's Radio Address. Retrieved on 8 July 2006 from: http://www.whitehouse.gov/news/releases/2006/06/20060603.html

Butler, J. (1990). *Gender Trouble: Feminism and the Subversion of Identity*. London: Routledge.

Cahill, S. (1995). Welfare Moms and the Two Grooms: The Concurrent Promotion and Restriction of Marriage in US Public Policy. *Sexualities*, 8(2): 169-187.

Calhoun, C. (1994). Separating Lesbian Theory from Feminist Theory. *Ethics*, 104(3): 558-581.

Carey, B. (2005). Straight, Gay or Lying: Bisexuality Revisited. *New York Times* (5 July).

Card, C. (1996). Against Marriage and Motherhood. *Hypatia: A Journal of Feminist Philosophy*, 11(3): 1-23.

Connell, R. W. (1987). *Gender and Power: Society, the Person and Sexual Politics*. Cambridge: Polity Press.

Coontz, S. (2004). The World Historical Transformation of Marriage. *Journal of Marriage and Family*, 66(4): 974-979.

Coontz, S. (2005). *Marriage, a History: From Obedience to Intimacy, or How Love Conquered Marriage*. New York: Viking.

Deleuze, G., & Guattari, F. (1987). *A Thousand Plateaus: Capitalism and Schizophrenia*. Trans. B. Massumi. Minneapolis: University of Minnesota Press.

Derrida, J. (1976). *Of Grammatology*. Trans. G.C. Spivak. Baltimore: John Hopkins University Press.

Dobson, J. (2004). *Marriage Under Fire: Why We Must Win This Battle*. Sisters, OR: Multnomah Publishers.

Ehrhardt, A. A. (1979). "The Interactional Model of Sex Hormones and Behavior." In H.A. Katchadourian (Ed.), *Human Sexuality: A Comparative and Developmental Perspective* (pp. 150-160). Berkeley: The University of California Press.

Elshtain, J. B. (2003). Women and the Dilemma of Equality. *Logos: A Journal of Catholic Thought*, 6(4): 35-50.

Engels, F. (1986 [1884]). *The Origin of the Family, Private Property and the State*. New York: Penguin Books.

Epstein, S. (1994). A Queer Encounter: Sociology and the Study of Sexuality. *Sociological Theory*, 12(2): 188-202.

Fausto-Sterling, A. (2000). *Sexing the Body: Gender Politics and the Construction of Sexuality*. New York: Basic Books.

Fausto-Sterling, A. (2004). Refashioning Race: DNA and the Politics of Health Care. *differences: A Journal of Feminist Cultural Studies*, 15(3): 1-37.

Fracher, J., & Kimmel, M. S. (1995). Hard Issues and Soft Spots: Counseling Men About Sexuality. In M.S. Kimmel and M. Messner (Eds.), *Men's Lives* 3rd Ed. (pp. 365-374). Boston: Allyn and Bacon.

Fraser, N. (2000). Rethinking Recognition. *New Left Review*, 3: 107-120.

Fraser, N. (1995). From Redistribution to Recognition: Dilemmas of Justice in a 'Post-Socialist' Age. *New Left Review*, I(212): 68-93.

Fraser, N., & Nicholson, L. J. (1997). Social Criticism without Philosophy: An Encounter Between Feminism and Postmodernism. In D.T. Meyers (Ed.), *Feminist Social Thought: A Reader* (pp. 132-146). New York: Routledge.

Foucault, M. (1990 [1978]). *The History of Sexuality: An Introduction*. Trans. R. Hurley. New York: Knopf.

Garfinkel, H. (1967). *Studies in Ethnomethodology*. Englewood Cliffs, NJ: Prentice Hall.

Grindstaff, D. (2003). Queering Marriage: An Ideography Interrogation of Heteronormative Subjectivity. *Journal of Homosexuality*, 45(2): 257-275.

Halperin, D. M. (1990). *One Hundred Years of Homosexuality: And Other Essays on Greek Love*. New York: Routledge.

Hird, M. J. (2000). Gender's Nature: Intersexuals, Transsexuals and the 'Sex'/'Gender' Binary. *Feminist Theory*, 1(3): 347-364.

Hird, M. J. (2002). Welcoming Dialogue: A Further Response to Out/Performing Our Selves. *Sexualities*, 5(3): 362-366.

Hird, M. J. (2004a). *Sex, Gender and Science*. Basingstoke: Palgrave.

Hird, M. J. (2004b). Equal Marriage–Bill C268. *Private communication* (24 November).

Hird, M. J. (2006). Sex Diversity and Evolutionary Psychology. *The Psychologist*, 19(1): 30-32.

hooks, b. (1994). *Teaching to Transgress: Education as the Practice for Freedom*. New York: Routledge.

Hunter, A. (1991). Same Door, Different Closet: A Heterosexual Sissy's Coming-Out Party. *Feminism and Psychology*, 2(3): 367-385.

Jacobsen, J. P. (1994). *The Economics of Gender*. Malden, MA: Blackwell Publishers.

Kane, G. (2004). A Family Affair: The World Congress of Families Wants *Governments* to Decide What's Natural. *Ms. Magazine*, Fall: 57-58.

Katz, J. N. (1995). *The Invention of Heterosexuality*. New York: Dutton.

Keller, E. F. (1985). *Reflections on Gender and Science*. New Haven: Yale University Press.

Kinsey, A. C. (1948). *Sexual Behavior in the Human Male*. Philadelphia: W.B. Saunders.

Kinsey, A. C. (1953). *Sexual Behavior in the Human Female*. Philadelphia: Saunders.

Kutsche, P. (1997). A Mudfight in Same-Sex Research. *American Ethnologist*, 25(3): 495-498.

Laqueur, T. W. (1990). *Making Sex: Body and Gender from the Greeks to Freud*. Cambridge: Harvard University Press.

Lister, A. (2004). Marriage and Misogyny: The Place of Mary Astell in the History of Political Thought. *History of Political Thought*, 24(1): 44-72.

Mann, P. S. (1994). *Micro-Politics: Agency in a Postfeminist Era*. Minneapolis: University of Minnesota Press.

Martin, E. (1991). The Egg and the Sperm: How Science had Constructed a Romance Based on Stereotypical Female-Male Roles. *Signs: Journal of Women in Culture and Society*, 16(3): 485-501.

Moi, T. (2004). From Femininity to Finitude: Freud, Lacan, and Feminism, Again. *Signs: Journal of Women in Culture and Society*, 29(3): 841-878.

Monahan, P. (2005). Civil Union is Not Real Marriage. *Globe and Mail*, 26 January: A15.

Pateman, C. (1988). *The Sexual Contract*. Cambridge: Polity Press.

Peel, Elizabeth. (2001). Mundane Heterosexism: Understanding Incidents of the Everyday. *Women's Studies International Forum* 24(5): 541-554.

Petersen, A. (1998). Sexing the Body: Representations of Sex Differences in Gray's *Anatomy*, 1858 to the Present. *Body and Society*, 4(1): 1-15.

Prasad, A. (2005). Reconsidering the Socio-Scientific Enterprise of Sexual Difference: The Case of Kimberly Nixon. *Canadian Woman Studies*, 24(2/3): 80-84.

Prasad, A. (2006). *Identity without Corporeality: On the Etiology and Politics of Male Lesbians*. M.A. Thesis, Queen's University at Kingston.

Radicalesbians. (1973). The Woman Identified Woman. In A. Koedt, E. Levine, and A. Rapone (Eds.), *Radical Feminism* (pp. 240-245). New York: Quadrangle Books.

Rich, A. (1980). Compulsory Heterosexuality and the Lesbian Existence. *Signs: Journal of Women in Culture and Society*, 5(4): 631-660.

Rubin, G. (1992). Of Calamites and Kings: Reflections on Butch, Gender, and Boundaries. In J. Nestle (Eds.), *The Persistent Desire: A Femme-Butch Reader* (pp. 466-482). Boston: Alyson.

Schiebinger, L. (1989). *The Mind Has No Sex?: Women and Origins of Modern Science*. Cambridge: Harvard University Press.

Schowengerdt, D. M. (2002). Defending Marriage: A Litigation Strategy to Oppose Same-Sex 'Marriage.' *Regent University Law Review*, 14(2): 487-511.

Sinfield, A. (2002). Lesbian and Gay Taxonomies. *Critical Inquiry*, 29(1): 120-138.

Stacey, J. (1996). *In the Name of the Family: Rethinking Family Values in the Postmodern Age*. Boston: Beacon Press.

Waite, L. G., & Gallagher, M. (2000). *The Case for Marriage: Why Married People are Happier, Healthier, and Better off Financially*. New York: Broadway Books.

Weeks, J. (1985). *Sexuality and its Discontents: Meanings, Myths & Modern Sexualities*. London: Routledge.

Yuval-Davis, N. (1997). *Gender and Nation*. London: Sage.

Zita, J. (1994a). Male Lesbians and the Postmodernist Body. In C. Card (Ed.), *Adventures in Lesbian Philosophy* (pp. 112-132). Bloomington: Indiana University Press.

Zita, J. (1994b). Gay and Lesbian Studies: Yet Another Happy Marriage? In L Garber (Ed.), *Tilting the Tower: Lesbians Teaching Queer Subjects* (pp. 258-276). New York: Routledge.

COURT CASES CITED

Baker et. al. v. State of Vermont et. al. [1999] 170 Vt. 194, 744 A.2d 864.
Brown v. Board of Education. [1954] 347 U.S. 483.
Hyde v. Hyde. [1866] L.R. 1 P. & D. 130.
Loving v. Virginia. [1967] 388 U.S. 1
M. v. H. [1999] 2 S.C.R. 3.
Reference re Same-Sex Marriage. [2004] 3 S.C.R. 698, SCC 79.

RESEARCH PERSPECTIVES: ATTITUDES TOWARD BISEXUALITY AND SAME-SEX MARRIAGE

Bias Toward Bisexual Women and Men in a Marriage-Matching Task

Angela L. Breno
M. Paz Galupo

Past research on bisexuality has often served to increase stereotypes and myths about bisexual individuals and their relationships. The majority of research about bisexuality has focused on relationships, with a particular emphasis on non-monogamous relationships (Klesse, 2005; Mclean, 2004; Mint, 2004; Rambukkana, 2004; Rust, 1996; Yescavage & Alexander, 2003), promiscuity and sexually transmitted diseases (STDs) (Bailey, Farquhar, Owen & Whittaker, 2003; Bevier, Chiasson, Heffernan & Castro, 1995; Danzig, 1990; Doll, Meyers, Kennedy & Allman, 1997; Einhorn & Polgar, 1994), and sexual behavior (Boulton, Hart, & Fitzpatrick, 1992; Carrier, 1989; Connell, Crawford, Dowsett, Kippax, et al. 1990; Doll & Beeker, 1996; Goldbaum, Perdue, & Wolitski, 1998; Matteson, 1997; Weatherburn & Reid, 1995). When bisexuality is examined in the context of marriage, the focus is usually negative, concentrating on conflict and "crisis" (Buxton, 1994, 2001, 2004). Most of this research focuses on bisexual individuals who come out following marriage to other-sex partners (Buxton, 1994, 2000, 2001, 2004; Coleman 1981/1982; Gochros, 1989; Hays & Samuels, 1988; Matteson, 1985; Whitney, 1990; Wolf, 1985).

ATTITUDES TOWARD BISEXUAL INDIVIDUALS

Attitudes toward bisexual individuals often reflect a marked sex difference. While men view bisexual women and lesbians no differently, women view bisexual men more negatively than gay men (Steffens &

Wagner, 2004). Overall, bisexual men are perceived more negatively than bisexual women, gay men, and lesbians (Eliason, 1997; 2001).

Bisexual individuals often experience stigmatization and discrimination (Barrios, Corbitt, Estes, & Topping, 1976; Herek, 2002; Mohr, Israel, & Sedlacek, 2001). A study conducted by the Kaiser Family Foundation found that 60% of bisexual women and men experienced discrimination, 52% were targets of verbal abuse, and 26% were not accepted by their families of origin because of their bisexual identity (Kaiser Family Foundation, 2001).

Among the negative attitudes toward bisexual individuals is the belief that bisexuality is synonymous with promiscuity and nonmonogamy (Rust, 1996; Spalding & Peplau, 1997). Heterosexual individuals tend to associate bisexuality with higher rates of HIV infection and other STDs, believing that bisexual women and men are more likely than heterosexual, lesbian, and gay individuals to expose a partner to STDs (Spalding & Peplau, 1997). During the early years of the HIV epidemic when it was primarily associated with the lesbian, gay, bisexual and transgender (LGBT) community, people feared that bisexual women and men would spread HIV to heterosexuals (Stokes, Taywaditep, Vanable & McKirnan, 1996). In reality, HIV transmission via bisexuality has been estimated as being nominal (Kahn, Gurvey, Pollack, & Catania, 1997), estimating that only 1% of the annual HIV infections can be attributed to bisexual men infecting female sexual partners.

Bisexual individuals are often subjugated to double discrimination or biphobia, which Ochs (1996) defines as discrimination from not only heterosexual individuals, but also includes hostility and distancing from lesbians and gay men (Blumstein & Schwartz, 1974, 1977; Eliason, 1997; Herdt, 2001; Herek, 2002; Mulick & Wright, 2002; Rust, 1993, 1995, 1996; Weinberg, Williams, & Pryor, 1994). While heterosexual attitudes toward bisexuality are generally related to a belief in the stereotypes about bisexual individuals, lesbians' and gay men's negative attitudes may have different origins. Lesbians and gay men tend to view bisexual individuals as less oppressed than other sexual minorities (Ochs, 1996).

BISEXUAL EXPERIENCE OF MARRIAGE AND RELATIONSHIPS

Bisexual identity remains largely invisible within the context of relationships as sexual orientation is often presumed based on whether the coupling is same- or other-sex (Ochs, 1996). This may lead to a feeling of disconnect between communities and increased isolation, especially when bisexual individuals change partners (Galupo, Sailer, & St. John, 2004). Bisexuality tends to be visible typically during "negative" transitions. For example, a woman's bisexual identity is acknowledged when she leaves her husband for a woman, or when she leaves her woman partner for a man.

When bisexuality is examined in the context of marriage, the focus is usually negative, concentrating on conflict and "crisis" (Buxton, 1994, 2001, 2004) and focusing on individuals who are disproportionately drawn from therapeutic environments. Most of this research focuses on experiences within cross-sex cross-orientation marriages where a bisexual individual is married to a heterosexual spouse (Buxton, 1994, 2000, 2001, 2004; Coleman 1981/1982; Gochros, 1989; Hays & Samuels, 1988; Matteson, 1985; Whitney, 1990; Wolf, 1985).

BISEXUALITY AND THE SAME-SEX MARRIAGE DEBATE

How society conceptualizes bisexuality plays a fundamental role in its portrayal within the same-sex marriage debate. Whereas lesbians and gay men are the focal point in the same-sex marriage debate, bisexual individuals have remained largely invisible. While bisexual invisibility is far from a new phenomenon (Galupo, Sailer, & St John, 2004; Ochs, 1996; Weinberg, Williams, & Pryor, 1994, 2001), there are several possible explanations for bisexual invisibility within the context of the same-sex marriage. Among them may include a belief that bisexual women and men do not wish to marry because marriage would restrict bisexual individuals to a monogamous lifestyle (Rust, 1995, 1996, 2002; Weinberg, Williams, & Pryor, 1994). However, in a recent study by Lannutti (2007) on same-sex marriages in Massachusetts, bisexual-lesbian couples expressed that their marriage itself helped subside fears about the bisexual partner's ability and desire to make a marriage commitment.

Another possible explanation for bisexual invisibility within the context of same-sex marriage is the general belief that bisexual individuals who do commit to a monogamous relationship will choose the relationship type that is most socially acceptable, namely a cross-sex relationship (Rust, 1995, 1996). In addition, bisexual women and men are perceived as committing to either a heterosexual orientation or lesbian/gay orientation based on the sex of their partner (Rust, 1995,

1996). For example, when a bisexual woman is monogamously coupled with a man, she is perceived as committing herself to heterosexuality and when she is monogamously coupled with a woman, she is perceived as committing herself to a lesbian identity. Another reason for bisexual invisibility in the same-sex marriage debate is the belief that bisexuality does not represent a stable and valid sexual orientation identity; rather it is viewed merely as a step toward eventual lesbian and gay identity development (Rust, 1995; Weinberg, Williams, & Pryor, 1994).

As same-sex marriage receives increased attention, the debate about what characterizes long-term, healthy relationships has become increasingly fierce. Central to this debate are people's beliefs about the characteristics that contribute to successful relationships and healthy families. Although supporters of same-sex marriage identify marriage as a civil right, attitude patterns of same-sex marriage may not parallel attitudes regarding other civil rights legislation. This may be due, in part, to religious institutions historically defining marriage (Herman, 1997; Warner, 1999). Therefore it is likely that more religiously affiliated individuals have morality-based attitudes toward same-sex marriage (Barclay & Fisher, 2003; Wald, Button, & Rienzo, 1996). A recent study by Pearl and Galupo (2007) provides the first measure of attitudes towards same-sex marriage (ATSM) and demonstrated that ATSM scores were inversely related to religious conservatism.

Several factors complicate the issue of people's perceptions about whom a bisexual individual should be partnered with. Among these factors include (1) bisexual individuals often being viewed by heterosexual individuals more negatively than lesbians and gay men, (2) bisexual individuals often experience hostility from lesbians and gay men, and (3) prevailing myths regarding bisexual individuals harboring HIV and other STDs.

STATEMENT OF THE PROBLEM

The goal of the current study was to examine the characteristics that people believe essential to a stable, long-lasting, and healthy marriage. The purpose of the current research was three-fold: (1) to develop an indirect measure of attitudes toward same-sex marriage; (2) to examine bisexual invisibility in a marriage-matching task; and (3) to examine the role of HIV status on the marriage-matching.

Participants were presented with a marriage-matching task where they read twelve profiles of fictitious individuals. Profiles varied in sex (female and male), sexual orientation (lesbian/gay, bisexual, and heterosexual) and HIV status (positive and negative). For each profile, participants created the ideal match for a fictitious individual using a fixed set of characteristic options relating to appearance, identity, and behavior.

METHOD

Participants

Participants were recruited via the Internet through the Social Psychology Network and Hanover College Psychological Research on the Net, two websites designed for academic research and participant recruitment. Most people who access these websites are students and faculty in the social sciences, but they are accessible to the public through search engines. Participants ranged in age from 18 to 96 years of age ($M = 24.85$, $SD = 9.57$). Participants represented all regions of the United States, residing in 34 states and the District of Columbia. Participants ranged in education from having an 8th grade education to having a post-graduate degree, with 4 not having graduated from high school (2.6%), 20 with a high school diploma (12.9%), 72 having some college education (46.5%), 12 having an A.A. Degree (7.7%), 31 with a B.A./B.S. Degree (20.0%), 12 having a post-graduate education, and 4 (2.6%) participants with either a vocational school education or other.

The survey was accessed a total of 594 times. Out of the 594 times the survey was accessed, 119 participants dropped out of the study immediately after reading the consent form. A total of 298 surveys were not used because of missing data. Of the 177 participants who completed the survey, 22 were not used because the participants identified either as a sexual minority or as having an HIV positive status. The resulting sample ($N = 155$) included heterosexual women and men who were HIV negative.

Of the 155 participants, 132 were female (85.2%) and 23 male (14.8%). The racial/ethnic composition of the sample was relatively diverse where participants self-identified as 71.7% ($n = 111$) White, 11.6% ($n = 18$) Black, 7.7% ($n = 12$) Hispanic, 2.6% ($n = 4$) Asian American, 1.3% ($n = 2$) Native American, and 5.2% ($n = 8$) identified as Other. The religious composition of the sample included participants who self-identified as 54.2% ($n = 84$) Christian, 21.9% ($n = 34$) Catholic, 16.1% ($n = 25$) none, 3.9% ($n = 6$) Jewish, 1.3% ($n = 2$) Buddhist,

1.3% ($n = 2$) Muslim, and 1.3% ($n = 2$) other. With regard to participants' religiosity, 24.5% ($n = 38$) identified themselves as being not religious, 55.5% ($n = 86$) as being somewhat religious, and 20.0% ($n = 31$) as being very religious.

RESEARCH DESIGN

Questionnaires were completed on a secure website and participant responses were completely anonymous. No contact or identifying information was collected. Participants were told they were completing a questionnaire that assesses the traits of a person they believe contribute to a stable, long-lasting relationship like marriage. They were also told that part of the questionnaire would assess their attitudes and ask some basic demographic information.

Data was collected using a marriage-matching task. Participants read twelve profiles and created an ideal match for each profiled person. Profiles followed a similar format to profiles on *Out In America*, a national lesbian, gay, bisexual, transgender, questioning (LGBTQ) website. Each profile consisted of a short description of the person in the form of a personal advertisement. Each description was accompanied by additional characteristics based on the following categories: sexual orientation, ethnicity, religion/spirituality, age, HIV status, hair/eye color, height, weight, body type, smoking and drinking habits, drug use, political affiliation, and education. After participants read each profile, they created an ideal match that they felt would result in a long-lasting marriage. To create a marriage match, participants selected characteristics from a drop down menu based on the same categories of descriptors previously listed.

MATERIALS

Marriage matching task. The marriage-matching task was created specifically for the current study. Each participant reviewed twelve profiles. To ensure that participants knew that same-sex couples could be included as an option for an ideal marriage match in this study, all participants first viewed a profile of a gay man who could only be paired with another male. This controlled for individual definitions of marriage. While participants viewed a total of twelve profiles, data from eight profiles were used for the analyses to allow for comparisons across race (Black / White), sex (female / male), and HIV status (positive/negative). Three versions of the survey were used to counterbalance sexual orientation, resulting in each profile being viewed as gay/lesbian, bisexual, and heterosexual. Participants only saw one version of each profile. Table 1 provides the name of each profile and summarizes the sex, HIV status, and race of the fictitious person characterized in the profile.

General demographic questionnaire. Participants were asked to respond to a series of demographic questions that included whether they were in a relationship, how they define that relationship, and their sexual orientation. They were also asked some basic demographic information that included religion, religiosity, age, sex, race, state of residence, and how they heard about the study.

DATA ANALYSIS

As a result of the eight profiles being counterbalanced for sexual orientation, there were a total of 24 different profiles used for the analysis. The first three Chi-Square analyses focused on whether the sexual orientation identity of the profile influenced the sexual orientation of the ideal match provided by the participants. Specifically, analyses focused on: (1) whether participants were more likely to choose a bisexual partner for bisexual profiles versus non-bisexual profiles; (2) whether participants were more

TABLE 1. Profle Demographics as it Appeared to Every Participant

Profile Name	Profile Race	Profile Sex	Profile HIV Status
Kya	Black	Female	Negative
Alana	White	Female	Negative
Abbie	Black	Female	Positive
Nicole	White	Female	Positive
Kevin	Black	Male	Negative
Clark	White	Male	Negative
Camran	Black	Male	Positive
Konner	White	Male	Positive

likely to choose a bisexual partner for heterosexual profiles versus les-bian/gay profiles; and (3) whether the participants were more likely to pro-vide an ideal same-sex or other-sex match for bisexual profiles.

The second set of analyses focused on the role HIV status played in par-ticipants' creation of ideal matches. The first analysis focused on whether participants made HIV concordant matches for positive and negative pro-files. Additional Chi-Square analyses focused on whether the sexual orien-tation identity of the profile influences the HIV status of the ideal match created by the participant. A final analysis was conducted to examine the role of same-sex versus other-sex pairings on the HIV status of matches.

HYPOTHESES

In examining whether the sexual orientation identity of the profiles influenced the sexual orientation of the ideal match, two predictions were made. First, it was predicted that participants would pair bisexual profiles significantly more frequently with bisexual matches than non-bisexual matches. Second, it was predicted that there would be no significant differences in bisexual matches for heterosexual and lesbian/gay profiles. Third, it was predicted that, overall, participants would match bisexual profiles significantly more frequently with other-sex matches rather than with same-sex matches.

In examining participants' perceptions of HIV concordance in ideal matches, three predictions were made. First, it was predicted that partic-ipants would create matches that are concordant with each profile's HIV status. Second, it was predicted that sexual orientation of the pro-file would influence the HIV status of the ideal match created by the participant. Specifically, it was predicated that significantly more HIV positive matches would be created for bisexual profiles compared to HIV negative matches. Third, in examining the influence of bisexual HIV related stereotypes on participants' match creations, it was pre-dicted that HIV positive matches as opposed to negative matches would be made significantly more frequently with other-sex pairings versus same-sex pairings for bisexual matches.

RESULTS

Bisexual Matches Depend Upon Profile Sexual Orientation

Two Chi-Square analyses focused on whether the sexual orienta-tion identity of the profile influenced the sexual orientation of the ideal match provided by the participants. In particular, analyses focused on: (1) whether participants were more likely to choose a bisexual partner for bisexual profiles versus non-bisexual profiles (see Table 2); and (2) whether participants were more likely to choose a bisexual partner for heterosexual profiles than lesbian/gay profiles (see Table 3).

As illustrated in Table 2 and consistent with predictions, participants were significantly more likely to make a bisexual match for bisexual versus non-bisexual profiles. This was true across profile sex (female and male), race (Black and White), and HIV status (positive and negative). An additional analysis compared the number of bisexual matches for heterosexual and lesbian/gay profiles. Overall participants did not often make bisexual matches for heterosexual and lesbian/gay profiles. However, when bisexual matches occurred a different pattern emerged for male and female profiles (see Table 3). For female profiles, participants were significantly more likely to make bisexual matches for lesbian versus heterosexual profiles. In contrast, for male profiles there were no significant differences in the number of bisexual matches for heterosexual and gay male profiles.

Sex Matches Resulting From Bisexual Profiles

Overall, there was no significant difference across the eight profiles between the number of same-sex and other-sex matches for bisexual profiles, with one exception. Specifically, participants created other-sex matches significantly more frequently than same-sex matches for Clark's profile. It is worth noting that Clark is the only White male profile with an HIV negative status. For the remaining seven profiles, participants were no more likely to pair a bisexual profile with a same-sex versus other-sex match.

Overall, Profiles Were Paired with HIV Concordant Matches

HIV status was investigated through a direct analysis of the profiles' HIV status versus the HIV status of the match participants created. Table 4 summarizes the results, which clearly show that participants are significantly more likely to pair a profile with a match that is HIV concordant. This was true across profile sex (female and male) and race (Black and White). For this analysis data were collapsed across sexual orientation of the profile.

TABLE 2. Bisexual Profiles are Sigifcantly More Likly than NonBisexual Profiles to hae Bisexual Matches ($N = 15$

	Race	HIV Status	Sexual Orientation	Bisexual Matches		Chi-Square
				Yes	No	
Female						
Kya	Black	HIV -	Bisexual	27	23	30.64
			Not Bisexual	13	92	
Alana	White	HIV -	Bisexual	24	31	29.77
			Not Bisexual	7	93	
Abbie	Black	HIV +	Bisexual	37	13	58.85
			Not Bisexual	13	92	
Nicole	White	HIV +	Bisexual	30	25	23.68
			Not Bisexual	17	83	
Male						
Kevin	Black	HIV -	Bisexual	40	15	72.55
			Not Bisexual	7	93	
Clark	White	HIV -	Bisexual	31	19	77.05
			Not Bisexual	1	104	
Camran	Black	HIV +	Bisexual	32	23	35.16
			Not Bisexual	13	87	
Konner	White	HIV +	Bisexual	34	16	35.75
			Not Bisexual	20	85	

Note: All Chi-Square analyses significant at the .001 level

Additional analyses were conducted to consider these data separated out by sexual orientation (bisexual, lesbian/gay, heterosexual) for HIV positive and HIV negative profiles. In all cases, participants were more likely to make HIV concordant matches. An additional set of analyses was conducted for bisexual profiles, comparing the HIV status assigned for same- and other-sex matches, and again no significance differences were found. Consistent with previous analyses, matches were made based on HIV concordance. This was also true for same- and other-sex matches.

TABLE 3 Lesbian Profiles are More Likely than Heterosexual Profiles to have Bisexual Matches

	Race	HIV Status	Sexual Orientation	Bisexual Matches		N	Chi-Square
				Yes	No		
Female							
Kya	Black	HIV -	Lesbian	12	43	105	9.48*
			Heterosexual	1	49		
Alana	White	HIV -	Lesbian	7	43	100	7.53*
			Heterosexual	0	50		
Abbie	Black	HIV +	Lesbian	10	40	100	5.11*
			Heterosexual	3	52		
Nicole	White	HIV +	Lesbian	11	39	100	1.77
			Heterosexual	6	44		
Male							
Kevin	Black	HIV -	Gay	4	46	100	0.15
			Heterosexual	3	47		
Clark	White	HIV -	Gay	1	49	105	1.11
			Heterosexual	0	55		
Camran	Black	HIV +	Gay	5	45	100	0.79
			Heterosexual	8	42		
Konner	White	HIV +	Gay	12	43	105	0.58
			Heterosexual	8	42		

Note: *Significant results found at the .05 level.

DISCUSSION

The marriage-matching task used for this research allowed for a subtle measurement of attitudes towards bisexual women and men within the context of marriage. While past research has used more straightforward survey techniques to assess attitudes toward bisexual individuals (Israel & Mohr, 2004), this is the first study that allows for an assess-

TABLE 4 Overall Participants Rate Concordant Matches (N = 5

	Race	HIV Status	HIV Matches		Chi-Square
			Negative	Positive	
Female					
Kya	Black	HIV -	149	6	131.93
Alana	White	HIV -	149	6	131.93
Abbie	Black	HIV +	38	117	40.27
Nicole	White	HIV +	42	113	32.52
Male					
Kevin	Black	HIV -	151	4	139.41
Clark	White	HIV -	151	4	139.41
Camran	Black	HIV +	36	119	44.45
Konner	White	HIV +	40	115	36.29

Note: All Chi-Square analyses are significant at the .001 level.

ment of attitudes regarding bisexuality and marriage. Presented with a marriage-matching task, heterosexual participants created ideal matches for profiles that differed across sexual orientation and HIV status. Importantly this task assessed how bisexual individuals were considered in the context of both "traditional" and same-sex marriage.

Who Should Bisexual Women and Men Marry?

Overall, when making marriage matches there was a clear perception that bisexual partners were best suited to other bisexual individuals (whether those individuals were of the same- or other-sex). Bisexual partners were mostly chosen for bisexual profiles and were infrequently chosen when profiles were presented as lesbian, gay, or heterosexual. These findings represent a clear bias in perception toward bisexual women and men in that they are not seen as viable partners in cross-orientation marriages with heterosexual, lesbian and gay individuals.

When bisexual partners were chosen for cross-orientation pairings a different pattern emerged across sex of the profile. Bisexual women were matched with lesbian profiles more often than bisexual men were matched with heterosexual women. There was no difference in bisexual matches between gay and heterosexual men. These findings did not support the general prediction that bisexual individuals would be paired more often in a same-sex, rather than cross-sex context. Rather, these findings seem to parallel research showing greater social acceptance for women's non-heterosexuality and for women's sexuality as flexible (Baumeister, 2000; Diamond, 2003; Rust, 2002).

Role of HIV Status

Very little research has been dedicated to examining HIV-discordant couples (Moore et al., 1998; Remien, Carballo-Dieguez, & Wagner, 1995; Remien, Wagner, Dolezal, & Carballo-Dieguez, 2001). This research represents the first study to consider the perceptions of HIV-concordant and disconcordant couples while simultaneously considering sexual orientation within the context of marriage. Overwhelmingly the present results emphasize the belief that HIV concordant pairings are ideal and this belief is extended to sexual minority individuals.

Through a series of analyses, HIV concordance was further established as a dominant factor in participants' perceptions of ideal matches. Although it was predicted that sexual orientation (specifically bisexuality) would play a role in the way in which matches were made according to HIV status, these predictions were not supported. The results clearly showed that sexual orientation played little to no role in participants' assignment of HIV positive matches to profiles.

At first glance, these findings appear inconsistent with previously documented heterosexual beliefs that bisexual women and men are more likely to give an STD to a partner than heterosexual, lesbian, and gay individuals (Spalding & Peplau, 1997). It is possible that sexual orientation played such a minor role in the HIV status of matches because of the research methods of this study. Because the marriage matching task presented the profiled individuals as desiring marriage, participants may have been less likely to think of these individuals as promiscuous (even when they presented as bisexual). That is, considering bisexual women and men within a marriage context required participants to disengage from prevailing stereotypes of bisexuality.

Limitations and Directions for Future Research

This sample represents a convenience sample of individuals who self-identify as heterosexual and should be interpreted in light of this limitation. While the sample is geographically diverse and represents a cross-section of educational experiences, the participants largely represented a more educated cohort of the general population. This limitation is salient, as education has been tied to more positive attitudes toward sexual minority individuals (Herek & Capitanio, 1995; Lewis, 2003; Simoni, 1996).

Given that this research integrates participants' attitudes toward bisexuality and same-sex marriage, two areas in which women report more positive attitudes than men (Eliason, 1997, 2001; Pearl & Galupo, 2007) an important consideration when interpreting these data is that 85.2% of the participants were women. Future research should seek more gender balance in the sample and allow for comparison of response across sex of participants. Because negative attitudes about bisexuality are not limited to heterosexual individuals (Ochs, 1996) future research should pursue the issue of how sexual minorities (including bisexual individuals) would respond in a similar marriage-matching task.

The marriage-matching task developed for this research provides a solid method of inquiry for assessing subtle attitudes regarding sexuality and marriage. Given the changing legal definitions of marriage as they relate to sexual minorities, this method may prove useful in documenting attitude change across time and locale.

REFERENCES

Bailey, J. V., Farquhar, C., Owen, C., & Whittaker, D. (2003). Sexual behaviour of lesbians and bisexual women. *Sexually Transmitted Infections, 79,* 147-150.

Barclay, S., & Fisher, S. (2003). The states and the differing impetus for divergent paths on same-sex marriage. *Policy Studies Journal, 31*(3), 331-352.

Barrios, B. A., Corbitt, L. C., Estes, J. P., & Topping, J. S. (1976). Effect of a social stigma on interpersonal distance. *The Psychological Record, 26,* 343-348.

Baumeister, R. F. (2000). Gender difference in erotic plasticity: The female sex drive as socially flexible and responsive. *Psychological Bulletin, 126,* 347-374.

Bevier, P., Chiasson, M., Heffernan, R., & Castro, K. (1995). Women at sexually transmitted disease clinics who reported same-sex contact: Their HIV seroprevalence and risk behaviors. *American Journal of Public Health, 85,* 1366-1371.

Blumstein, P. W. & Schwartz, P. (1974). Lesbianism and bisexuality. In E. Goode (Ed.), Sexual Deviance and Sexual Deviants, (pp. 278-295). New York: Morrow.

Blumstein, P. W. & Schwartz, P. (1977). Bisexuality: Some social psychological issues. *Journal of Social Issues, 33,* 30-45.

Boulton, M., Hart, G., & Fitzpatrick, R. (1992). The sexual behaviour of bisexual men in relation to HIV transmission. *AIDS Care, 4*, 165-175.

Buxton, A. P. (1994). *The Other Side of the Closet: The Coming-Out Crisis for Straight Spouses and Families.* New York: John Wiley & Sons.

Buxton, A. P. (2000). The best interest of children of lesbian and gay parents. In R. Galatzer-Levy & L. Kraus (Eds.), *The Scientific Basis for Child Custody Decisions,* (pp. 319-346). New York: John Wiley & Sons.

Buxton, A. P. (2001). Writing our own script: How bisexual men and their heterosexual wives maintain their marriages after disclosure. In B. Beemyn & E. Steinman (Eds.), *Bisexuality in the Lives of Men: Facts and Fiction,* (pp. 157-189). New York: Harrington Park Press.

Buxton, A. P. (2004). Works in progress: How mixed-orientation couples maintain their marriages after the wives come out. *Journal of Bisexuality, 4*, 57-82.

Carrier, J. M. (1989). Sexual behavior and the spread of AIDS in Mexico. *Medical Anthropology Quarterly, 10*, 129-142.

Coleman, E. (1981/1982). Bisexual and gay men in heterosexual marriages: Conflicts and resolutions in therapy. *Journal of Homosexuality, 7*, 93-103.

Connell, R. W., Crawford, J., Dowsett, G. W., Kippax, S. et al. (1990). Danger and context: Unsafe anal sexual practice among homosexual and bisexual men in the AIDS crisis. *Australian and New Zealand Journal of Sociology, 26*, 187-208.

Danzig, A. (1990). Bisexual women and AIDS. In The ACT UP/New York Women & AIDS Book Group (Eds.), *Women, AIDS, and Activism.* Boston: South End Press.

Diamond, L. M. (2003). Was it a phase? Young women's relinquishment of lesbian/bisexual identities over a 5-year period. *Journal of Personality and Social Psychology, 84*, 352-364.

Doll, L. S., & Becker, C. (1996). Male bisexual behavior and HIV risk in the United States: Synthesis of research with implications for behavioral interventions. *AIDS Education and Prevention, 8*, 205-225.

Doll, L. S., Meyers, T., Kennedy M., & Allman, D. (1997). Bisexuality and HIV risk: Experiences in Canada and the United States. *Annual Review of Sex Research, VIII*, 102-147.

Einhorn & Polgar, (1994). HIV-risk behavior among lesbians and bisexual women. *AIDS Education & Prevention, 6*, 514-523.

Eliason, M. J. (1997). The prevalence and nature of biphobia in heterosexual undergraduate students. *Archives of Sexual Behavior, 26*, 317-325.

Eliason, M. (2001). Bi negativity: The stigma facing bisexual men. *Journal of Bisexuality, 1*, 137-154.

Galupo, M. P., Sailer, C. A., & St John, S. C. (2004). Friendships across sexual orientations: Experiences of bisexual women in early adulthood. *Journal of Bisexuality, 4*, 37-53.

Gochros, J. S. (1989). *When Husbands Come Out of the Closet.* New York: Harrington Park Press.

Goldbaum, G., Perdue, T., & Wolitski, R. (1998). Differences in risk behavior and sources of AIDS information among gay, bisexual, and straight-identified men who have sex with men. *AIDS & Behavior, 2*, 13-21.

Hays, D. & Samuels, A. (1988). Heterosexual women's perceptions of their marriages to homosexual or bisexual men. *Journal of Homosexuality, 17,* 81-100.

Herdt, G. (2001). Social change, sexual diversity, and tolerance for bisexuality in the United States. In A. R. D'Augelli, & C. J. Patterson (Eds.), *Lesbian, Gay, and Bisexual Identities and Youth: Psychological Perspectives,* (pp. 267-283). New York: Oxford University Press.

Herek, G. M. (2002). Heterosexuals' attitudes toward bisexual men and women in the United States. *Journal of Sex Research, 39,* 264-274.

Herek, G. M., & Capitanio, J. P. (1995). Black heterosexuals' attitudes toward lesbians and gay men in the United States. *Journal of Sex Research, 32*(2), 95-105.

Herman, D. (1997). *The Antigay Agenda: Orthodox vision and the Christian Right.* Chicago: University of Chicago Press.

Israel, T. & Mohr, J. J. (2004). Attitudes toward bisexual women and men: Current research, future directions. *Journal of Bisexuality, 4,* 117-134.

Kahn J. G., Gurvey J,, Pollack L. M, & Catania J. A. (1997). How many HIV infections cross the bisexual bridge? An estimate from the United States. *AIDS, 11,* 1031-37.

Kaiser Family Foundation. (2001). *Inside-Out: A Report on the Experiences of Lesbians, Gays, and Bisexuals in America and the Public's View on Issues and Politics Related to Sexual Orientation.* Retrieved January 10, 2006, from http://www.kff.org.

Klesse, C. (2005). Bisexual women, non-monogamy and differentialist anti-promiscuity discourses. *Sexualities, 8,* 445-464.

Lannutti, P. J. (2007). "This is not a lesbian wedding": Examining same-sex marriage and bisexual-lesbian couples. *Journal of Bisexuality, 7,* 237-260.

Lewis, G. B. (2003). Black-White differences in attitudes toward homosexuality and gay rights. *Public Opinion Quarterly, 67,* 59-78.

Matteson, D. R. (1985). Bisexual men in marriage: Is a positive homosexual identity and stable marriage possible? *Journal of Homosexuality, 11,* 149-173.

Matteson, D. R. (1997). Bisexual and homosexual behavior and HIV risk among Chinese-, Filipino- and Korean-American men. *Journal of Sex Research, 34,* 93-104.

Mclean, K. (2004). Negotiating (non)monogamy: Bisexuality in intimate relationships. *Journal of Bisexuality, 4,* 83-97.

Mint, P. (2004). The power dynamics of cheating: Effects on polyamory and bisexuality. *Journal of Bisexuality, 4,* 55-76.

Mohr, J. J., Israel, T., & Sedlecek, W. E. (2001). Counselors' attitudes regarding bisexuality as predictors of counselors' clinical responses: An analogue study of a female bisexual client. *Journal of Counseling Psychology, 48,* 212-222.

Moore, J., Harrison, J. S., Vandevanter, N., Kennedy, C., Padian, N., Abrams, J., Lesondar, I. M. & O'Brien, T. (1998). Factors influencing relationship quality of HIV serodiscordant heterosexual couples. In Derlega, V. J. & Barbee, A. P. (Eds), *HIV and Social Interaction.* Thousand Oaks, CA: Sage.

Mulick, P. S., & Wright, L. W. Jr. (2002). Examining the existence of biphobia I the heterosexual and homosexual populations. *Journal of Bisexuality, 2,* 45-64.

Ochs, R. (1996). Biphobia: It goes more than two ways. In B.A. Firestein (Ed.), *Bisexuality: The psychology and politics of an invisible minority,* (pp. 217-239). Thousand Oaks, CA: Sage.

Pearl, M. L., & Galupo, M. P. (2007). Development and validation of the attitudes toward same-sex marriage scale. *Journal of Homosexuality*, 53(3), 117-134.

Rambukkana, N. P. (2004). Uncomfortable bridges: The bisexual politics of outing polyamory. *Journal of Bisexuality, 4,* 141-154.

Remien, R. H., Carballo-Dieguez, A., & Wagner, G. (1995). Intimacy and sexual risk behavior in serodiscordant male couples. *AIDS Care, 4,* 429-438.

Remien, R. H., Wagner, G., Dolezal, & Carballo-Dieguez, A. (2001). Factor associated with HIV sexual risk behavior in male couples of mixed HIV status. *Journal of Psychology & Human Sexuality, 13,* 31-48.

Rust, P. (1993). Neutralizing the political threat of the marginal women: Lesbians' beliefs about bisexual women. *Journal of Sex Research, 30,* 214-229.

Rust, P. (1995). Bisexuality and the challenge to lesbian politics: Sex, loyalty, and revolution. New York: NYU Press.

Rust, P. (1996). Monogamy and polyamory: Relationship issues for bisexuals. Firestein (Ed.), *Bisexuality: The psychology and politics of an invisible minority,* (pp. 127-148). Thousand Oaks, CA: Sage.

Rust, P. (2002). Bisexuality: The state of the union. *Annual Review of Sex Research, 13,* 180-240.

Simoni, J. M. (1996). Pathways to prejudice: Predicting students' heterosexist attitudes with demographics, self-esteem, and contact with lesbians and gay men. *Journal of College Student Development, 37*(1), 68-78.

Spalding, L. R., & Peplau, L. A. (1997). The unfaithful lover: Heterosexuals' perceptions of bisexuals and their relationships. *Psychology of Women Quarterly, 21,* 611-625.

Steffens, M. C., & Wagner, C. (2004). Attitudes Toward Lesbians, Gay Men, Bisexual Women, and Bisexual Men in Germany. *Journal of Sex Research, 41,* 137-149.

Stokes, J. P., Taywaditep, K., Vanable, P. & McKirnan, D. J. (1996). Bisexual men, sexual behavior, and HIV/AIDS. Firestein (Ed.), *Bisexuality: The Psychology and Politics of an Invisible Minority,* (pp. 149-168). Thousand Oaks, CA: Sage.

Wald, K. D., Button, J. W., & Rienzo, B. A. (1996). The politics of gay rights in American communities: Explaining antidiscrimination ordinances and policies. *American Journal of Political Science, 40,* 1152-1178.

Warner, M. (1999). Normal and normaller. *GLQ: A Journal of Lesbian & Gay Studies, 5,* 119-171.

Weatherburn, P., & Reid, D. (1995). Survey shows unprotected sex is a common behaviour in bisexual men. *British Medical Journal, 311,* 1163-1164.

Weinberg, M. S., Williams, C. J., & Pryor, D. W. (1994). *Dual Attraction: Understanding Bisexuality.* New York, NY: Oxford University Press.

Weinberg, M. S., Williams, C. J., & Pryor, D. W. (2001). Bisexuals at midlife: Commitment, salience, and identity. *Journal of Contemporary Ethnography, 30,* 180-208.

Whitney, C. (1990). *Uncommon lives: Gay men and straight women.* New York, Plume Books.

Wolf, T. J. (1985). Marriages of bisexual men. *Journal of Homosexuality, 11,* 135-148.

Yescavage, K. & Alexander, J. (2003). Seeing what you want to see: Searching for bisexual representation in threesome' films. *Journal of Bisexuality, 3,* 109-127.

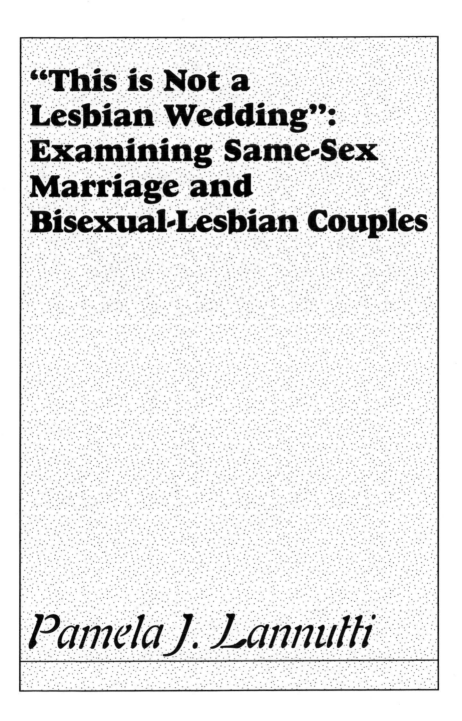

"This is Not a Lesbian Wedding": Examining Same-Sex Marriage and Bisexual-Lesbian Couples

Pamela J. Lannutti

During the past decade, various forms of legal recognition of same-sex partnerships have developed in some parts of the United States (see Purcell, 1998 and Human Rights Campaign, n.d., for overviews) and in other countries (see Gay-Civil-Unions, n.d. and Goransson, 1998 for overview). Although these marriage-like unions were available in selected locations, the civil benefits of these forms of legal recognition remained unequal to those granted to different-sex couples. A change occurred when Massachusetts became the first of the United States to recognize same-sex marriages (SSM) in May 2004. Since then, over 7,800 same-sex couples have been married in Massachusetts (Massachusetts Department of Public Health [MDPH], personal communication, August 24, 2006). Although these marriage rights are not federally recognized or reciprocated in other U.S. states, legal recognition of SSM in Massachusetts has afforded same-sex couples an opportunity to gain the same public recognition and protection for their relationships as their different-sex counterparts.

Although the civil benefits of SSM are straightforward and the battle for and against SSM continues to challenge same-sex couples in the political and legal arenas, it is less clear how SSM is benefiting and challenging same-sex couples on the individual and interpersonal levels. Although previous research has begun to examine how legally recognized SSM as a civic institution (Lannutti, 2005; Lannutti, 2007) and as a specific form of expressed commitment (Lannutti, 2006) has impacted the lives of gay, lesbian, bisexual, transgender, and queer (GLBTQ) people, the majority of this research has focused on individuals who identify as gay or lesbian and are members of couples in which both partners share the same sexual orientation. Thus, little is known about the influence of SSM on the relational experiences of members of the GLBTQ community who identify as something other than gay or lesbian or may be members of cross-sexual orientation couples. The current study attempts to address this gap in the previous research by examining the ways that SSM, as a civic institution and a specific form of expressed commitment, affects the relational experiences bisexual-lesbian couples.

PREVIOUS RESEARCH ON SAME-SEX MARRIAGE

Previous research examining same-sex relationships suggests many similarities between committed same-sex relationships and their heterosexual counterparts. For example, research has shown little difference in the experience of jealousy (Bevan & Lannutti, 2002), attractions and constraints to commitment (Kurdek, 2000), and relational maintenance behaviors (Haas & Stafford, 1998) for same-sex and different-sex couples. Yet, one consistent difference found between the relational experiences of different-sex and same-sex couples has been the stigmatized and non-institutionalized status of same-sex couples (see Patterson, Ciabattari, & Schwartz, 1999). Although same-sex couples often compensated for the lack of institutional recognition for their relationships through commitment ceremonies and other rituals (Stiers, 1999; Suter, Bergen, Daas, & Durham, 2006), these forms of expressed commitment could do little to give couples the wide-spread societal recognition and legal protection afforded to different-sex couples through civil marriage.

The legal recognition of SSM in Massachusetts marks a possible shift in the status for same-sex relationships within the state from non-institutionalized to institutionally recognized. Because people's understandings of themselves (Massey, 1986) and their relationships (Parks & Eggert, 1991) are influenced by the social context, same-sex relationships need to be re-examined in the changing social context marked by the introduction of legally recognized SSM. To that end, I have conducted several studies using web-based open-ended surveys to examine the ways in which SSM has impacted experiences of the GLBTQ people.

Lannutti (2005) examined the ways in which GLBTQ people were assigning meaning to legally recognized SSM as a new civil institution. Participants from across the United States indicated that legally recognized SSM in Massachusetts was an important indicator of increased civic equality for GLBTQ people, but there were also dialectical tensions (Baxter & Montgomery, 1996), or simultaneous contradictory forces, within participants' understanding of SSM. Participants saw the institution of SSM as a means for same-sex couples to become more serious and more fanciful, for the GLBTQ community to become both stronger and weaker, and for the relationship between the GLBTQ community and heterosexual others to become more healing and injurious. This study revealed the complex and contradictory nature of GLBTQ peoples' understanding of SSM, and highlighted the interconnections between same-sex relationships and the GLBTQ community and heteronormative social structure.

A further study (Lannutti, 2007) more closely examined the ways in which the institution of legally recognized SSM influenced GLBTQ people's view of their romantic relationship or romantic relationships in general. Results indicated that SSM impacted participants' understanding of romantic relationships by making existing relationships seem more real and by serving as a tool through which participants realized their desires for ideal potential partner and relationship characteristics. This study demonstrated that the institution of SSM changed the way that GLBTQ people saw themselves and their relationships, but also suggested that further research to more fully describe the experience of couples in the context of SSM was needed.

A further study focused more specifically on the experiences of same-sex couples as they considered SSM as a new vehicle for expressing their commitment. Lannutti (2006) asked GLBTQ people who were married or engaged to be married to a same-sex partner to report their attractions to marriage and the obstacles they faced when considering marriage. Gaining civil and social network recognition for their relationship were among the attractions to marriage, while civil limitations of marriage, social network disapproval, and practical and symbolic issues with weddings and the institution of marriage were among the obstacles. This study again showed that SSM had positive and negative aspects for GLBTQ people. It also highlighted the interdependence between the couple and their social network (Parks & Eggert, 1991) and the particularly powerful challenge that an unsupportive social network can present to same-sex couples (Caron & Ulin, 1997; Rostosky et al., 2004).

Taken together, this research shows that the SSM, both as an institution and as a specific form of expressing commitment, has complex and contradictory implications for the relational experiences of GLBTQ people and same-sex couples. The studies show that SSM influenced participants' perspectives on their society, GLBTQ community, and personal relationships. Yet, these studies are limited in three ways. First, the studies used survey methods, therefore forcing participants' responses to pre-determined questions and limiting the descriptive richness of the data. Second, although Lannutti (2006) focused on the experiences of couples, only one member of the couple participated in the study. Finally, GLBTQ community members who identify as something other than gay or lesbian are under-represented in the samples. The current study is part of an ongoing research project that attempts to further the understanding of SSM through interviews with married or engaged same-sex couples. To better understand the experiences of GLBTQ members who identify as something other than gay or lesbian, the current study focuses on bisexual-lesbian couples.

BISEXUAL-LESBIAN COUPLES

Although approximately 63% of the SSMs that have occurred in Massachusetts are between women (MDPH, personal communication, August 24, 2006), there is no data available regarding the sexual orientations of the partners in these marriages. Yet, to assume that all of these marriages are between women who identify as lesbian would continue the trend of ignoring the uniqueness of bisexual identity when discussing same-sex relationships (Burleson, 2005; Hutchins, 1996). Those who identify as bisexual are often challenged by both heterosexual and homosexual people, (Mulick & Wright, 2002; Ochs, 1996). Negative attitudes towards bisexuals often suggest that bisexuality is a phase, bisexuals are actually gay or lesbian, or bisexuals can not commit to a relationship (Hutchins, 1996; Israel & Mohr, 2004). Rust (1995, 2000) suggests that lesbians' negative attitudes towards bisexual women are particularly complex due to women's political struggles. According to Rust (2000), the biphobia displayed by some lesbians towards bisexual women includes two types of beliefs: "explanatory" beliefs that challenge the existence of bisexuality as a true sexual orientation, and "depoliticizing" beliefs that bisexual women are politically dangerous to lesbians because they lack loyalty to the lesbian community.

Given the larger social context of identity politics, bisexual-lesbian couples may have relational experiences that are unique to cross-sexual orientation same-sex relationships between women. Yet, relationships between bisexual-lesbian couples are understudied. To better understand legally recognized SSM, this study examines the experiences of bisexual-lesbian couples. To understand the experience of SSM as both a civil institution and a specific way of expressing relational commitment, the study examines the experiences of married or engaged couples. Specifically, the study examines the ways in which married or engaged bisexual-lesbian couples experience the impact of their marriage or decision to marry on their relational lives.

METHOD

Semistandardized interviews were conducted with couples using the three-way chat function of a popular instant messaging (IM) program. Participant recruitment, theoretical sampling, and data analysis occurred simultaneously until saturation was reached (Strauss & Corbin, 1998).

Participant Recruitment and Sampling

Participant recruitment took place in two phases. As part of a larger study, participation was first sought from couples who met the following criteria: both partners were female, the couple was legally married or engaged to be married, and both members of the couple were 18 or over. Announcements about the study were distributed through the newsletters and listservs of several Massachusetts GLBTQ social organizations. Interested participants were asked to contact the researcher by email for more information about the study and to pass the study information on to other couples who met the study criteria and may be interested in participating. From this initial sample, twelve bisexual-lesbian couples were interviewed.

The second phase of participant recruitment, theoretical sampling, took place after the 12 initial interviews were analyzed. Theoretical sampling (Charmaz, 2000; Strauss & Corbin, 1998) is used to refine the data analysis process by comparing new data to the analysis of previously collected data. The recruitment criteria and procedures for the theoretical sample remained the same as that for the initial sample except that participation was sought from bisexual-lesbian couples only. Saturation was reached after 14 additional interviews.

Participants

Twenty-six bisexual-lesbian couples were interviewed ($N = 52$). All participants were residents of Massachusetts and lived in 15 towns within the state. Most participants were Caucasian ($n = 37$) while 6 were Asian, 5 were African American, and 4 were Hispanic. Participant ages ranged from 24 to 57 years ($M = 35.71$, $Mdn = 34$, $SD = 8.54$).

All participants lived full-time with their partner and had an exclusive relationship. The average age difference between partners was 2.73 years ($Mdn = 1.5$, $SD = 3.44$). The majority of the couples (85%, $n = 22$) had married since Massachusetts started legally recognizing SSMs in May 2004. The remaining four couples were engaged to be married and were planning weddings during the 8 months following the interviews. The length of time that participants had been in their relationships ranged from 2.5 to 15 years ($M = 6.42$, $Mdn = 5.75$, $SD = 3.21$). Six of the couples had a commitment ceremony prior to the legal recognition of SSM in Massachusetts. None of the participants had a marriage or commitment ceremony with a previous same-sex partner, but three of the bisexual participants had been previously married to a man. Five of the couples were interracial couples. Four of the couples were currently raising children together.

Interview Procedure

The recruitment announcement instructed those who were interested in the study to contact the researcher by email. When emails from potential participants were received, the researcher responded by sending a consent form with details about the study to the potential participant and indicated that to participate in the study, each member of the couple would need to send informed consent back to the researcher in separate emails. Participants were also asked to indicate whether they would prefer a face-to-face interview at the location of their choice, or an interview using the chat function of a popular IM program that was available for free to all participants. All of the participants who consented to participate in the study indicated that they would prefer an IM format interview. After informed consent was received from both members of the couple, an interview time was scheduled. Participants were also sent a link and instructions for downloading the IM program (most participants indicated that they already had the program on their computers). To protect the participants' confidentiality, they were asked to create a new IM screen name to be used exclusively for the purposes of the interview.

The IM chat room function allowed for three people to send and receive instant messages from each other in an exclusive environment. The entire chat is visible to all people participating in it. IM interviews offer several advantages over face-to-face interview methods such as the ability to save the interview without transcribing and less scheduling and resource strain. Disadvantages of IM interviewing compared to face-to-face interviewing include some brief time-lagging associated with typing and posting a response during an ongoing conversation and the inability to include nonverbal communication beyond simple emoticons in the conversation.

The researcher and participants logged on to the IM program at the agreed upon interview time and the researcher established a three-way chat environment for the interview. Interviews were semistandardized such that an interview guide with some predetermined questions and topics was used for all interviews, but each interview ultimately developed in reaction to participants' responses (Berg, 1995). All interviews began with questions about participant demographic information and background information about their relationship which were answered by all participants. During the remaining interview, participants were asked about their decision to marry and the impact of their marriage or decision to marry on their romantic relationship and their relationship with others. Interviews lasted between 45 and 90 minutes.

Analysis

The data from the initial set of interviews was analyzed using an inductive method informed by grounded theory. When using this type of data-driven approach, themes emerge from the participants' responses rather than a priori conceptual categories (Boyatzis, 1998). Using procedures recommended by Strauss and Corbin (1998), the first step in analyzing the initial interviews was open coding. Open coding was performed for each of the participants' responses to questions or each other's statements during the interview to identify key concepts and organize them into categories. Axial coding was then performed to identify links among categories and identify themes.

The goals of the second set of interviews using theoretical sampling (Charmaz, 2000; Strauss & Corbin, 1998) were to refine the data analysis process such that categories and themes were well explicated and that saturation, meaning that no new categories or themes emerged, was reached. Participants' responses to the interviewer's questions and to each other's comments were analyzed using a constant comparative method (Strauss & Corbin, 1998) to understand the relationship between these responses and the categories and themes identified in the initial interviews.

Steps were taken to verify the credibility of the data analysis (Lincoln & Guba, 1985; Miles & Huberman, 1994). To ensure the validity of the coding procedure, a colleague with expertise in qualitative methods reviewed the transcripts and analysis of 6 randomly selected interviews and agreed with the fittingness of the data to the categories and themes. To check the external credibility of the coding, two of the couples were asked to review the categories and themes that emerged from data analysis, and they confirmed that the descriptions fit with their lived experiences regarding SSM.

RESULTS AND DISCUSSION

Participants discussed the impact of SSM on their lives along four distinct, but interconnected themes: their self-images, their romantic relationships, their relationships with social network members, and their relationship with GLBTQ community. Each theme was comprised of two conceptual categories. The results presentation relies upon directly quoted excerpts from the interviews to give priority to the participants' voices. The quotes presented were edited to replace any IM slang, such as "u" for "you," with the standard English translation and punctuation. Although participants' were identified by their screen names during the interviews, pseudonyms are used here to further protect participant identities.

Same-Sex Marriage and Self-Image

The first theme that emerged from the interviews describes the participants' perspectives on the impact of SSM on views of themselves. Two conceptual categories pertain to SSM and self-image: SSM as an affirmation of bisexual identity and thoughts about being and having a "wife" in a SSM.

Affirming bisexual identity. Many of the bisexual participants discussed how their decision to marry a female partner caused them to reflect on their own bisexual identity in the context of SSM. These participants saw SSM as an affirmation of their bisexual identity. First, participants saw the legal recognition of SSM as a sign of recognition and acceptance for those who are not heterosexual, resulting in a sense of support for their bisexual identity. For example, "I wanted to get married because the legal recognition of SSM isn't just for gay and lesbian people, it's for all of us who love a same-sex partner. It made me feel proud to be bi and with Jess."

Other participants explained that being able to have the same legal recognition of their relationship with a woman as they could for a relationship with a man removed a barrier to their relational freedom. For example, "Now that I could marry a woman, I didn't feel like in being with a woman I had to give anything up anymore. I could be married and have everything I would want in a committed relationship." The idea of SSM allowing for true freedom of choice was expressed by many participants. For example:

> I was so excited that marriage was being recognized for everybody. I mean, for me, being bi has always been about making my own choices and not having society or whatever make them for me. I could choose who to love. Now, I could choose who to marry.

Thus, legally recognized SSM was seen as a means of affirmation for bisexual identities and the relational freedom of choice participants associated with bisexuality.

Being a (and having) a "wife." The second way in which participants discussed the relationship between SSM and their self-images was by reflecting on what it meant to be (and have) a wife within the context of SSM. While some participants expressed excitement and comfort with the institution of marriage (e.g. "I always wanted to get married." and "We were already acting like we were married before it was legal."), others discussed the ways in which they sought to find a fit between their self-image and their understanding of marriage. Many participants commented on their initial reluctance to getting married due to political and philosophical issues with the institution of marriage. For example:

> Jasmine: "We were both nervous about getting married. We didn't want to seem like we were acting straight. And we didn't want to be our parents."
> Laura: "Yeah, marriage is so main-stream. I never wanted to get

married even when I thought I was straight. It just wasn't me."
Jasmine: "And we both hated the history of marriage. Women be-
ing property and all that. We couldn't see ourselves as wives."
Laura: "We had to think about it in a different way."

Many participants explained that they dealt with misgivings about heteronormative marriage by defining or redefining marriage-related terms in a way that fit better with their self-concepts. For example, participants avoided the term "wife" and instead used terms such as "spouse" and "partner" to refer to each other. Other participants resisted negative images of wives in marriages by co-opting traditional language through tongue-in-cheek references to each other as "my bitch" or "my old lady." Participants also spoke of their definition of marriage verses what they perceived as a heteronormative definition of marriage. For example,

Candace: "I'd been married to a man before. He was really controlling, and I guess I thought that was what marriage was like. I
couldn't be that person again, so we talked about it."
Stephanie: "We talked about it a lot."
Candace: "Yeah, and I realized that it wasn't that I wasn't the marriage-type, I just wasn't the controlling marriage-type."
Stephanie: "Right. We had to be sure to have a marriage that fit
who we were. For me, too."

Participants' concerns with marriage as a mainstreaming and hetero-normative institution echoed the concerns of GLBTQ participants in previous research examining SSM (Lannutti, 2005, 2006). Although previous research (Lannutti, 2006) indicated that same-sex couples, especially female-female couples, had reservations about legally recognized marriage based in feminist critiques of marriage (e.g., Steil, 2000), the current research offers additional insight into this aspect of SSM by describing in more detail how couples dealt with their concerns. Through targeted conversations about the meaning of marriage and redefinition of terms associated with marriage, participants sought to align their self-image and beliefs with the institution of marriage.

Same-Sex Marriage and the Primary Relationship

The second theme that emerged from the interviews was the effect of SSM on the couples' relationship with each other. Two categories comprised this theme. The first category includes descriptions of how marriage strengthened the couples' relationships, while the second category describes the ways in which marriage challenged the couples' relationships.

Strengthening relationships. All of the couples expressed some way in which SSM improved or strengthened their romantic relationship. Many couples discussed feeling that their relationship was stronger because it now had legal protections. For example, "Getting married helped us because we didn't have to worry anymore about what would happen if something horrible happened to one of us. I know she will be taken care of now because of the legal protections." Another participant stated, "I think because we are more legally secure now, we feel more secure in our relationship."

Other couples expressed the ways in which SSM contributed to a closer emotional bond between them. Many couples expressed greater feelings of love as a result of getting married. For example, "Obviously, we loved each other or we wouldn't have gotten married. But actually being married has made our love deeper I think." Another participant stated, "Having made those vows in front of our family and friends made me realize how much I really cared for her and how much I really did want to spend my life with her."

Couples also discussed how SSM strengthened their relationship by creating the opportunity to reflect on their relational goals and values with one another. For example:

> Carly: "We didn't just get married right away because we could. We really thought and talked about it."
> Melissa: "It was a serious decision for us. We talked about what we thought was important in a relationship. What our strengths and weaknesses were. We hadn't done that much before.
> Carly: "Well, we didn't have intense conversations like that before thinking about getting married."
> Melissa: "That's true. It really helped make us closer. And feel more confident about marriage."

The discussion of relational values and goals was sometimes explicitly related to one partner's bisexual identity. For example, "When we talked about getting married, I made it really clear to Emily that even though I would always think of myself as bi, I was making a lifelong monogamous commitment to her and I expected the same from her." Another bisexual participant expressed how marriage strengthened their relationship by showing her partner the depth of her commitment: "Right after we got married, Jen told me that she felt a lot happier in our relationship. She confessed that she worried deep down that I wouldn't be able to ever fully commit to her because I was bi. Getting married made her forget that stupid idea." Although all of the couples discussed how SSM made their relationship stronger, many also discussed how SSM challenged their relationship.

Challenging relationships. Couples' discussed the stress that was introduced into their relationship through either their marriage decision process or planning their weddings. While the discussions during their decision to get married were a means to a stronger emotional bond for some couples, others expressed hurt feelings and relational distancing during their marriage decision-making process. For example:

> Coryne: "It was kind of a struggle for us to decide to get married. I wanted to right away, but she was unsure."
> Gram: "Well, I was sure I loved her, but I wasn't sure if we were ready for marriage. I didn't want to do it just cause it was legal."
> Coryne: "Neither did I. But, I really wanted to marry her cause I loved her and I thought the protections would help us."
> Gram: "We fought about it. I actually moved out for a short time."
> Coryne: "It was horrible. But, we worked it out. We both needed to grow-up I think."

Other couples discussed challenges in deciding the terms of their marriage. For example, "I wanted us to be married, but have an open marriage. She wanted no parts of that." Another participant explained, "We were all excited about getting married, but when it came down to pooling our financial resources, I became less sure. We almost broke-up over money before I realized how untrusting and unfair I was being."

In addition to challenges to the relationship presented as part of the marriage decision making process, couples also discussed how planning their wedding ceremonies introduced stress into their relationships. For example:

> Diane: "I had been married to a man before. I didn't want anything that was like that wedding."
> Marie: "But, I wanted some of the traditional things. Like a formal reception and stuff like that. I didn't see why her straight wedding before should mean we couldn't have some of those nice things, too."

Many couples expressed problems with planning their wedding ceremonies because they lacked support from their families-of-origin. For example, "I really didn't want to have a big wedding at first because I knew my parents wouldn't come. In the end, we had the wedding, but it was bittersweet for me."

The idea that SSM helps strengthen same-sex relationships, especially through legal protection, is consistent with previous research on SSM (Lannutti, 2005). However, the present data is also consistent with previous research (Lannutti, 2005) in that SSM is also seen as challenging to couples. Like the couples interviewed for this study, same-sex couple often report struggling with the symbolism involved in commitment rituals and ceremonies (Stiers, 1999). Suter et al. (2006) discuss how lesbian couples may struggle with the public-private dialectic in their commitment ceremonies because members of the couple's families-of-origin are unsupportive of the relationship. Thus, the couples' experience of SSM as both a relationship bolstering and stressing phenomena is consistent with previous research. The relationship between SSM, the couples, and their families and friends is explored further as part of the third theme.

Same-Sex Marriage and Social Networks

The third theme that emerged from the interviews describes the influence of SSM on couples' relationships with their social network members. Couples' discussions of their social networks comprised two categories. First, couples discussed the support and resistance to their marriage from their families-of-origin. The second category describes the pressure some couples felt from their lesbian friends regarding marriage.

Support and resistance from families-of-origin. All of the couples discussed how the legal recognition of SSM or their specific decision to marry affected their relationships with their families-of-origin. The most frequently discussed family-of-origin members were the participants' parents. Some couples discussed the support they felt from their families for SSM in general. For example:

> Jody: "The whole marriage debate really helped my relationship with my parents. They were so upset at how the anti-marriage people acted."
> Cynthia: "Her parents never were really supportive of us before."
> Jody: "They weren't unsupportive. It's more like they didn't take our relationship very seriously before I guess."

Cynthia: "But they got really involved in the fight against the anti-marriage amendments."

Other couples also explained the support they felt from family members for their marriage. For example, "My parents were happy we could get married because it made us so happy." Some participants explained how their parents were surprised by their decision to marry because of their bisexual identity, but were supportive of the decision nonetheless. For example:

When I told my mom that Diane and I were getting married, I wasn't sure how she was going to react. But, she just started laughing and saying she was glad I was going to finally going to marry some-body. I asked her why she said that, and it turns out she was worried that because I was bi I was never going to have a secure lifelong re-lationship with someone. I have no idea why she thought that. It's not like I even dated around that much!

Although some couples described how one partner's bisexual iden-tity was associated with surprised, yet supportive reactions to their mar-riage plans from family members, others described family members who where both surprised and unsupportive. Participants explained how their family members, particularly parents, seemed to view their bisexuality as reason to hope that they would someday choose to marry a man. For example:

Kali: "My parents, especially my mom, lost it when I told them we were engaged."
Carmen: "It was a nightmare. They were never really happy about us, but they were coping. But, this did it for them."
Kali: "I was surprised. When they finally spoke to me, they told me that they thought that being with Carmen was a phase . . . that I would find a man someday."
Carmen: "Imagine, I'm a 4 year phase!"
Kali: "I asked them why after all this time they would think that, and they said 'you call yourself bi, not a lesbian.' Anyway, they are still upset. They say they won't come to the wedding."

Another participant explained, "My sister was totally against us getting married. She could accept me dating a woman, but not marrying one.

We had this fight and she said that I've dated men before and that I should wait to marry a man."

For other couples, families were simply unsupportive of their marriage because it was a SSM, regardless of the participants' individual sexual orientations. For example, "My parents were so embarrassed that I was marrying a woman. They had told people we were roommates all this time." Participants also mentioned that their families were unsupportive of their marriage for religious reasons.

In previous research examining same-sex couples considering marriage, lack of family approval for the union was the most frequently identified obstacle to marriage (Lannutti, 2006). Although the struggle for same-sex couples to gain acceptance and support from families-of-origin is a commonly reported stressor (e.g. Kurdek & Schmitt, 1987; Rostosky et al., 2004; Smith & Brown, 1997), the current data highlight the role that misperceptions about bisexuality play in increasing this stress. Family members' attitudes reflect belief that bisexual women can not fully commit to another woman. Ironically, the families hold on to this stereotypical belief as a "ray of hope" that their bisexual family member may reconnect to the heterosexual world, while ignoring the fact that believing in this myth creates greater stress and distance in their relationship with her.

Marriage pressure from lesbian friends. The second category describing how SSM impacted couples' relationships with their social networks demonstrates a tension between some couples and their lesbian friends. Some couples described the ways in which their lesbian friends pressured them to consider marriage. For example, "As soon as it became clear we could get married legally, it seemed like all of our lesbian friends started asking us when we were getting married. And they persisted. It became annoying after a while because we wanted to really think about it seriously." Another couple describes how a lesbian friend seemed to challenge one partner's bisexuality while pressuring them to marry:

> Susan: "This one friend, Patty, she was kind of over supportive."
> Teressa: "I wouldn't describe it as supportive. She was almost like a bully about it. She kept saying 'you should get married.' Then, when we would say we were thinking about it, she would say 'Well, why not, Teressa? If you can be bi and live with a woman, you can be bi and marry a woman, can't you?'"
> Susan: "It bothered Teressa . . .throwing the bi thing at her like it was something wrong. I think she was just being protective of me, though. She wanted Teressa to make a commitment to me."

Teressa: "Fine. But I never said I wouldn't marry you and it had nothing to do with being bi. Patty was really pushy and rude. I mean, I did marry you. I wanted to."

Other couples described how some lesbian friends attempted to assert their influence on the ways in which the couples defined their marriages and themselves. Some couples described how a lesbian friend asked specific questions about the terms of their marriage. For example, "My friend Allie, she kept asking, 'Is it a monogamous marriage? She won't be able to date men will she?'" Many lesbian friends seemed to take the marriage as a sign that the bisexual partner no longer identified as bisexual. For example, "Deciding to get married actually started some fights with our friends, our lesbian friends. They would make a joke like, 'Well, I guess Quinn grew out of that bi thing, huh?' and eventually we had to come back at them." Another couple explained:

Lisa: "Sometimes when we told people we were getting married, they would say, 'So, you're giving up on guys for good?' or something like that. I got really mad, especially when lesbian friends would say it. It was like they had won a game or something."
Liz: "It was annoying because she had never been with a guy while with me. We were exclusive. She was making a commitment to me, not 'women.'"
Lisa: "It was really because they resented me being bi I think. It made me sorry I ever labeled myself as anything."

The pressure felt by bisexual-lesbian couples to marry and to define the terms of their marriage in ways that their lesbian friends approved of reflects the tension between lesbian and bisexual women described by Rust (1995; 2000). Couples' descriptions of how lesbian friends sought for signs of loyalty to the lesbian partner, a proxy for the lesbian community, through a monogamous marriage is reflective of Rust's (2000) "depoliticizing" aspect of biphobia. "Explanatory" biphobia (Rust, 2000) is evident in lesbian friends' direct challenges to their friends' bisexual identity now that she had decided to marry a same-sex partner. The intersection between bisexual-lesbian SSM and the GLBTQ community is explored further in the next theme.

Same-Sex Marriage and the GLBTQ Community

The fourth theme that emerged during the interviews explained how SSM influenced couples' relationship with the larger GLBTQ community. Two conceptual categories comprised this theme. The first category relates how couples felt a stronger sense of belonging to the GLBTQ community as a result of the political fights over legally recognized SSM and their own marriage. The second category describes how many, particularly bisexual participants, expressed a sense of increased invisibility for their relationship as a result of SSM.

Belonging to the GLBTQ community. The first way in which SSM was relevant to the couples' relationship to the larger GLBTQ community was by encouraging the couples to feel more a part of the community. Couples described feeling more united with the GLBTQ community in two ways. First, many couples described feeling more a part of the community as the community struggled to maintain their marriage rights. Although Massachusetts began recognizing SSM in May 2004, there have been several attempts at overturning these rights through amendments to the state constitution. At the same time, there has been the continuous threat of federal legislation that would eliminate SSM in the United States. Some participants described a renewed sense of belonging with the community as it continued its political struggle over SSM. For example, "We got really involved in all the political stuff to protect marriage. Going to the state house, stuff like that. It reminded me how great the queer community can be, and how much I had drifted away from queer events." Other participants described feeling a part of the GLBTQ community for the first time as a result of the struggle over SSM. For example, "I'd never been into any type of community action stuff. I mean, I'm not the kind of person who wears t-shirts about being bi or anything. Everyone got together to fight to protect it . . . . it didn't matter to me whether I belonged before."

In addition to feeling an increased sense of belonging to the GLBTQ community because of the political struggle over SSM, couples discussed feeling more united with the community because of their marriage itself. Several couples described a sense of "being counted" as part of the community through their marriage. For example, "Because we are married we are officially registered as a same-sex couple. It made us realize that our marriage isn't just about us, it's a part of something bigger that couldn't happen before the law changed." Other couples felt that in getting married, they were more accepted as a couple by the larger GLBTQ community. For example, "There is kind of a pride in the married couples, I think. Like, our gay friends, they are always introducing us as their 'married' friends and people are instantly excited about that." While many couples ex-

pressed feeling a stronger sense of belonging to the GLBTQ community, others expressed a sense that SSM made them more invisible
within the GLBTQ community.

Increased invisibility. Some couples explained how the political
struggle over SSM made them feel that their relationship was invisible
in the GLBTQ community. Couples discussed how getting married
made them little more than a statistic to the GLBTQ community. For example, "I think that to some people, all that matters is that as many people as possible get married and stay married. Who cares who you are . . .
we need numbers!" Other couples discussed how their relationship became defined by the community as a "lesbian marriage" and erased the
uniqueness of their relationship, especially one partner's bisexuality.
One couple's discussion shows how frustrated this sense invisibility
may become:

> Carla: "All you ever hear about is 'lesbian and gay marriages.' It
> makes me mad that we don't use the term 'same-sex marriage.' I
> mean, it's like we don't want to complicate things or some-
> thing."
> Paula: "It shouldn't really matter I guess. But it seems like how we
> see ourselves doesn't matter right now or something."
> Carla: "I just didn't want to hear about our 'lesbian wedding' any-
> more. Everybody, even our very gay florist who we've known for
> years kept calling it a 'lesbian wedding.' Sometimes I wanted to
> yell, 'This is not a lesbian wedding!' but then again, do labels really
> matter? It only matters that we are married and can stay married. So,
> we put up with it."

Thus, SSM affected the intersection between the couples and the
larger GLBTQ community in two ways. As in previous research
(Lannutti, 2005), couples described feeling a part of a united GLBTQ
community struggling to protect the civil institution of SSM. Couples
also felt that by specifically expressing their commitment through
SSM, they had an opportunity to be affirmed by the GLBTQ community. In contrast, other couples explained how expressing their commitment through SSM increased their sense of being ignored by the
GLBTQ community because SSM cloaked the uniqueness of their relationship and self-images. This function of SSM serves as another example of the way that bisexual experiences and concerns become
invisible as they are subsumed under the GLBTQ banner (e.g.,
Hutchins, 1996).

CONCLUSION

This study examined the ways in which bisexual-lesbian couples experience legally recognized SSM. Examining the SSM experiences of bisexual-lesbian couples contributes the emerging SSM literature by focusing on the unique experiences of cross-sexual orientation couples. The study also widens the scope of the bisexuality in marriage literature, which has mostly focused on the experiences of bisexual individuals in different-sex marriages (e.g., Buxton, 2005; Coleman, 1985).

This study showed that SSM impacted the lives of bisexual-lesbian couples as both a civil institution and a specific way of expressing relational commitment. Couples discussed how the political battle over the institution of same-sex marriage, both inside and outside of the GLBTQ community, made them experience their own identities and relationship in new ways. They also discussed the challenges of integrating the institution of marriage, which many viewed as philosophical and political problematic, with their own identities and relationship. Couples also discussed how choosing to express their commitment through marriage impacted their lives. Participants expressed the ways that becoming a married couple influenced how they and others viewed their relationship and their individual identities. Thus, legally recognized SSM is taking on two roles in impacting the lives of same-sex couples.

While previous research has examined the way that GLBTQ people and couples understand and experience SSM (Lannutti, 2005, 2006, & 2007), this study is different in that it specifically examines the experiences of bisexual-lesbian couples. This study showed that bisexual-lesbian couples experienced SSM in ways similar to other same-sex couples. As in previous research on same-sex couples and SSM (Lannutti, 2006), the couples interviewed for this study also experienced SSM as a complex, and often contradictory, phenomena that both benefited and challenged their primary relationship and their relationships with their social networks and the larger GLBTQ community. However, this study also described the unique experience of bisexual-lesbian couples regarding SSM. For example, participants explained how lesbian friends displayed biphobia in discussing the couples' marriage and marriage-decision process and the way in which getting married seemed to cloak the couples' identity as a *bisexual*-lesbian couple within the GLBTQ community. Thus, this study highlights the need to consider the experiences of GLBTQ people who identify as something other than gay or lesbian, and the need to further examine the experiences of cross-sexual orientation same-sex couples.

While this study describes the SSM experiences of bisexual-lesbian couples, several limitations of this study should be noted. The couples' interviewed for the study were all married or engaged to be married in Massachusetts, and their experiences may differ from bisexual-lesbian couple in other geographical regions and from bisexual-lesbian couples who have not chosen to marry. The experiences of these couples may also differ from the experiences of male-male cross-sexual orientation couples. Future research should examine the ways in which legally recognized SSM influences the relational experiences of bisexual-gay male couples and non-married bisexual-lesbian couples.

REFERENCES

Baxter, L. A., & Montgomery, B. M. (1996). *Relating: Dialogues and dialectics.* New York: Guilford Press.

Berg, B. L. (1995). *Qualitative research methods for the social sciences, 2nd Ed.* Boston, MA: Allyn and Bacon.

Bevan, J. L., & Lannutti, P. J. (2002). The experience and expression of romantic jealousy in same-sex and opposite-sex romantic relationships. *Communication Research Reports, 19,* 258-268.

Boyatzis, R. E. (1998). *Transforming qualitative information: Thematic analysis and code development.* Thousand Oaks, CA: Sage.

Burleson, W. E. (2005). *Bi America: Myths, truths, and struggles of an invisible community.* Binghamton, New York: Harrington Park Press.

Buxton, A. P. (2005). A family matter: When a spouse comes out as gay, lesbian, or bisexual. *Journal of GLBT Family Studies, 1,* 49-70.

Caron, S. L., & Ulin, M. (1997). Closeting and the quality of lesbian relationships. *Families in Society: The Journal of Contemporary Human Services, 78,* 413-419.

Charmaz, K. (2000). Grounded theory: Objectivist and constructivist methods. In N. K. Denzin & Y.S. Lincoln (Eds.), *Handbook of qualitative research* (pp. 509-535). Thousand Oaks, CA: Sage.

Coleman, E. (1985). The integration of male bisexuality and marriage. *Journal of Homosexuality, 11,* 189-208.

Gay-Civil-Unions.com (n.d.). *World watch: International status of same-sex unions.* Retrieved August 24, 2006 from http://www.gay-civil-unions.com/HTML/International.htm.

Goransson, L. (1998). International trends in SSM. In R. J. Cabaj & D. W. Purcell (Eds.), *On the Road to Same-Sex Marriage: A Supportive Guide to Psychological, Political and Legal Issues.* (pp. 141-164). San Francisco: Jossey-Bass Inc.

Haas, S. M., & Stafford, L. (1998). An initial examination of maintenance behaviors in gay and lesbian relationships. *Journal of Social and Personal Relationships, 15,* 846-855.

Human Rights Campaign (n.d.). *Marriage.* Retrieved August 24, 2006 from http://www.hrc.org/Template.cfm?Section = Center&Template = /TaggedPage/ TaggedPageDisplay.cfm&TPLID = 63&ContentID = 15110.

Hutchins, L. (1996). Bisexuality: Politics and community. In B. Firestein (Ed.), *Bisexuality: The Psychology and Politics of an Invisible Minority* (pp. 240-259). Thousand Oaks, CA: Sage.

Israel, T., & Mohr, J. J. (2004). Attitudes toward bisexual woman and men: Current research, future directions. In R. C. Fox (Ed.), *Current research on bisexuality* (pp. 117-134). Binghamton, NY: Harrington Park Press.

Kurdek, L. A. (2000). Attractions and constraints as determinants of relationship commitment: Longitudinal evidence from gay, lesbian, and heterosexual couples. *Personal Relationships, 7,* 245-262.

Kurdek, L. A., & Schmitt, J. P. (1987). Perceived emotional support from family and friends in members of homosexual, married, and heterosexual cohabitating couples. *Journal of Homosexuality, 14,* 57-68.

Lannutti, P. J. (2005). For better or worse: Exploring the meanings of same-sex marriage within the lesbian, gay, bisexual and transgendered community. *Journal of Social and Personal Relationships, 22,* 5-18.

Lannutti, P. J. (2006). Attractions and obstacles while considering legally recognized same-sex marriage. Manuscript submitted for publication.

Lannutti, P. J. (2007). The influence of same-sex marriage on the understanding of same-sex relationships. *Journal of Homosexuality* 53, 135-151.

Lincoln, Y. S., & Guba, E. G. (1985). *Naturalistic inquiry.* Beverly Hills, CA: Sage.

Massey, R. (1986). What/who is the family system? *American Journal of Family Therapy, 14,* 23-39.

Miles, M. B., & Huberman, A. M. (1994). *Qualitative data analysis: An expanded sourcebook.* Thousand Oaks, CA: Sage.

Mulick, P. S., & Wright, L. W. (2002). Examining the existence of biphobia in the heterosexual and homosexual populations. *Journal of Bisexuality, 2,* 45-64.

Ochs, R. (1996). Biphobia: It goes more than two ways. In B. Firestein (Ed.), *Bisexuality: The psychology and politics of an invisible minority* (pp. 217-239). Thousand Oaks, CA: Sage.

Parks, M. R., & Eggert, L. L. (1991). The role of context in the dynamics of personal relationships. In W. H. Jones & D. Perlman (Eds.), *Advances in Personal Relationships* (pp. 1-34). London: Jessica Kingsley Publishers.

Patterson, D. G., Ciabattari, T., & Schwartz, P. (1999). The constraints of innovation: Commitment and stability among same-sex couples. In J. M. Adams & W. H. Jones (Eds.), *Handbook of Interpersonal Commitment and Relationship Stability: Perspectives on Individual Differences* (pp. 339-359). Dordrecht, Netherlands: Kluwer Academic Publishers.

Rostosky, S. S., Korfhage, B. A., Duhigg, J. M., Stern, A. J., Bennett, L., & Riggle, E. D. B. (2004). Same-sex couples perceptions of family support: A consensual qualitative study. *Family Process, 43,* 43-57.

Rust, P. C. (1995). *Bisexuality and the Challenge to Lesbian Politics: Sex, Loyalty, and Revolution.* New York: NYU Press.

Rust, P. C. R. (2000). Neutralizing the political threat of the marginal woman: Lesbians' beliefs about bisexual women. In P. C. R. Rust (Ed.), *Bisexuality in the United States: A Social Science Reader* (pp. 471-495). New York: Columbia University Press.

Smith, R. B., & Brown, R. A. (1997). The impact of social support on gay male couples. *Journal of Homosexuality, 33,* 39-61.

Steil, J. M. (2000). Contemporary marriage: Still an unequal partnership. In C. Hendrick & S.S. Hendrick (Eds.), *Close Relationships: A Sourcebook* (pp. 125-136). Thousand Oaks, CA: Sage.

Stiers, G. (1999). *From this Day Forward: Commitment, Marriage, and Family in Lesbianand Gay Relationships.* New York: St. Martin's Press.

Strauss, A., & Corbin, J. (1998). *Basics of Qualitative Research, 2nd Ed: Techniques and Procedures for Developing Grounded Theory.* Thousand Oaks, CA: Sage.

Suter, E. A., Bergen, K. M., Daas, K. L., & Durham, W. T. (2006). Lesbian couples' management of public-private dialectical tensions. *Journal of Social and Personal Relationships, 23,* 349-365.

Make Love, Not Law: Perceptions of the Marriage Equality Struggle Among Polyamorous Activists

Hadar Aviram

I know it's unconventional
Radical but practical
Why can't the three of us live together?
It's a culture shock
But it's the only hope we've got
Tell me, why can't the three of us live together?

–Olivia Newton John, *Culture Shock*

The strong controversy in the gay, lesbian, bisexual and trans (GLBT) community regarding the struggle for marriage equality is hardly news. While many organizations and individuals invest political and financial resources in the fight for marriage rights for same-sex couples, others vehemently oppose these efforts (see especially Kim, 2006). At its core, this controversy concerns the meaning we attach to the institution of marriage, be it legal, religious, economic, social or a combination of these (Coontz, 2005). Different parties to the debate refer to different aspects of marriage to explicate the importance, irrelevance, or shortcomings of marriage equality as the GLBT community's center-stage struggle. Some have highlighted the instrumental aspects of marriage benefits, arguing for and against the importance of these material rights and the possibility to mimic them through private law institutions (Kotulski, 2004). Others have stressed the political components of the struggle, mentioning its importance for group action and collective empowerment, or cautioning about the alienation of various subcultures within the GLBT community (Goldberg-Hiller, 2002). Finally, many focus their arguments on the cultural, symbolic meaning of marriage: an indicator of full citizenship, social respect and recognition, or a mechanism perpetuating patriarchal, limited relationship patterns (Hull, 2006; Kim, 2006; Pinello, 2006). These three aspects–instrumental, political, and cultural–are not endemic to marriage, and feature in various activist attempts to mobilize for legal rights (Kostiner, 2003; also see Crenshaw, 1988; McAdam, 1996; McCann, 1986, 1993).

This paper offers a fresh and unusual perspective on these three aspects of marriage: instrumental, political and cultural. Rather than examining them from the perspectives of gays and lesbians, for whom the struggle for same-sex marriage is a tangible part of their lives, it observes them through the eyes of the polyamorous community in the San Francisco Bay Area. "Polyamory", a term coined in the early 1990s to replace the term "responsible nonmonogamy" (Anapol, 1997; Easton & Liszt, 1997; Munson & Stelboum, 1999; Nearing, 1992), is used in various ways by community activists (Michael, 2005), but in general describes "the practice, state or ability of having more than one sexual [or, for some, romantic] loving relationship at the same time, with the full knowledge and consent of all partners involved" (Anapol 1997). Polyamory can exist within heterosexual, homosexual and bisexual relationship frames.

For people in polyamorous relationships and families, a public legal structure acknowledging their relationships has not, so far, been a likely possibility. Contrary to the conservative "slippery-slope" argument against same-sex marriage (made famous in comments by Rick Santorum, R-Pa, in an interview with Associated Press on April 7, 2003), discussing the possibility of marrying gay and lesbian couples has not, so far, led bigamists, polygamists and polyamorists to ask for plural marriages (nor has it led bisexuals to ask for them in order to fully and simultaneously experience their relationship choices). Since 1854 (and in later amendments in 1882 and 1887), Federal law prohibits any marriage between more than two persons, and there have been no attempts, certainly not outside the context of Mormon polygamy, to revise the legal status of multiple marriages–and even in that context, the Church of Latter-Day Saints only renounced the practice in 1890 (Firmage, 1989; Gordon, 2001; also see *Reynolds v. U.S.*, 98 U.S. 145 (1878)). In polyamorous circles, which are often associated with the other end of the American political map, there have been no attempts to struggle for marriage. The only known case in which community resources were used to contest the monogamous legal order–a child custody battle in Tennessee, between a polyamorous mother, April Divilbiss, and the paternal grandmother–ended in the mother's loss of custody (Emens, 2004).

This lack of legal activism cannot be fully attributed to the nonexistence or marginality of the community, least of all in the San Francisco Bay Area, where there is a vibrant, active presence of polyamorous people. The Bay Area polyamorous community shares the area's legacy of progressive struggles for civil rights in general, and strongly supports GLBT, and particularly bisexual, pride and activism. The community's history can be traced to the 1960s' traditions of free love (Zientara & Rila, 2005), and many of its members sympathize with utopian, idealistic and visionary perspectives through the subculture of science fiction and fantasy fandom and the alternative spirituality milieu (Anderlini-d'Onofrio, 2004; Robins, 2004). Today, the community Internet list, SfBay-Poly, has 519 subscribers; polyamory-oriented and polyamory-friendly parties, as well as sex-positive workshops and regional polyamory conferences, are attended by hundreds of participants; and the national polyamory magazine, Loving More, reports a readership of 10,000 subscribers (Emens, 2004). The lack of focus on marriage as an important goal is even more intriguing in light of the deep sympathies held by polyamorous activists toward the GLBT community and its struggles. The polyamorous community regularly participates in San Francisco's annual Pride March, sharing a truck with the bisexual contingent. Several community members believe that polyamory is closely related to bisexuality and offers an opportunity to live a bisexual identity to its fullest extent; in fact, one could expect that the conservative labeling of bisexuality as polyamory, and of both bisexuality and polyamory as promiscuity, would propel the two communities to support a common struggle for marriage rights of all kinds. The community's activist organizations, such as Love and Politics, emphasize their sex-positive focus and regularly protest against homophobia, and particularly biphobia, in the media.

In light of the curious lack of mobilization for public status, this paper explores how polyamorous activists perceive marriage. In particular, the following research questions were considered: Is plural marriage an attainable goal for the activists? How do they perceive marriage? Do they consider it a worthy cause?

METHODS

Research Design

The research questions were approached through an ethnographic research design. Between December 2004 and September 2005, I attended a variety of political and social events in the Bay Area polyamorous community: meetings, workshops, parties, and the annual World Polyamorous Association conference. In addition to the explicitly polyamorous events, I attended events for "poly-friendly" audiences in science fiction conventions and bookstores, leather stores and GLBT community centers. While the Bay Area's character as a politically progressive milieu could lead to a bias in sampling validity in a different type of study, it was an ideal site for conducting a study focusing on progressive activism.

I also conducted a series of in-depth, semi-structured interviews with 35 active and salient members of the community. The project was not designed to provide a representative sample of the community, but rather to observe these particular activists' approaches toward marriage. Since the project examined attitudes toward mobilization, I chose to focus on activists as those who would be most heavily involved in such initiatives and would therefore constitute the "purest cases" (Luker 1984: 250; also see Kostiner, 2002).

Participant Recruitment

For purposes of the project, I defined "active and salient" community members as people who were organizers, presenters, or vocal participants in polyamory conferences, workshops, online lists (particularly activist lists, such as "love + politics") or polyamory (and "poly-friendly") social events. Other interviewees had written books and articles on polyamory for diverse audiences. I also interviewed people who were mentioned by other members of the community as having had polyamorous relationships for a substantial amount of time (several years) and who were well-known and established "old-timers". A few of the interviewees did not occupy any official role in the community, but who were often mentioned as "social butterflies" that were well-connected within the community and well-versed on its issues.

The recruitment of participants was conducted using several methods. I emailed people who organized or actively and vocally participated in polyamorous events and forums, or approached them in person, and invited them to participate. I also used a snowball technique, asking each interviewee to mention names of people who were, in her or his opinion, active and important names in the community; after a certain point, virtually all names were cross-mentioned by most interviewees.

Participants

The demographics of my sample were concurrent with activists' assessment of the community's profile (Doleshal, 2004). Interviewees' ages ranged between 21 and 70, with an average age of 44. Only 2 of the 35 did not have a university background; 2 were students, 16 had a bachelor's degree, and 15 had advanced degrees. Nine of the interviewees (24%) worked in computer science and technology jobs; 6 (19%) were involved in various aspects of health care and therapy; 4 (12%) were lawyers; 3 (9%) were artists; 4 (12%) were full-time, or close to full-time, activists for progressive causes; the remaining 11 (27%) held different professional, clerical and retail positions. Politically, all interviewees strongly identified with left-wing ideology and policies, though two of them had originally come from right-wing, fundamentalist Christian backgrounds. Seven of the interviewees were either Pagan, or closely identified with Earth-reverent spirituality; most of the others were nonreligious Jews and Christians, with the exception of one Unitarian Universalist who was active in promoting understanding of polyamory in the church (UUPA, 2004). Fifteen of the interviewees self-identified as bisexual; 6 as "straight but not narrow"; and the remaining 14 chose to keep their sexual identity fluid and unlabeled.

Interview Procedure

Interviews ranged between one and two hours and included both personal and general issues. Interviewees were asked to elaborate on the way they structured their past and current relationships, and then to talk about the community in general, its institutions, culture and goals (at this point, I did not mention marriage or public status). The subjects of same-sex marriage and marriage activism were explicitly introduced about halfway through the interview, unless they had previously come up unprompted by me. The interviews were coded manually; the names and identifying details have been changed, for reasons of confidentiality.

RESULTS

From the interviews, workshops and activities, it was clear that pursuing marriage, or a marriage-like structure, was nowhere on the polyamorous agenda. While the community entertained various utopian visions of a world without patriarchy, jealousy, homophobia and possessiveness were mentioned, these were not to be achieved through marriage. In fact, the institution of marriage was often seen as a counter-effective tool for social change. When asked, "how would your world change if one could marry more than one person?" only two of the interviewees, a married couple, replied "we'd go to lots of weddings". The remaining interviewees said that their lives would more-or-less remain the same, and while they acknowledged that the option of marriage might have a symbolic meaning, they did not consider it a desirable path for social activism. Similarly, workshops and activities organized by the community never focused on the marriage struggle per se. Most of them were geared toward improving the relationships themselves, or toward sex-positive politics aimed for receiving social acceptance by other means.

The interviewees' reservations about marriage referred to the three aspects mentioned earlier: the instrumental benefits to be achieved, the political issues, and the cultural and symbolic meanings. It is important to mention that all three aspects were mentioned by each of the interviewees, though personal opinions differed and different people emphasized different aspects.

Marriage as a Vehicle of Material Rights: Practical Doubts and Private Law Mimicry

Steve and Jessica met in the sixties, in a commune in the North Bay. They fell in love, and when they left the commune, disenchanted with the politics and interpersonal drama, they got married. Steve got his graduate degree in the sciences and started working in the IT industry; Jessica completed a graduate degree in behavioral sciences and went on to a position in research administration. In the mid-eighties, Jessica met Doug at work, and they fell in love. Steve and Doug met and forged a strong friendship. After a few years, Doug moved in with Steve and Jessica, as Jessica's "co-husband". Doug paid for the building of the top floor in their shared house, which is owned by Steve and Jessica. All three have made wills which leave each household member's property to the two others, in equal share. None of them is interested in any political activity aimed at obtaining public status for their relationship.

Pragmatic designs for living: Mimicking marriage. Only a few interviewees were as thorough as Steve, Jessica and Doug, in planning the instrumental and financial aspects of their relationships. Nevertheless, all of them found ways to organize the household and make their lives work, materially, without plural marriage. These alternative structures were considered superior to marriage by interviewees of all ages and income levels. Marcy, a pregnant woman in her early twenties who shared her life with her live-in girlfriend and their mutual boyfriend, was unenthusiastic about the possibility of marrying both, or either: "If I got married I'd lose my benefits as a single mom". Roger, a retired professional in his seventies, lives alone; he is committed to his girlfriends, two of whom live nearby, but manages his finances by himself and prefers it that way. Luca, in her early forties and mother to two children, shares her life with Elijah and Elaine, a married couple and parents to a child; all three of them have lived together for the last five years. They had a symbolic commitment ceremony in their back yard, and share rearing responsibilities for the children, but none of them holds a power-of-attorney document in regard to children who are not biologically theirs. Luca, who comes from a less privileged background, explains: "I feel better if I don't owe anyone anything".

For several others, the lack of plural marriage structures is not a problem, because they live their public and financial lives, ostensibly and practically, in couple structures. The earlier versions of polyamorous families, which included a "primary" partner and several "secondary" and "tertiary" partners, are no longer in vogue, because of their rigidity, but are still quite popular in practice; eight of the interviewees, and many other activists I met in workshops, shared the household with just one partner, leading a material life much like that of a monogamous couple.

The activists are well aware of the implications their lifestyle might have on issues such as child custody or property disputes in case of separation, but prefer to lead their lives "under the radar", and to avoid encounters with the law, rather than start an open struggle for public status. The few writers and workshop facilitators on "polyamory and the law" recommend low visibility, and quiet dispute resolution, when such difficulties arise. One popular tool for managing such possible disputes is an agreement on various aspects of the relationship; virtually every polyamorous person I spoke with, in interviews and in workshop,

mentioned the importance of discussing issues of household management, child rearing and responsibilities, fidelity, safe sex, and conflict
resolution methods. One of the most popular workshops in poly conferences and gatherings is titled "On Agreements". Participants are taught
to examine all the important issues of the relationship (household
management, child rearing and responsibilities, fidelity, safe sex, etc.)
and create a quasi-contractual document, which, while not legally
binding, has to be formulated in a clear language in order to create
commitment and resolve misunderstandings. About a third of the interviewees reported having written agreements of this sort, while others verbalized them. Two families with written agreements reported that
these agreements were later disregarded, renegotiated or simply violated by mutual, implicit agreement.

Doubts about the suitability of marriage for securing material rights.
While all these methods, which mimic the material institutions of marriage through private law and extra-legal mechanisms, are very much
in use in the community, polyamorous activists appear to be quite hesitant about insisting on obtaining the full "original package" of material benefits through marriage. Some of them express serious doubts
about the possibility of drafting a workable, practical framework
which would not limit their lives. Emily, a 25-year-old woman in multiple relationships, comments:

> We often talk about how we would do [poly marriage], but there's
> lots of problems that we really have no answer for. See, if I want to
> ask, say, for insurance for any of my partners; obviously the em-
> ployer won't want to pay for five, or twenty people, right? So we
> have to come up with something that's reasonable. I mean, reason-
> able to them. And I personally really don't have the drive to do it.

Deborah's comments, and similar ones from other activists, reflect
an understanding of the type of negotiation that would be necessary if
polyamory were to seek public status through the mainstream legal system. The activists are well aware of the need to compromise with mainstream society if seeking to establish an acknowledged status; these
compromises might require limiting the number of partners who can be
parties to such a marriage, or giving up a certain portion of the material
benefits offered to married couples. As the following sections show,
such compromises are very difficult due to the fluid, pluralist nature of
the community.

Marriage Activism as a Political Issue:
Narrow Coalitions and Strategic Concerns

George is a poly and sex-positive activist, who has recently left a polyamorous relationship. In designing the organization he helped found, he consciously tried to avoid "vanilla" activism and to be "in your face". For example, recently, the organization flooded a well-known gay online magazine with furious letters, protesting a homophobic article written by one of the gay columnists. In addition, the organization has several topical groups, offering discussions and workshops on poly-related subjects. The possibility of a struggle for plural marriage is not on the agenda, at all.

For the gay and lesbian community, the struggle for same sex marriage has become a "front" for a larger struggle for equality and rights, which has become the most salient (albeit not necessarily the most important for everyone) issue in community activism. The interviews reveal that, for the polyamorous community, a similar struggle would not serve the same function. Polyamorous activists lean toward a framework that rejects identity politics and strives to go beyond it.

Beyond identity politics. The interviewees see identity politics–asking for "poly rights" in themselves, as poly people–as a strategic, or even tactical, type of activism they wish to avoid. In his essay "Poly Politics: Lessons from Queer Liberation" (Mint, 2005), Pepper Mint, a bisexual, polyamorous activist, mentions the problems of using fixed identities as a platform for requesting civil rights. These reflections characterize some of the younger interviewees, who developed their lifestyle in the light (or shadow) of the same-sex marriage struggle. The liberal argument, according to which gay people are "born gay" and therefore do not have the choice to marry someone from the other sex, seems, to some poly activists, problematic, and resembles, to a great extent, arguments made by several bisexual activists as to the validity of sexual choice regardless of genetic predispositions (Hutchins and Kaahumanu, 1991). Regardless of whether they believe they are genetically "wired poly", or whether they chose their lifestyle, they argue that, if their relationships are to be recognized, it is not because they have been born "different" or "defective". As Claire explains, bringing to mind Foucault (1977) and Butler (1990),

[t]here are poly people who argue they were born like this. I think it's not a good idea. I agree it's a defensive strategy you have to

take against the right wing, but if you actually believe in it you create a trap–it become politically-driven essentialism, but empowering thinking would be that we have choices and we choose what's
good for us. There's more: I believe that bi, poly and spirituality
are epistemologies, paths to knowledge, modalities of knowledge
through which we experience the world and learn, and that's how
they are empowering . . . I don't discount identity. Identity is important in the political sense, but freedom lies in epistemology.

Kathy, a member of a triad in her forties, argues along the same lines,
and adds a pragmatic reason for avoiding identity politics. Discussing
benefits and support, she argues for a broad definition of family, based
on actual connections rather than identities:

[It's important to] to make it easier to define family more broadly,
so that would get addressed at in terms of what people actually
need. As human beings. [Family would be] predicated upon acknowledgment that there is a significant . . . ah . . . economic interdependence. (interview #26)

The post-identity approach sees polyamorous marriages as merely
creating yet another limiting, difficult category. George argues: "If you
just legalize pluralized marriage in America today, it would be a really
reactionary institution". And Kathy, seeking freedom from categories
rather than the creation of another category, uses the symbolic example
of official forms to explain the importance of a post-identity approach:

[J]ust say we look at each other as more than single/divorced/
widow–you know, because I have to fill out these squares where . . .
it's like . . . I don't do it any more. I don't say I'm single, I don't say
I'm divorced, I don't say I'm married. There's never a square that
says "other". I'm "other".

*Reasons for eschewing identity politics: Lack of stigma, pluralism, and
the concern over narrow coalitions.* Poly activists' rejection of identity
politics stems from various characteristics of their community. One of
these is the fact that polyamory has not, historically, suffered the social
stigma associated with homosexuality. In *History of Sexuality* (1977),
Foucault argues that "homosexuality", as an identity, was created by a
process of social medicalization, a definition as medical perversion rather
than a lifestyle. Sedgwick (1991) connects between this social process

and the development of gay identity. The polyamorous community hasn't gone through a similar process. As Greg, a thirty-three year old activist, puts it, "we're just not pissed off enough. Remember Stonewall? Why do you think that happened? Folks were furious. Now they were at the end of their rope, there. We're not there yet".

In addition, polyamorous people are less likely to adopt common labels that encompass the entire community, because of their strong preference for individualism, pluralism and fluidity. All polyamorous books and publications emphasize that there are many ways to "do polyamory right" (Anapol, 1997; Easton, 1997; Millstine, 2002). One of my interviewees told me she had agreed to the interview because I introduced the subject of my interest as "polyamory lifestyles" rather than "lifestyle". Virtually all interviewees expressed antagonism toward "other" polyamorous activists, who were trying to dictate different choices and methods. George, for example, criticized other activists: "they present their views on polyamory as if that's the only way to make your family work. That really pisses me off". Under these circumstances, developing a common "model of marriage" does not seem a realistic prospect.

Some of the complexities regarding a common identity have to do with the fact that some subcultures in the community might be more difficult to "market" to the mainstream. George illustrates the difficulties in choosing "poster children" for a common struggle:

> There is a lot of crossover with kink [BDSM, kinky sex practices]
> ... it'll be a challenge to make this more palatable for the public ...
> so you wouldn't want to exclude them, but you wouldn't exactly
> make them into the poster children of the movement, either.

Certainly, such issues have come up in the GLBT rights struggle as well (Armstrong, 2002), and various groups oppose the focus on marriage because of its lack of appeal for less privileged subgroups with more pressing concerns (Pinello, 2006). However, the poly community seems to ascribe more importance to pluralism than to common activism.

Issues of diversity and solidarity come up in the context of cooperation with other social groups–mainly the GLBT rights movement and Mormon polygyny. Despite their lack of enthusiasm about a poly marriage struggle, the interviewees were supportive of GLBT rights and of the same-sex marriage struggle. In fact, some of them expressed an unwillingness to raise their public profile, in fear that such a move might, as Fay mentions, "sabotage[e] the case of for our gay and lesbian brothers and sisters". Fay, a forty-two year old woman in a "quad"–a relationship between two men and two women–said that supporting gay and lesbian rights from afar would be, in the long run, better for the polyamorous community as well: "It's a gradual thing. If we let the gays and lesbians have their moment in the sun and get their rights, society may be more prepared to give us rights when the time comes".

Mormon polygyny seldom comes up in the conversation as a potential partner for activism. While polyamory and Mormon polygyny share an interest in nonmonogamous lifestyles, they are on opposite sides of the socio-political map on nearly any other aspect. This situation makes a narrow coalition between the two groups highly improbable. George analyzes the situation:

> Yes, we and [the Mormons] believe in multiple partnership, but everything else about how they do it is something I can't feel real kinship with. The patriarchy, the way the relationships are one sided–you can only have wives, a woman can't have husbands–it would make any cooperation very difficult, if not impossible.

All other interviewees concurred that there was no communication, and no initiative to communicate, between the two communities. Karen, a twenty-four year old volunteer in a local feminist/queer bookstore, supported the possibility of an alliance with Mormons. Jessica, Steve and Doug's "wife", commented that, although several aspects of Mormon life seemed unacceptable to her, she "empathized with Mormon women and their lack of jealousy". She also believed that Mormon lifestyle could have feminist, liberating implications (Emens, 2004; Gordon, 1996; Iversen, 1984). However, other interviewees felt that the political, ideological and religious chasm between them and Mormon polygynists prevented any possibility of cooperation on a political platform.

Marriage as a Cultural/Symbolic Artifact: Mistrust of Government, the Emphasis on Love, and the Double-Edged Sword of Utopia

> My research notes from the summer of 2005 tell of my experiences at the World Polyamorous Association's annual conference, where poly people from California and other states attended a variety of workshops. Most of the workshops focused on relationship enhancement techniques: communication, conflict resolution, jealousy management, polyamory in science-fiction-fantasy culture, and . . . tantric lovemaking. No one brought up marriage as a viable option to pursue; the focus was love, not politics.

A few months after the conference, I was invited to speak to poly-amorous activists, where these priorities were echoed by Norm, a conflict-resolution workshop facilitator. He told me about the im-portance of developing strong, healthy, long-term polyamorous relationships; working on love is more important than mobilizing for marriage. He and his primary partner had gone through highs and lows on their path to developing a good method for communi-cating. Without such investment in the quality of the relationships themselves, "marriage", he said, was "a moot point".

The supporters of the same-sex marriage struggle emphasize the ways in which the possibility of marriage symbolizes cultural and social acceptance. For the polyamorous activists I interviewed, however, mar-riage has different cultural associations. Marriage entails a submission to government and bureaucracy, normalization and stagnation of fluid, creative, visionary lifestyles. These sentiments contribute to the reser-vations about the possibility of marriage-oriented activism. To under-stand where they stem from, it is important to sketch the cultural milestones that shaped the polyamorous community.

Sources of cultural reservations about marriage: The counter-cultural scene as a double-edged sword. The lack of enthusiasm about marriage equality and other forms of public legal mobilization in the polyamorous community stems, to a great extent, from its cultural roots. The community's cultural heritage hails from the sixties, when many of the older interviewees came to this lifestyle through the alternative, counter-cultural scene (Robins, 2004; Zientara & Rila, 2005). The uto-pian visions of intentional communities and nonexclusive loves are still very present in the community's publications and activities. *Loving More*, the community's magazine, devotes countless articles to various forms of communal living. A recently published anthology of texts about polyamory and bisexuality included a utopian piece about a triad of artists. When asked to describe their ideal world, the interviewees of-ten spoke of peaceful, loving communities, reminiscent of the ideals in the sixties.

Many of these utopian models were influenced by the science fiction and fantasy literature, of which many polyamorous people are fans (Doleshal, 2004), and particularly by the works of Robert Heinlein, es-pecially *Stranger in a Strange Land* (1961). In this novel, a man born on Mars returns to Earth and teaches the people he meets to love uncondi-tionally and without possessiveness. George recounts:

I'll have to say [my fascination with polyamory] started by reading a book–*Stranger in a Strange Land*. I was twelve. And I know this for a fact because . . . I recently found a book review that I wrote at that age, saying how wonderful it was. That vision of a community, a loving community, imprinted itself on me when I was still a virgin and would remain as such for some time to come.

For the twenty-first century reader, *Stranger in a Strange Land* appears dated, sexist and homophobic. Nevertheless, in the years immediately following its publication the book was considered revolutionary, and even led to the formation of a religious polyamorous organization, the *Church of All Worlds (CAW)*. "Living the Dream", a group connected with CAW and with its magazine, *Green Egg*, is currently considering ideas on how to create a commune based on Heinlein's premises in the Los Angeles area. Daniel, a conference organizer and workshop facilitator, explains the appeal of science fiction to polyamorists in broader terms:

There is something different about science fiction literature compared to, say, standard or mainstream literature, and it has to do with the ideas about change, and about future and what if things were different than they were. What if people lived to be 900 years old instead of 90? What if technology was different, what if there were creatures here from other planets . . . the kind of mind that is attracted to these things tends to be visionary and . . . active imagination, more open to alternative possibilities . . . they can look at the world and imagine it real different.

Indeed, many activists are drawn to spiritual and literary subcultures that encourage them to envision unconventional, alternative lifestyles. Raven, a child of the 1980s, came to polyamory through the Society for Creative Anachronism (SCA), which reconstructs battles and scenes from Greco-Roman, Medieval and other historical periods (O'Roarke, 1996). Caroline was drawn to it through the Punk scene and, like many other interviewees, through Neo-Pagan, Earth-based spirituality (Anderlini-D'Onofrio, 2004; Millstine, 2002).

[my]thesis is that there are a thousand ways to make love, there isn't just one way, and we tap into our creative and our imagination, on how do we become better lovers. If there's thousands of ways . . . I mean in takes us to an environmental level, I mean eco-poli-

tics is really important to me. Part of how I make love to the planet is that I compost.

Claire, a long-time bisexual activist, adds:

> There is a connection between polyamory and Earth-based spirituality. That's actually what interests me in [being] poly. It's the missing link between being bisexual and being Pagan. Bisexuality comes from focusing on sexuality, and the whole idea of sexuality defines erotic expression as something you can study scientifically, while polyamory is less about sex and more about love, more related to spirit, so it's less explored scientifically and more experienced and expressed, like art, music, an expression form that is erotic. And that's what happens with Earth-based spirituality. It's knowledge that comes from a humanist tradition.

The sci-fi/fantasy, alternative spirituality and countercultural scenes intersect, today, on the internet–the best resource for newcomers to polyamory and a Petri dish for online discussion groups such as "bi-poly-pagan-goth".

This utopian, visionary background acts as a double-edged sword for poly community activism. On one hand, the nonconventional realms and spiritualities provide strong encouragement and support to think outside the box and "boldly go where no one has gone before", relationship-wise. On the other hand, they create a convenient milieu where polyamorous lifestyles are accepted and respected, discouraging activists from making an effort to seek mainstream acceptance through frameworks such as marriage.

Dislike for government. One of the ways in which activists express their lack of enthusiasm about interacting with the mainstream is their contempt for, and dislike of, governmental involvement in personal life. This was particularly evident in interviews with older interviewees, who were young adults in the 1960s. Bruce's comment is typical:

> When I figured out that none of this [monogamous marriage] stuff made sense to me I developed a fairly strong aversion to the idea that . . . the government should be involved in deciding who I did and didn't love.

The interviewees expressed suspicion that there was "too much government" involved in private matters. While none of the interviewees were libertarians in matters of national economy, they made a sharp distinction between welfare policies and the business of regulating feelings. Some of the interviewees acknowledged that government involvement in "who they did and didn't love" could work in two directions: it could be exclusionary, or guarantee rights and protection. However, the potential benefits were not seen as worth the problems involved in presenting the government with a strategy for recognizing polyamorous relationship. The earlier quote from Emily regarding the impracticality of asking for partner benefits for twenty partners reflects these problems.

When describing a life of disengagement from government bureaucracy, many interviewees used the expression "under the radar". Living "under the radar" means that one's lifestyle, household management, sexual life, and childrearing practices, are all designed to be lived unnoticed by anyone or anything "official". This attitude characterized not only the unwillingness to fight for multiple marriages, but also the reticence from legal separation agreements and, particularly, custody battles. In its one and only article on legal matters, Loving More, the national polyamorous magazine, recommends avoiding bringing up polyamory issues during child custody disputes, reminding the readers of the aforementioned unfortunate custody case (White, 2002), in which April Divilbiss, a woman in Tennessee, lost custody of her daughter, in part, because of her partnership in a polyamorous triad. Jerry, a community activist, broke up with Moira, while they were both involved in other relationships. They did their very best to divide their assets–including their house–on their own, despite the emotional difficulties and negotiation. Why did they not get a lawyer, or go to court? "We don't do that", Jerry explains, in a way reminiscent of Engel's "ethos of self-sufficiency" (1994). "The court is not a solution to the problem. Any issue I have, I'd rather resolve it by myself". (also see Bumiller, 1986)

Make love, not law. The interviewees' dislike for government involvement is closely related to another reservation against mobilizing for marriage: the strong belief that law is an unsuitable tool for organizing feelings and relationships. Polyamorous self-help books (Anapol, 1997; Easton & Liszt, 1997; Millstine, 2002) contain plenty of advice for conflict resolution and jealousy management, and virtually none on legal issues. As mentioned above, *Loving More* published only one article about legal matters in its forty issues (White, 2002). Any discussion of the future revolves around utopian scenarios rather than actual steps for mobilization. Most workshops offered in the community provide tools for managing relationships. There are two exceptions I am familiar with are occasional presentations on "polyamory and the law" by polyamorous attorneys, which mostly deal with issues of custody and zoning, and the aforementioned workshop on "relationship agreements", which advocates written quasi-contracts between romantic partners, for the purpose of clarifying expectations and resolving conflicts, rather than establishing public status. The World Polyamorous Association annual conference in 2005 included a myriad of workshops dealing with relationships and sexuality. Only one workshop dealt with a pragmatic subject (cohousing). This minimal discussion of law–and mobilization-related topics has much to do with the way the interviewees perceive law. As can be seen from Kathy's words about "checking boxes", law is perceived as a rigid structure. While providing protection and rights, it also confines, regulates, and is inflexible. Relationships, on the other hand, are fluid, ever-changing entities, which cannot be truly encapsulated in a legal right or duty. Reflecting again on Bruce's words, the government not only shouldn't tell its subjects who to love, it is actually unable to do so. Love is perceived to be beyond the reach of any regulative apparatus, and helping loving relationships to grow and thrive is more important than tailoring them so they are palatable to lawmakers.

DISCUSSION

Why does the polyamorous community not seek plural marriage as an objective? This is a difficult, and perhaps impossible, question to answer. As the findings show, the answer may lie in any of several factors: the availability of private-law instruments which provide adequate material tools, the uncertainty about how to frame requests for polyamorous legal rights, the pluralism of poly organizations and their disagreement on political moves, the lack of enthusiasm about identity politics, the lack of stigma, the concern that mainstream public may not be "ready" yet to acknowledge multiple, simultaneous romantic relationships, or the concern over the stifling, confining outcomes of the institution of marriage. Obviously, the heart of the matter cannot be reduced to a single factor, and law, as a tool for social justice, is rejected both due to its instrumental inefficiency (Rosenberg 1992, 1993) and lack of symbolic value (McCann, 1992). The different meanings of marriage, and the different rationales for the lack of enthusiasm for marriage, are present, side-by-side, in the interviewees' "cultural toolkits", and each interviewee invoked several of them (Ewick & Silbey, 2000; Kostiner, 2003; Swidler, 1986).

It is important to point out, however, that all these reservations and hesitations were present for social movements that did, eventually, mobilize and struggle for legal rights. First-wave feminism was plagued by multiple factions and organizations, a situation that only became more complex when radical feminism appeared on the scene (Flexner & Fitzpatrick, 1996; Messer-Davidow, 2002). The story of GLBT liberation is also a complex one, which involved reconciling differences between several factions on the path toward developing a "GLBT identity" (Armstrong, 2002; S. M. Engel, 2001; Marcus, 2002). The GLBT example is particularly instructive, because, in the era before civil unions, same-sex couples, just like today's polyamorous families, used similar private-law arrangements to mimic marital situations. In both the feminist and GLBT examples, there were concerns on whether the public was "ready" for a revolution, and there were voices arguing for incremental, rather than revolutionary, approaches. Despite these factors, the feminist and GLBT movements eventually did "move" in the legal direction–and, in the GLBT case, by engaging in a struggle for marriage equality, despite the strong internal controversy about the struggle's value and importance.

In light of the histories of these struggles, we might ask ourselves whether polyamory will, eventually, seek public status through marriage. It is, of course, possible that if there is a polyamorous social movement (McAdam, 1996) it has not "moved" yet, and might be waiting to benefit from the achievements of the gay and lesbian struggle and use an incremental tactic to obtain plural marriage when the time comes. On the other hand, it is not unreasonable to suggest that in the polyamorous case there are special considerations, which inhibit polyamorous activists from framing their agenda in the language of legal rights.

Whether or not a polyamorous marriage struggle will take place in the future, I believe that the cultural background which has shaped the community for the last forty years has created a priority for certain ways of thinking, which, while fruitful for creativity in relationships, are not conducive to pro-marriage activism. The strongest manifestations of these thought patterns are the strong opinions against government involvement and for fluidity and pluralism in the definition of relationships.

The cultural background of the movement impacts the willingness to struggle for recognition in two main ways. First, it supports a visionary perspective based on utopianism. Science fiction literature and alternative spirituality provide inspiration for a free, nonpossessive relationship style, but do not readily supply strategies for universalizing this style and making it accessible to all. Polyamorous activists are propelled to "think outside the box", and to dream of a better world, where love is egalitarian, free from patriarchy and hypocritical constraints. However, they do not feel it necessary, at present, to provide a practical platform for immediate steps to be taken in an imperfect world.

The second way in which the cultural background influences polyamorous activism is related to the cultural encouragement for freedom, fluidity and individualism. Geek culture, sci-fi/fantasy fandom and alternative spirituality are good options for people who are willing to live some aspects of their lives outside the mainstream culture. All of these subcultures encourage individuals to shape their lives in any way that works for them. The outcome—for better or worse—is a community that largely focuses on enabling originality, individual solutions and tolerance, rather than on finding common ground. A short Internet search of popular polyamory websites reveals much resistance to any activist who offers suggestions on "how to do polyamory right". The community's self-help books also create much resistance and controversy. Many of the interpersonal disagreements uncovered in the interviews stem from the interviewees' perception that others are trying to "enforce" a "correct" way of living in polyamorous relationships. This cultural mindset of individualism is very conducive for experimental lifestyles, but not as conducive to group empowerment and tighter definitions of objectives, which are perceived as required for legal mobilization.

Naturally, polyamorous people are not isolated from mainstream society, and, in addition to their own "cultural milestones", share cultural ideas from society's cultural tool-kit (Swidler, 1986). They are not oblivious to ideas of mobilization and rights, to the struggles of the feminist and gay liberation movements, or (at least in the Bay Area) to the local heritage of the Free Speech Movement. As mentioned earlier, it may well be that the time for using these "tools", rather than the ones provided by the community's birth, has simply not yet come, and that we might see future attempts for mobilization. However, at this point in time it is possible to conclude that the law, and the language of rights and obligations, is not "all over" for the polyamorous activists (Sarat, 1990); they decline law's promise to organize and govern their lives. Apparently, there are realms, like the realm of feelings and emotions, where the rigid, pragmatic character of law makes people push it aside and construct their lives around alternative concepts (also see Aviram, 2006; Levine & Mellema, 2001).

Should this reluctance to pursue public legal status be seen as resistance to law, to marriage, or to social conformism? The answers to these questions depend largely on our definitions of these terms. It is evident from the interviews, however, that the interviewees equate the public, official aspects of marriage, with legal rights. It is not that law does not matter to polyamorous activists; on the contrary, it matters very much, and its perceived logical mechanisms are exactly the features they seek to avoid by not pursuing marriage as an objective. The interviewees seem to perceive law as a Luhmannian system which "thinks" in a certain rigid, coercive way (Luhmann, 2004; Teubner, 1983, 1989) that does not fit the way in which they would like to conceptualize their relationships. Among other factors, this contrast–the contrast between the perceived features of marriage as a legal arrangement and the fluid, visionary construction of relationships–hinders polyamorous activists from hopping on the marriage equality train, or from seeking other forms of public recognition for their families.

CONCLUSIONS AND FUTURE AGENDA

This paper hopes to contribute to the discussion of same-sex marriage by discussing the meaning of marriage for a community in which the prospect of marriage is (still?) a dream. The choice to make marriage the focus of a social struggle is valid and understandable, but there are equally valid counterarguments whose logic is, in my opinion, supported by the polyamorous example. The concern over the negative aspects of struggling for polyamorous marriage is extremely relevant to the same-sex marriage issue. Particularly, the argument that marriage can lead to a submission to an archaic, rigid, undesirable social order, often referred to by objectors to the same-sex marriage agenda within the community, is extended to its logical conclusion in the polyamory example. The polyamorous understanding of marriage as an imposition of limits on the fluidity and versatility of relationship is an argument that many bisexuals (and many gays and lesbians) might identify with.

I would like to end by suggesting two arenas in which future research can examine some of the topics discussed in this paper. One of them is to seek other new communities that could potentially struggle for public legal recognition–not necessarily marriage–and compare the different cultural backgrounds and impact on mobilization. One such community may be that of the obese and overweight, in which some individuals have used law to trace the lines of rights and discrimination with varying degrees of success (Colker, 1996; Kirkland, 2003). Another could be returning to the polyamorous community in a few years, in order to observe whether the reservations about marriage activism were "growing pains" which eventually led to activist initiatives, or genuine characteristics of the movement, which make the institution of marriage an undesirable objective.

REFERENCES

Anapol, D. M. (1997). *Polyamory: The New Love Without Limits*. San Rafael: Intinet Resource Center.

Anderlini-D'Onofrio, S. (2004). *Plural Loves: Designs for Bi and Poly Living*. Binghamton: Harrington Park Press.

Armstrong, E. A. (2002). *Forging Gay Identities: Organizing Sexuality in San Francisco, 1950-1994*. Chicago: University of Chicago Press.

Aviram, H. (2004). When the Saints Go Marching In: Legal Consciousness and Prison Experiences of Conscientious Objectors to Military Service in Israel. In L. B. Nielsen & B. D. Fleury-Steiner (Eds.), *The New Civil Rights Research, Dartmouth:*Ashgate.

Baldwin, M. L. (1997). Can the ADA Achieve Its Employment Goals? *Annals of the American Academy of Political and Social Science, 549*, 37-52.

Bernstein, M. (1997). Celebration and Suppression: The Strategic Uses of Identity by the Lesbian and Gay Movement. *American Journal of Sociology, 103*(3), 531-565.

Bumiller, K. (1986). Victims in the Shadow of the Law. *Signs: Journal of Women in Culture and Society, 12*(3), 421-439.

Burstein, P. (1991). Legal Mobilization as a Social Movement Tactic: The Struggle for Equal Employment Opportunity. *American Journal of Sociology, 96*, 1201-1225.

Burstein, P., & Edwards, M. (1994). The Impact of Employment Discrimination Litigation on Racial Disparity in Earnings. *Law and Society Review, 28*, 79-108.

Butler, J. (1990). *Gender Trouble: Feminism and the Subversion of Identity*. New York: Routledge.

Chambers, D. L. (1996). What If? The Legal Consequences of Marriage and the Legal Needs of Lesbian and Gay Male Couples. *Michigan Law Review, 95*(2), 447-491.

Colker, R. (1996). *Hybrid: Bisexuals, Multiracials and Other Misfits under American Law*. New York: New York University Press.

Coontz, S. (2005). *Marriage, a History: From Obedience to Intimacy, or How Love Conquered Marriage*. New York: Viking.

Crenshaw, K. (1988). Race, Reform and Retrenchment: Transformation and Legitimation in Antidiscrimination Law. *Harvard Law Review, 101*, 1131-1287.

Doleshal, D. (2004). *What is Polyamory?* Flier for distribution: World Poyamorous Association.

Easton, D., & Liszt, C. A. (1997). *The Ethical Slut: A Guide to Infinite Sexual Possibilities*. San Francisco: Greenery Press.

Emens, E. F. (2004). Monogamy's Law: Compulsory Monogamy and Polyamorous Existence. *Forthcoming: New York University Review of Law and Social Change, 29*, 277-376.

Engel, D. M. (1994). The Oven Bird's Song: Insiders, Outsiders, and Personal Injuries in an American Community. In Greenhouse & Yngverson & Engel (Eds.), *Law and Community in Three American Towns*. Ithaca: Cornell University Press.

Engel, S. M. (2001). *The Unfinished Revolution: Social Movement Theory and the Gay and Lesbian Movement*. Cambridge: Cambridge University Press.

Eskridge, W. N. (1993). A History of Same-Sex Marriage. *Virginia Law Review, 79*(7), 1419-1513.

Ewick, P., & Silbey, S. S. (2000). *The Common Place of Law: Stories from Everyday Life*. Chicago: University of Chicago Press.

Firmage, E. B. (1989). Free exercise of religion in nineteenth century America: The Mormon cases. *Journal of Law and Religion, 7*(2), 281-313.

Flexner, E., & Fitzpatrick, E. (1996). *Century of Struggle: The Womans Rights Movement in the United States, Enlarged Edition*. Cambridge: Belknap Press.

Foucault, M. (1977). *The History of Sexuality, Volume I: An Introduction* (R. Hurley, Trans.). New York: Pantheon.

Francis, E. (2004). From Self to Self: Masturbation as the Future of Sex. In S. Anderlini-D'Onofrio (Ed.), *Plural Loves: Designs for Bi and Poly Living* (pp. 167-176). Binghamton: Harrington Park Press.

Goldberg-Hiller, J. (2002). *The Limits to Union: Same-Sex Marriage and the Politics of Civil Rights (Law, Meaning, and Violence)*. Ann Arbor: University of Michigan Press.

Gordon, S. B. (1996). The liberty of self-degradation: Polygamy, woman suffrage, and consent in nineteenth-century America. *The Journal of American History 83*(3), 815-847.

Gordon, S. B. (2001). *The Mormon Question: Polygamy and Constitutional Conflict in Nineteenth-Century America*. Chapel Hill: University of North Carolina Press.

Haslam, K. (1997). Confessions of a Polyamorous Geezer.

Heinlein, R. (1961). *Stranger in a Strange Land*. New York: Ace Books.

Hull, K. (2006). *Same Sex Marriage: The Cultural Politics of Love and Law*. New York: Cambridge University Press.

Hutchins, L., & Kaahumanu, L. (eds.). (1991). *Bi Any Other Name: Bisexual People Speak Out,* Los Angeles and New York: Alyson Books.

Iversen, J. (1984). Feminist implications of mormon polygyny. *Feminist Studies, 10*(3), 505-522.

Jenness, V. (1995). Social movement growth, domain expansion, and framing processes: The gay/lesbian movement and violence against gays and lesbians as a social problem. *Social Problems, 42*(1), 145-170.

Kim, R. (2006). Beyond Same-Sex Marriage. Retrieved Aug. 1, 2006, from the World Wide Web: http://www.beyondmarriage.org/.

Kirkland, A. (2003). Representations of Fatness and Personhood: Pro-Fat Advocacy and the Limits and Uses of Law. *Representations, 82*, 24-51.

Kostiner, I. (2002). Evaluating Legality: Activists' Understandings of the Role of Law in Social Change. *Law and Society Review, 37*(2), 323-368.

Kotulski, D. (2004). *Why Should You Give a Damn About Gay Marriage*. New York: Advocate Books.

Levine, K., & Mellema, V. (2001). Strategizing the street: How law matters in the lives of women in the street-level drug economy. *Law and Social Inquiry, 26*(1), 169.

Luhmann, N. (2004). *Law as a Social System* (K. A. Ziegert, Trans.). Oxford and New York: Oxford University Press.

Luker, K. (1984). *Abortion and the politics of motherhood*. Berkeley: University of California Press.

Marcus, E. (2002). *Making Gay History: The Half Century Fight for Lesbian and Gay Equal Rights*. Perennial Currents.

Marovitch, M. (2004). Exploring the great divide–swinging vs polyamory. *Loving More, 33*.

Matthesen, E. (1997, June 10). *alt. Polyamory Frequently Asked Questions*. Retrieved May 23, 2005, from the World Wide Web: http://www.faqs.org/faqs/polyamory/faq/

McAdam, D., McCarthy, J., & Zald, M. (1996). *Comparative Perspectives on Social Movements: Political Opportunities, Mobilizing Structures, and Cultural Framings*. Cambridge University Press.

McCann, M. (1993). Reform litigation on trial. *Law and Social Inquiry, 17*(4), 715-744.

McCann, M. W. (1986). *Taking Reform Seriously: Perspectives on Public Interest Liberalism*. Ithaca: Cornell University Press.

McCann, M. W. (1994). *Rights at work: Pay Equity Reform and the Politics of Legal Mobilization*. Chicago, IL: University of Chicago Press.

Merry, S. E. (1990). *Getting Justice and Getting Even: Legal Consciousness among Working Class Americans*. Chicago: University of Chicago Press.

Merry, S. E. (1995). Going to court: Strategies of dispute management in an American urban neighborhood. In R. L. Abel (Ed.), *Law and Society Reader*. New York and London: New York University Press.

Messer-Davidow, E. (2002). *Disciplining Feminism: From Social Activism to Academic Discourse*. Durham: Duke University Press.

Michael, J. (2005). *Poly Definitions* [Website]. NYC Poly. Retrieved May 22, 2005, from the World Wide Web: http://www.poly-nyc.com/definitions.html

Millstine, W. (Wendy-O Matic). (2002). *Redefining Our Relationships: Guidelines for Responsible Open Relationships*. Oakland: Defiant Times Press.

Mint, P. (2005a). Border Wars: Swinging and Polyamory.

Mint, P. (2005b). Poly Politics: Lessons from Queer Liberation.

Munson, M., & Stelboum, J. P. (Eds.). (1999). *The Lesbian Polyamory Reader: Open Relationships, Non-Monogamy, and Casual Sex*. New York and London: Harrington Park Press.

Nearing, R. (1992). *Loving More: The Polyfidelity Primer* (3rd ed.). New York: Pep Publishing.

Nelson, R. L., & Bridges, W. P. (1999). *Legalizing Gender Inequality*. Cambridge: Cambridge University Press.

O'Roarke, S. (1996). What is the SCA? Retrieved June 18, 2006, from http://www.sca.org/sca-intro.html

Pinello, D. R. (2006). *America's Struggle for Same-Sex Marriage*. New York: Cambridge University Press.

Robins, S. (2004). Remembering the kiss. In S. Anderlini-D'Onofrio (Ed.), *Plural Loves: Designs for Bi and Poly Living* (pp. 101-108). Binghamton: Harrington Park Press.

Rosenberg, G. N. (1992). Hollow Hopes and Other Aspirations: A reply to Feeley and McCann. *Law and Social Inquiry, 17*(4), 761-778.

Rosenberg, G. N. (1993). *The Hollow Hope: Can Courts Bring About Social Change?* (Pbk. ed.). Chicago: University of Chicago.

Sarat, A. (1990). The law is all over: Power, resistance and the legal consciousness of the welfare poor. *Yale Journal of Law and the Humanities, 2,* 343.

Scheingold, S. A. (1975). *The Politics of Rights: Lawyers, Public Policy and Political Change*. New Haven: Yale University Press.

Sedgwick, E. K. (1991). *Epistemology of the Closet*. Berkeley: University of California Press.

Skrentny, J. D. (2002). *The Minority Rights Revolution*. Cambridge: Harvard University Press.

Smart, C. (1989). *Feminism and the Power of Law*. London: Routledge Press.

Swidler, A. (1986). Culture in action: Symbols and strategies. *American Sociological Review, 51*(2), 273-286.

Teubner, G. (1983). Substantive and reflexive elements in modern law. *Law and Society Review, 17,* 239.

Teubner, G. (1989). How the law thinks: Toward a constructivist epistemology of law. *Law and Society Review, 23*(5), 727-758.

UUPA. (2004). *Understanding Polyamory: Unitarian Universalists and Responsible Non-Monogamy*. Flier for distribution: Unitarian Universalists for Poly Awareness.

White, D. (2003, December 10). *Celebrate Friendship*. Retrieved May 22, 2005, from the World Wide Web: http://www.celebratefriendship.org

White, V. (2002). Polyamory and the law. *Loving More, 28,* 7-10.

Zell-Ravenheart, O., & Zell-Ravenheart, M. G. (2006). *Church of All Worlds*. Retrieved June 18, 2006, from http://www.caw.org/articles/WhatIsCaw.html

Zientara, J., & Rila, M. (2005, May 6). *Scenes from the Late 60's Sexual Culture in the Bay Area*. Paper presented at the Society for the Scientific Study of Sexuality Annual Meeting: Unstudied, Undestudied and Underserved Sexual Communities, San Francisco

Bisexual Attitudes Toward Same-Sex Marriage

M. Paz Galupo
Marcia L. Pearl

Research related to attitudes toward same-sex marriage is increasingly important given the shifting landscape of same-sex marriage legislation in the U.S. and Canada. The *Attitudes Toward Same-Sex Marriage Scale* (ATSM) is a recently developed measure that has been shown to be a psychometrically sound measure of heterosexual attitudes (Pearl & Galupo, 2007). The current research was designed to extend the usage of the ATSM in order to investigate sexual minority attitudes toward same-sex marriage in general, with a focus on the attitudes of bisexual women and men.

ATTITUDES TOWARD SEXUAL MINORITIES

Past research indicates that sex is the greatest predictor of heterosexual attitudes toward lesbians and gay men. Heterosexual men report stronger negative attitudes than do their female counterparts (D'Augelli & Rose, 1990; Herek, 2002; Herek & Capitanio, 1999; Kite, 1984; LaMar & Kite, 1998; Pearl & Galupo, 2007) and both heterosexual women and men hold stronger negative attitudes toward gay men than toward lesbians (Herek, 1988, 2000, & 2002). Negative attitudes toward lesbians and gay men are related to religious conservatism (Herek, 1984; Herek & Capitanio, 1995; Horvath & Ryan, 2003; Newman, Dannenfelser, & Benishek, 2002; Pearl & Galupo, 2007). Additionally, positive attitudes are most likely to be reported in younger participants and individuals with post-secondary education (Herek, 1984; Herek & Capitanio, 1995; Lewis, 2003; Simoni, 1996). Heterosexual attitudes toward bisexual women and men follow similar patterns with regard to sex, race, and religiosity (Mohr & Rochlen, 1999). However, while heterosexual men report similar attitudes toward bisexual women and lesbians, heterosexual women view bisexual men more negatively than gay men (Steffens & Wagner, 2004). Overall, bisexual men are perceived more negatively than bisexual women, gay men, and lesbians (Eliason, 1997; 2001).

Attitudes Toward Same-Sex Marriage

The increased public visibility of LGBT individuals within the context of the same-sex marriage debate, presents a new and culturally salient direction for understanding attitudes toward sexual minority individuals. The *Attitudes Toward Same-Sex Marriage Scale* (ATSM) was developed and demonstrated to be a psychometrically robust measure of attitudes toward same-sex marriage (Pearl & Galupo, 2007). Data collected using the ATSM reveals that women hold more positive attitudes toward same-sex marriage than men and positive attitudes are related to a higher level of educational attainment. Additionally, religiosity and political conservatism are negatively correlated with attitudes toward same-sex marriage. As this research included only heterosexual participants, little is known about the factors relating to attitudes toward same-sex marriage for sexual minority individuals.

A recent study by Lannutti (2005) used narrative methods to explore the meanings of same-sex marriage within the LGBT community. While this was not a quantitative assessment of attitudes, the results are informative. Specifically, Lannutti found that all of her LGBT participants discussed same-sex marriage and its relation to legal equality. Other themes were expressed in dialectical ways–participants reported that the legal recognition of same-sex marriage will lead LGBT individuals to view same-sex partnerships in both more serious, and more "fanciful" ways (Lannutti, 2005). Same-sex marriage was discussed as both strengthening and weakening the LGBT community. The relation between the LGBT community and heterosexual others was discussed as being affected in both healing and injurious ways through same-sex marriage. These results emphasize the complex ways in which LGBT individuals conceptualize the meanings associated with same-sex marriage and the diversity of perspectives that exist toward same-sex marriage in the LGBT community.

Bisexuality and the Same-Sex Marriage Debate

Although Lannutti (2005) included bisexual individuals in her sample, her analysis did not allow for a discussion of whether bisexual individuals regarded same-sex marriage in unique ways from lesbians and gay men. In her more recent study, Lannutti (2007) interviewed bisexual-lesbian couples who were either married or were engaged to be married in the state of Massachusetts. This research highlighted the ways in which bisexual identity was affirmed and challenged in the context of (cross-orientation) same-sex marriage. Importantly, this research expands the discussion of bisexuality in the marriage literature as past research has focused on bisexual experience in different-sex marriages and specifically emphasizes experiences of bisexual men (Buxton, 1994, 2004; Hays & Samuels, 1988; Matteson, 1985; Whitney, 1990; Wolf, 1985). In order to gain a more comprehensive understanding of bisexuality in the context of same-sex marriage, qualitative research (see Lannutti, 2005, 2007) should be complemented with additional research employing quantitative attitude assessment.

Statement of the Problem

The purpose of the current research was to expand the usage of the ATSM. Two studies were conducted in order to (1) establish the psychometric properties of the ATSM with a sexual minority population; (2) compare bisexual women and men's ATSM scores with those of lesbian and gay male participants; and (3) explore the relation between demographic and relationship factors with ATSM scores for bisexual participants. Using two separate and non-overlapping samples, Study 1 included sexual minority participants (lesbians, gay men, bisexual women and men) and Study 2 included exclusively bisexual women and men.

METHOD

General Participants and Procedure

Participants in both studies were self-identified sexual minority women and men. All participants completed Pearl and Galupo's (2007) *Attitudes Toward Same-Sex Marriage Scale,* as well as a basic demographic questionnaire. Participants individually completed the study in an on-line, anonymous format through a secure server. Participation required approximately 10-15 minutes. Upon completing the study, participants were free to ask any questions generated by the research process by emailing the primary researcher. All participants were treated in accordance with the ethical standards of the American Psychological Association (APA, 2002).

Materials

Attitudes Toward Same-Sex Marriage Scale (ATSM). The ATSM measured participants' individual attitudes toward same-sex marriage. Developed by Pearl and Galupo (2007), this 17-item scale measures general attitudes toward same-sex marriage. Participants choose a number on a five-point Likert-type scale (1 = strongly disagree to 5 = strongly agree) to denote their level of agreement with each of the 17 statements. Possible scores ranged from 17 (highly negative attitudes) to 85 (highly positive attitudes). A copy of the ATSM questions can be found in the Appendix.

STUDY 1

Purpose

The purpose of Study 1 was to establish the psychometric properties of the ATSM for use with a sexual minority population. Factor structure and reliability were considered. A secondary purpose of Study 1 was to determine whether ATSM scores differed across sex and sexual orientation for sexual minority participants.

Participants

The sample consisted of 112 participants (89 women and 23 men) recruited from postings on two web pages devoted to listing links for on-line Psychological Studies. All participants self-identified as sexual minorities, specifically 26 identified as bisexual and 86 identified as lesbian or gay. Participants represented all regions of the United States including 28 states and Washington D.C. Participants ranged in age from 17 to 72 years, with a mean age of 34.11 years ($SD = 10.66$). Participants identified themselves as African American/Black (6.3%, $n = 7$), White/Non-Hispanic (87.5%, $n = 98$), Hispanic/Latino/a (1.8%, $n = 2$), Multiracial (2.7%, $n = 3$), or Not Identified (1.7%, $n = 2$). With regard to the highest level of education completed, 1 participant (0.8%) had completed Some High School, 33 (29.4%) were High School Graduates or had completed their GED, 37 (32.8%) had College Degrees, and 41 (36.6%) had Master's or Doctoral Degrees.

Results

Results for Study 1 demonstrated a successful replication of Pearl and Galupo's (2007) previous research with a sexual minority population. The Principal Components Analysis with oblimin rotation revealed one factor (eigenvalue = 7.42), where all 17 items loaded on this factor and accounted for 46.51% of the variance in the data. In this sample, the ATSM yielded a high level of internal consistency, where $\alpha = .89$ ($N = 112$).

A 2-way ANOVA was conducted and indicated that there was a significant interaction between sex and sexual orientation for ATSM scores, $F(1) = 4.14, p < .05$. Table 1 includes the mean ATSM scores by sex and sexual orientation. While lesbians and gay men did not significantly differ in their attitudes toward same-sex marriage, bisexual women reported significantly higher ATSM scores than bisexual men.

TABLE 1. Mean ATSM Scores by Sex and Sexual Orientation

	Women $n = 89$	Men $n = 23$
Bisexual $n = 26$	79.00	71.40
Lesbian/Gay $n = 86$	78.81	81.22

STUDY 2

Purpose and Hypotheses

The purpose of Study 2 was to consider factors related to ATSM scores for bisexual participants. Initially the psychometric properties for the ATSM with an exclusively bisexual sample were considered. Subsequent analyses explored the relation between demographic and relationship variables with ATSM scores among bisexually identified individuals.

Consistent with Pearl & Galupo's (2007) findings for heterosexual participants and the preliminary data from Study 1, it was predicted that among bisexual individuals, women would have higher ATSM scores than men. For this study, participants rated their religious identification and political conservatism using a single item scale (see Morrison & Morrison, 2002). Following past research (Pearl & Galupo, 2007) it was predicted that there would be a negative correlation between ATSM and religiosity, as well as ATSM and political conservatism. Individuals who indicate being more religious and more politically conservative are expected to have lower ATSM scores. It was expected that these trends would also hold true for both bisexual women and men.

Exploratory analyses were also conducted to determine whether relationship variables for bisexual individuals affect ATSM scores. Relationship type (monogamous, non-monogamous, no relationship), relationship status (married, single, divorced, partnered) and parental status were considered.

Participants

The sample consisted of 125 adult women and men who self-identified as bisexual and who were currently residing in the United States ($n = 105$) or Canada ($n = 20$). Participants were recruited from postings on two web pages devoted to links for on-line Psychological Studies as well as two list-serves specifically geared toward bisexually identified individuals. Participants ranged in age from 17 to 63 years, with a mean age of 37.7 years ($SD = 10.85$). Participants resided in Canada and all regions of the U.S., including 28 states and Washington D.C. Participants identified themselves as African American/Black (4.1%, $n = 10$), Asian American (1.6%, $n = 2$), White/Non-Hispanic (72.87%, $n = 91$), Hispanic/Latino/a (1.6%, $n = 2$), Multiracial (12%, $n = 15$), or Not Identified (2.1%, $n = 5$).

With regard to sex, 79 participants reported their birth sex as female, and 45 as male. One participant self-identified as intersex. When asked what gender they were raised, 79 participants were raised as female and 46 as male. In terms of current gender identity, 75 participants indicated female, 39 indicated male, and 5 indicated androgynous. The remaining 6 self-described their gender identity in the following way: 2 "fluid" gender identity, 2 "genderqueer", 1 "agender or genderless", and 1 "both female and male, and neither female and male". Of the 125 participants, 5 identified as MTF Transgender.

Results

Psychometric properties of the ATSM scale for a bisexual sample. A Principal Components Analysis with an oblimin rotation was conducted for the ATSM scale. All 17-items loaded on one factor (eigenvalue = 10.09) and accounted for 59.36% of the total variance. With this sample the ATSM scale yielded high levels of internal consistency where α = .94 (N = 112).

Sex differences in ATSM scores. Independent sample t-tests were conducted to determine whether bisexual women and men differed in their attitude scores on the ATSM. As predicted, results indicated that bisexual men (M = 72.89, SD = 15.03) had significantly less positive attitudes toward same-sex marriage than bisexual women (M = 79.51, SD = 6.59), t (123) = 3.40, p < .001. These mean scores are similar to the mean scores reported for bisexual women and men in Study 1 (see Table 1).

ATSM scores and demographic factors. As hypothesized, there were significant negative correlations between ATSM scores and political conservatism by gender (r = −.39, p < .001 for participants raised as women, and r = −.60, p < .001 for participants raised as men). There was a gender difference for the relationship between ATSM scores and self-described religiosity where a significant negative correlation was found for participants raised as male (r = −.33, p < .05), but not for those raised as female (r = .04, p > .05).

ATSM scores and relationship factors. Three analyses were conducted to examine the effect of relationship variables on ATSM scores. There was no significant effect of current relationship type (monogamous, non-monogamous, not in a relationship) on ATSM scores, $F(118)$ = .98, p > .05.

A two-way ANOVA revealed no significant interaction between gender and relationship status (married, single, divorced, partnered) on ATSM scores. However, there was a significant main effect for gender raised, $F(1) = 7.55$, $p < .01$, where women had higher ATSM scores. There was also a significant main effect for relationship status, $F(1) = 4.94$, $p < .01$. Mean scores for relationship status can be found in Table 2. Post hoc Bonferroni comparisons confirmed that participants who were partnered ($p < .01$) and single ($p < .05$) had significantly higher ATSM scores than married participants. No other pair-wise comparisons were significant.

A two-way ANOVA between gender and parental status on ATSM scores revealed no significant interaction. However, a significant main effect was found for gender, $F(1) = 7.56$, $p < .01$ (means reported above). And a significant main effect was found for parental status, $F(1) = 4.46$, $p < .05$, where Non-Parents ($M = 79.19$, $SD = 8.14$) had significantly more positive ATSM scores than Parents ($M = 73.55$, $SD = 13.8$).

GENERAL DISCUSSION

Use of the ATSM Scale in Sexual Minority Populations

The results of these two studies support the contention that the ATSM is a psychometrically robust measure of attitudes toward same-sex marriage for use with sexual minority populations. The factor structure and reliability of the scale were consistent across a general sexual minority population, as well as with an exclusively bisexual pop-

TABLE 2. Mean ATSM Scores by Gender Raised and Relationship Status

| | Bisexual Women | | Bisexual Men | |
| | n = 77 | | n = 45 | |
	M	SD	M	SD
Married	76.62	9.55	66.31	18.96
Single	80.28	4.87	74.69	14.03
Divorced	81.28	3.40	74.50	12.83
Partnered	81.06	3.92	80.90	3.93

ulation. This research, then, extends the utility of the ATSM scale in future research.

Comparing Attitudes Toward Same-Sex Marriage Across Sexual Orientation and Sex

It is not surprising that sexual minorities report more positive attitudes toward same-sex marriage than heterosexual individuals. In the original ATSM research (Pearl & Galupo, 2007), heterosexual participants ($N = 467$) reported mean ATSM scores of 66.57 and 55.96 for women and men respectively, where higher values indicate more positive attitudes. Reported mean ATSM scores for Study 1 were 78.85 and 79.10 for sexual minority women (lesbians and bisexual women) and men (gay and bisexual men). Study 2 yielded mean ATSM scores of 79.51 and 72.89 for bisexual women and men respectively.

For sexual minorities, ATSM scores were simultaneously influenced by sex and sexual orientation. When using combined samples (including lesbians, gay men, and bisexual women and men) it is clear that considering the effects of sex or sexual orientation in isolation will provide a skewed understanding of attitudes toward same-sex marriage. The current research established that the sex difference in attitudes toward same-sex marriage found for heterosexuals holds true for bisexual women and men, where women have significantly more positive attitudes than men. Pearl & Galupo (2007) reported a 10.61-point spread in ATSM scores between heterosexual women and men. The current results reveal a smaller difference in ATSM scores between bisexual women and men (7.60-points and 6.62-points for Studies 1 and 2, respectively). The difference in ATSM scores between lesbians and gay men, in contrast, were not statistically significantly.

Heterosexual attitudes have consistently reflected a sex difference regarding lesbians and gay men (Herek, 2002; Herek & Capitanio, 1999; La Mar & Kite, 1998; Pearl & Galupo, 2007), as well as bisexual women and men (Eliason, 1997; 2001). It is not surprising then, that heterosexual attitudes toward same-sex marriage reflect this same pattern–where women hold more positive attitudes than men. Bisexual attitudes toward same-sex marriage also reflect a marked difference between women and men, although the difference is less pronounced. Although bisexual attitudes toward same-sex marriage were within the same (positive) range as those of lesbians and gay men, attitudes of lesbians and gay men do not show the same sex difference.

Overall, these results suggest that when studying sexual minority attitudes toward same-sex marriage, it is important to recognize that the attitudes of bisexual women and men may not neatly mirror those of lesbians and gay men. As seen in Study 2, additional demographic and relationship factors are related to bisexual attitudes toward same-sex marriage, such as relationship and parental status.

Understanding Bisexual Attitudes toward Same-Sex Marriage

As hypothesized, bisexual women reported more positive attitudes toward same-sex marriage than bisexual men, and attitudes were inversely related to religiosity and political conservatism. While relationship type (monogamous, non-monogamous, not in a relationship) did not impact bisexual attitudes toward same-sex marriage, married participants had more negative attitudes than did partnered or single participants and parents had more negative attitudes than non-parents. These findings underscore the fact that there is not a homogenous bisexual viewpoint regarding same-sex marriage.

Limitations of Present Study and Directions for Future Research

It is of interest that legal marital status (and not relationship type) influenced attitudes toward same-sex marriage for bisexual participants. Because the overwhelming majority of participants from Study 2 were U. S. residents and only 5 of those participants were residents of Massachusetts it is likely that most of those indicating "married" as their legal marital status were married to other-sex partners. Because of varied relationship configurations (including polyamorous and open relationships) and because of the way in which data were collected, participants' relationships could not be neatly categorized into either same- or other-sex pairings. Future research should investigate how current relationship status as it relates to same-sex, other-sex, and mixed-sex groupings inform attitudes towards same-sex marriage.

There was a marked difference in the way bisexual women and men regarded same-sex marriage. As a concept and institution, same-sex marriage reinforces the dichotomous perception of sex, gender, and sexual orientation (Hidalgo, Barber, & Hunter, 2007; Prasad, 2007); therefore, more research is needed which focuses on the varied ways bisexual individuals conceptualize and experience both sex and gender. For example, in Study 2 participants identified themselves on a series of dimensions related to sex and gender—including birth sex, gender raised, current gender identity, and trans identity. Answers to these questions reflected a more complex sense of sex and gender than the accepted standard "female" and "male" categories that are often used in social science research. Of the 125 participants, 11 (8.8%) did not select "female" or "male" as their descriptor for current gender identity. These participants' described their gender identity as "androgynous," "agender or genderless," "genderqueer," "fluid," and "both female and male, and neither female and male." With regard to birth sex, one individual was intersex, and with regard to transgender identity, 5 individuals identified as MTF. While these data were collected and are important in understanding the demographics of the sample, data were ultimately compared across two categories–those raised as women, and those raised as men. In order to allow for enough statistical power to conduct quantitative analyses, data were compared across "gender raised" as it was the only question where two clear categories emerged.

An important direction for future research is to explore how same-sex marriage is perceived by individuals who describe their gender identity outside of the traditional female/male binary, regardless of their sexual orientation identity. Quantitative approaches are limited in their ability to address these issues. More qualitative or narrative research (see Aviram, 2007; Lannutti, 2005, 2007) provides a model for investigating identity in the context of same-sex marriage in ways that capture the lived complexity of bisexual experience.

REFERENCES

American Psychological Association. (2002). Ethical principles of psychologists and code of conduct. *American Psychologists, 57*(12), 1060-1073.

Aviram, H. (2007). Make love, not law: Perceptions of the marriage equality struggle among polyamorous activists. *Journal of Bisexuality, 7*, 261-286.

Buxton, A. P. (1994). *The Other Side of the Closet: The Coming-Out Crisis for Straight Spouses and Families.* New York: John Wiley & Sons.

Buxton, A. P. (2004). Works in progress: How mixed-orientation couples maintain their marriages after the wives come out. *Journal of Bisexuality, 4*, 57-82.

D'Augelli, A. R., & Rose, M. L. (1990). Homophobia in a university community: Attitudes and experiences of heterosexual freshmen. *Journal of College Student Development, 31*, 484-491.

Eliason, M. J. (1997). The prevalence and nature of biphobia in heterosexual undergraduate students. *Archives of Sexual Behavior, 26*, 317-325.

Eliason, M. (2001). Bi negativity: The stigma facing bisexual men. *Journal of Bisexuality, 1*, 137-154.

Hays, D. & Samuels, A. (1988). Heterosexual women's perceptions of their marriages to homosexual or bisexual men. *Journal of Homosexuality, 17,* 81-100.

Herek, G. M. (1984). Beyond "homophobia": A social psychological perspective on attitudes toward lesbians and gay men. *Journal of Homosexuality, 10*(1/2), 1-21.

Herek, G. M. (1988). Heterosexuals' attitudes toward lesbians and gay men: Correlates and gender differences. *The Journal of Sex Research, 25*(4), 451-477.

Herek, G. M. (2000). Sexual prejudice and gender: Do heterosexuals' attitudes toward lesbians and gay men differ? *Journal of Social Issues, 56*(2), 251-266.

Herek, G. M. (2002). Gender gaps in public opinion about lesbians and gay men. *Public Opinion Quarterly, 66*(1), 40-66.

Herek, G. M., & Capitanio, J. P. (1995). Black heterosexuals' attitudes toward lesbians and gay men in the United States. *Journal of Sex Research, 32*(2), 95-105.

Herek, G. M., & Capitanio, J. P. (1999). Sex differences in how heterosexuals think about lesbians and gay men: Evidence from survey context effects. *Journal of Sex Research, 36*(4), 348-360.

Herman, D. (1997). *The Antigay Agenda: Orthodox Visions and the Christian Right.* Chicago: University of Chicago Press.

Hidalgo, D. A., Barber, K., & Hunter, E. (2007). The dyadic imaginary: Troubling the perception of love as dyadic. *Journal of Bisexuality, 7,* 171-189.

Kite, M. E. (1991). Psychometric properties of the Homosexuality Attitude Scale. *Representative Research in Social Psychology, 19,* 79-94.

LaMar, L., & Kite, M. (1998, May). Sex differences in attitudes toward gay men and lesbians: A multidimensional perspective. *The Journal of Sex Research, 35*(2), 189-196.

Lannutti, P. J. (2005). For better or worse: Exploring the meanings of same-sex marriage within the lesbian, gay, bisexual and transgendered community. *Journal of Social and Personal Relationships, 22,* 5-18.

Lannutti, P. J. (2007). "This is not a lesbian wedding": Examining same-sex marriage and bisexual-lesbian couples. *Journal of Bisexuality, 7,* 237-260.

Lewis, G. B. (2003). Black-White differences in attitudes toward homosexuality and gay rights. *Public Opinion Quarterly, 67,* 59-78.

Matteson, D. R. (1985). Bisexual men in marriage: Is a positive homosexual identity and stable marriage possible? *Journal of Homosexuality, 11,* 149-173.

Mohr, J. J., & Rochlen, A. B. (1999). Measuring attitudes regarding bisexuality in lesbian, gay male, and heterosexual populations. *Journal of Counseling Psychology, 36,* 353-339.

Morrison, M. A., & Morrison, T. G. (2002). Development and validation of a scale measuring modern prejudice toward gay men and lesbian women. *Journal of Homosexuality, 43*(2), 15-37.

Newman, B. S., Dannenfelser, P. L., & Benishek, L. (2002). Assessing beginning social work and counseling students' acceptance of lesbians and gay men. *Journal of Social Work Education, 38*(2), 273-288.

Pearl, M. L., & Galupo, M. P. (2007). Development and validation of the Attitudes Toward Same-Sex Marriage Scale. *Journal of Homosexuality, 53*(3), 117-134.

Prasad, A. (2007). On the potential and perils of same-sex marriage: A perspective from queer theory. *Journal of Bisexuality, 7,* 191-215.

Warner, M. (1999). Normal and normaller. *GLQ: A Journal of Lesbian & Gay Studies*, 5(2), 119-171.

Whitney, C. (1990). *Uncommon Lives: Gay Men and Straight Women.* New York, Plume Books.

Wolf, T. J. (1985). Marriages of bisexual men. *Journal of Homosexuality, 11*, 135-148.

APPENDIX

Attitudes Toward Same -Sex Marriage Scale (ATSM)

---

1. Same-sex marriage undermines the meaning of the traditional family.*
2. Two loving same -sex parents can provide the same quality of parenting and guidance as a man and a woman.
3. A primary purpose of marriage is to provide stability in a loving relationship. Same sex partners should have this legal right available to them.
4. The recognition of same-sex marriage poses a threat to society because public schools will be forced to teach that homosexuality is normal.*
5. Marital protections, such as social security and health care benefits, should be available to same-sex partners.
6. Same-sex marriage will strengthen the morals of society by supporting equality.
7. I support individuals who are not heterosexual seeking marriage rights.
8. Because more people will have the benefits of marriage, family will be strengthened by the recognition of same-sex marriages.
9. Men and women naturally complement one another, therefore a union between two men or two women should not be recognized in marriage.*
10. The legalization of same-sex marriage is an important step toward the acceptance of individuals who are not heterosexual.
11. A primary purpose of marriage is to raise children, therefore only a man and a woman should be married.*
12. Same-sex marriage ensures equal rights for all relationships regardless of sexual orientation.
13. The legalization of same-sex marriage will lead to unnecessary financial burdens, such as social security and health care benefits.*
14. The legalization of same-sex marriage will jeopardize religious freedom.*
15. Individuals should be free to enter into marriage with another same-sex consenting adult because God created all people and does not make mistakes.
16. Same-sex marriage will lead to the moral decay of society.*
17. I oppose the legalization of same-sex marriage.*

Note: Items with an asterisk require reverse scoring. Response key: 1 = strongly disagree; 2 = disagree somewhat; 3 = neither agree nor disagree; 4 = agree somewhat; 5 = strongly agree.

BISEXUAL PERSPECTIVES ON SAME-SEX MARRIAGE

Bisexuals are Bad for the Same Sex Marriage Business

ADVERTISING HOW BLAND WE CAN BE

We are just like you. We have families, vanilla sex, and fit into strict categories just like you. We are white or a non-threatening, mixed race, although not interracial couples. We want to raise 2.5 upstanding citizens while driving SUVs with 'Support Our Troops' magnetic ribbons and 'God Bless America' bumper stickers rather than those *in your face* rainbows and pride flags.

We are just like you. We do not have visible disabilities because those would be less than photogenic and could infer that if any 2 adults were able to legally marry that anyone could not only *become* Lesbian, Gay, Bisexual, Transgender (LGBT) but also acquire a disability, which of course is not currently the state of affairs. We oppose all things kinky and abnormal. We are middle to upper class, and we bake from scratch. We mean you no harm. We are just like you, and you, of course, are perfect.

The advertisements for gay marriage embody the above statements through consistently conservative images. Even the names 'same sex marriage' and 'gay marriage' are rather tame. They also leave out some folks who identify as a third gender, unless they happen to marry someone of the same third gender. Further, they exemplify the belief that either you are straight or gay. Why not use a more festive slogan like 'Trannie Marriage Rights' or "Bi-Whores Demand Marriage Equality'? Now those, I'd put on my hybrid . . . er, SUV. For the purposes of this article I will be using various terms to describe what is commonly re-ferred to as 'same sex marriage' and 'gay marriage.' I am confident you will be able to keep up.

THE LESS SEXY BDSM

We are bound to conservative standards. They dominate us. We in turn are sadistic to our brothers and sisters who do not fit. We masochis-tically cram ourselves into their teeny tiny, boxes of good and bad, in and out, us and them, which inevitably coincide with those with rights and those without.

It is the classic divide and conquer strategy enabling us to ultimately destroy ourselves. Many of us see what is occurring but may feel help-less to change it. It seems this is what typically occurs when oppressed groups work to obtain rights. The oppressed group attempts to show how similar they are to the dominant group and anyone who would hin-der that attempt is not welcome in their parade. Um, pardon me, I am so sorry to trouble you, but who the fuck wants to be like people who op-press other people? If this truly is a *human rights* campaign, then every-one's rights need to be fought for.

Then again, this debate begs, like a submissive, the question, who wants to play a game you can not win? Transgender players do not score touchdowns in the political arena even though those who fake it win Os-cars heroically. The same thing happened when fighting for hate crime legislation that is occurring with anti-discrimination policies. We say we will come back for Gender Identity once we get our rights in order, but in reality, most of us have not and will not. Intersexed folks are treated similarly. We do not care that they are more natural than apple pie, they need to choose a side (preferably the one that an arrogant or ignorant medical doctor prescribed for them at birth without their con-sent), or better yet get out of the way before you ruin this for the rest of us. While Bisexuals are on the outs often, we do fall under sexual ori-entation so we are allowed to come along for the ride for anti-discrimi-nation policies and hate crime legislation, but only if we sit on the back of the bus. In the case of marriage rights it is assumed that any two peo-ple will be able to marry regardless of gender or sex. Therefore, Transgender and Intersex people are not left out in that way. However, they, if they do not pass, certainly are not advertised either.

People have historically fit in with the mainstream culture enabling them to obtain the rights of the dominant group. I can not help but wonder if perhaps there are other ways to obtain rights as well. When I do this orally people discouragingly reply this is the way these things have always worked in the past. Rights do not happen overnight. Odd, that argument vaguely reminds me of another argument I heard . . . just recently . . . dang what was it . . . oh yeah, in "defense of marriage." *This is the way it has always been done. This is the way it works.* Wow! We should have those rights in no time. We sound just like them.

This is not to blame those without rights for the current situation. I do not. This is also not to say this issue is only good and bad, in and out, us and them. It simply is not that simple. But what happens if you betray part of your community, submit to the dominant culture, and you still do not get what you want? What are you left with? I argue less than you began with.

I have begun to wonder if marriage is opened to two adults, would Bisexuals be more accepted by the LG community. I mean if it was seen that we had the same opportunities for filing taxes together, insurance, etcetera, would that help relations between LG and B? Could we be closer than simply being placed together in an acronym? It is, at times, like a horribly dysfunctional family that sits at the same table but has nothing pleasant to say to one another at dinner. However, the LGBT community has also successfully worked together on a number of issues. I am advocating that we draw upon our strengths and not submit to the Top's ideologies. Even if we do not obtain the right to marry at least we would have more than what we began with.

PURPLE HIPPOPOTAMUS BUTTERCUP

The arguments on both sides are interesting. Often the right says marriage is sacred and then the left says, no, it is not so let us do it also, or yes, it is to us as well. We all know the truth is sometimes it is and sometimes it is not. That will be true no matter who is allowed to have an elaborate ceremony attempting to bring to fruition the American dream and driving themselves into debt, or who is allowed to drive thru a chapel in Vegas, or who can spend years and thousands of dollars for a divorce or a couple hundred dollars to have it annulled shortly after it began . . .

Taking a longer look at the debate, one can see that prisoners, in some cases, individuals who may be put to death or who have been stripped of their right to vote, may marry, while others may not marry because of their sexual orientation, which is no longer a crime. And the same groups, who argue that scenario is acceptable, argue that people who have abused their children should retain custody if they are straight. However based solely on one's sexual orientation, they may not adopt the same abused children even if a court has terminated the straight parents' parental rights. I know these arguments are not new to most, but think about the irrationality we are up against. We are not going to get through to some of these folks. Even if Wal-Mart (shiver) handled our advertising, they still would not see our side.

One of the groups against Marriage Rights for Flamers, Lezzies, Fence Sitters, and Genderfucks is Human Events Online: National Conservative Weekly. In May 2005 they ranked the "Top Ten Most Harmful Books of the 19th and 20th Centuries." Coming in at number one is *Communist Manifesto* by Karl Marx and Freidrich Engels. I did not really understand the reasoning behind it, but their number two ranking blew any possible comprehension out of the water, *Mein Kampf* by Hitler. Seriously?!?! Hitler at #2?!? Why because they dislike many of the same groups as him? Kinsey beat out many with his book *Sexual Behavior in the Human Male* coming in fourth place, just two baby steps away from Adolph Hitler. From where I am standing I am unable to see the logic in their rankings. What do you say to individuals who rank people who have not committed genocide's book as more harmful than someone who wrote a book serving as a blue print for genocide and then slaughtered thousands upon thousands of human lives?

It is as if we are not speaking the same language. If someone says to you (and believes what they are saying is right), "You do not deserve to have rights because of the gender of the consenting adult with whom you share your hopes, dreams, and life." What can you possibly say to them in return that would make more sense than, "Purple hippopotamus buttercup"?

MY PROTEST AGAINST THE HETEROSEXIST INSTITUTION OF MARRIAGE

In January 2003, I had recently graduated from a master's program with a number of student loans looming and without a job opportunity to assist me in silencing their demands while fulfilling my reasons for attending graduate school in the first place, to ensure world peace through a systematic use of *huggery* and social work. I found myself with a modest checking account balance and rather ostentatious bills. At the time, I was good friends with a man who lived with C-4 quadriplegia. He had a job and health insurance but did not possess long-term care disability insurance. Therefore, his mother assisted with his care and transportation, and truly, all of his needs. He was in his thirties and some time had passed since he acquired quadriplegia so he was looking for some help with his care. While his available income was modest, his house had plenty of room. We began discussing the possibility of me becoming one of his caregivers in exchange for room and board. There was a problem though. I desired health insurance for myself. We had spoken at length about my anger towards the heterosexist institution of marriage and my desire to protest them. We believed this situation served as an opportunity for our personal needs and my political ones. We were going to do what everyone was saying at the time would happen if marriage between any two people were legal. We used the system to our advantage and got married for insurance and tax purposes.

I did eventually get offered a job which allowed me to use my degree, although sadly, not my hugging abilities. Unfortunately, the pay was still only a slight upgrade from my pay as a bartender, and I had no choice but to claim all of it to the authorities. So I figured getting free room and occasion board would help me get a bit more financially stable. After speaking with my friend, we made an arrangement where I would still work part-time for him mostly on weekends when he wanted to go out with his friends (as it turns out having a relatively attractive 20-something year old as an aide is a lot sexier than your 70-something mom), and I still received a free place to stay and insurance benefits. We had this agreement for about 2 years, and it enabled me to save up enough money to buy my own place while paying off student loans. He in turn received help with his personal care needs and a tax break. When I had enough money and provided him sufficient notice I was quitting, we got a divorce. Our protest was a success! . . . er, sort of.

Perhaps because of my experiences as a Bi individual, I may have went a little over the top with my protest to prove my allegiance to the queer community, or maybe the anarchist in me won the mental coin toss that day. Regardless, some of my family and friends distanced themselves from me because of my choice of protest and because I stood up for my rights to marry the gender of my choice as a bisexual. They saw my actions as disrespectful to the institution of marriage, to their marriages, and their religion regardless of the conversations about separation of church and state, that love is love is love, and so on and so forth. Some were supportive, but others stopped speaking with me completely. One of my points was to prove that marriage in the eyes of the law is simply a contract, although not a simple contract. Even in my case it was still a business contract that bound my friend and I together in a serious way. I thought it was like going incorporated, of which I was unsure of the definition, but it sounded so catchy. How could it be bad?

Obviously, I was naive to how serious it was and also to my friend's eventually unfulfilled wishes for our arrangement to be realized as a *real* marriage. Ironically, I take the institution of marriage more seriously now than pre-protest but not in the manner right-wings might hope for. I now see how unrealistic the idea that anyone will get married just because they can is. If they do then they are as foolish as I was. When I was ready to end our arrangement, I provided my friend with a month's notice which turned into 6 months notice as he tried to squash my dreams of owning my own condo, and he had some substantial power to do since we were legally married. Through much discussion, he did finally step out of the way, but he and I are no longer friends.

Around the time I purchased my first home, the 2004 presidential election occurred simultaneously (probably some government conspiracy since I was distracted). I chose to vote for and publicly support Kucinch in the Democratic primaries in part because of his support for same sex marriage. He and Sharpton were the only two of the bunch who spoke acceptingly of gay marriage. When Kerry won, I moved onto Ralph Nader who again supported marriage equality rights, amongst other things I believe in strongly. At the time, I questioned a woman I was dating who identified as a lesbian and was wearing a Kerry pin with a rainbow on it, why she would settle for civil unions. She said it was better than nothing. How retro, separate but sort of equal. Another woman told me I was a fool for supporting Nader. About many things she was correct, but in this instance, I would have felt like a fool settling.

FEELS LIKE HOME . . .

Even with my self-proclaimed valiant efforts of protest and support for equality in marriage, when the first lesbian from the above story and I broke up, she claimed that I was unsure of my sexual orientation. Disgruntled, I spoke with another lesbian friend of mine about how she viewed bisexuals. She said that she had dated a bisexual in a 3 year long relationship, another for 2 years, and so on. She stated some of them were now in relationships with men and some with women. She laughed as she said, "I don't think they were faking." With the woman I dated I may have faked some things, but my sexual orientation was not one of them (she liked anime movies . . . never got into 'em).

So what does a *grrl* have to do to get some street cred with this LGBT crew? I have lost family. I have protested. I remain politically aware and active. I support LGBT owned and LGBT friendly companies. I'm an out and proud bisexual/multisexual/pansexual wommin . . . ah yes, that does complicate things a bit.

Today I have many fears. If marriage between any 2 consenting adults is legalized, will bisexuals continue not to fit in? Will people incorrectly assume that we have finally chosen a side? Or that we still can not remain monogamous (if we are in a monogamous relationship)? Will straight people find out what the blue, black, and white striped flag with the adorable little heart stands for? Despite my fears, I will continue to fight for the rights of all to marry other individuals of their choosing vigorously and with boundless enthusiasm. I do so with the knowledge that I am not real welcome on either side of the argument with my views and foul mouth. But what the fuck do they know?!?

A Bisex-Queer Critique of Same-Sex Marriage Advocacy

Hameed (Herukhuti) S. Williams

The issue of same-sex marriage (i.e., gay marriage and lesbian marriage) in the neo-imperial, post-modern, contemporary, capitalist United States is not a moral issue or a social issue but rather a political and economic issue. At the core of the issue is the management and distribution of political and economic resources. While same-sex marriage advocacy attempts an articulation of the expansion of the boundaries of the management and distribution of those political and economic resources, the assumptions upon which it is founded, such as the reification and (re)legitimization of the couple as an a priori relationship structure for marriage, fall short of advancing radical, queer politics or true marriage equality. Given this shortcoming of same-sex marriage advocacy, there is an opportunity to articulate an argument for marriage equality that is more consistent with radical, queer politics. Bisexuality, in particular the polyamorous practice of bisexuality, is one framework out of which a radical, queer argument for marriage equality can emerge. I am calling this framework a bisex-queer critique and it frames the following argument.

The concept of marriage and, a frequently dissociated concept, paternity have historically involved the resolution of property rights among those classes of people who had property in the patriarchal Western and European context (Cott, 2002; Goody, 1983). Who was getting what and how much of it they were getting have traditionally been answered, in part, through marriage, paternity, and birth order. So the issues of marriage-how it is defined, who has(n't) access to marriage as a device, its scope, limitations, and conditions, etc.-have been important elements of a larger arrangement and consolidation of wealth and power.

In the contemporary US context, the same factors exist alongside newer elements as consequences of the neo-imperial, post-industrial, post-modern, welfare state in a late-capitalist, globalized world. Health insurance and employee benefits are just as important in the same-sex marriage discussion as health proxy and patient visitation despite the lack of attention in the discussion to the former. With the cost of health care in the US rising (National Coalition on Health Care [NCHC], 2006a), the numbers of uninsured or underinsured rising (NCHC, 2006b), and the high numbers of unemployed or underemployed (having a job(s) that doesn't pay a living wage) (Howell, Madrick, & Mahoney, 2005), the redefining and reconfiguring of marriage could have a significant impact upon the distribution of health care insurance and employee benefits across the country thereby threatening the business interests of health insurance providers in particular and corporate business interests in general.

Mainstream same-sex marriage advocacy seeks something very short of that however. The efforts of this mainstream advocacy at best may result in the creation of opportunities for mostly middle-class and wealthy individuals to profit from a small modification (two persons of the same sex marrying) of the current marriage construct (two persons of different sexes, defined as male and female, marrying). But there's room for much more change and much more of a challenge to the privileged economic interests at work in the US.

The contemporary moment in which marriage equality is conceptualized as the legal ability of same-sex couples to marry and enjoy the same privileges of opposite-sex couples leaves room for a critical and radical conceptualization of marriage equality that queers the very concept of (legitimized) marriage. A practice of bisexuality that divorces legitimacy from the coupled structure of sexual-emotional-spiritual relationships, i.e., relationships between two people and de-essentializes monogamous marriage makes a significant contribution to the queering of marriage.

To illustrate the possibilities let me draw from my life to construct a scenario that I believe examples one of the many possibilities for real social justice intervention. I come from a poor and working class family background and I primarily socialize within black communities of a similar class consciousness–poor and working class. At the same time, I've been blessed by educational opportunities (e.g., a Ph.D.) that afford me access to resources. As I look toward the day when I'll have a faculty position at a university, I'm thinking about the benefits to which I will and won't have access because of the social organization and political economy of relationships in the US. As a faculty member at a university, I will have employee benefits including health insurance and educational benefits. If I had "a spouse," in this context defined as "a woman" (because I would be defined as a man) to whom I'm married, or if I had "a domestic partner" (at many but not all universities), in this context defined as "a woman" or "a man" with whom I've co-mingled certain resources/assets such as living space, savings, etc. for a period of time, then those individuals could share those employee benefits with me and their children, whether they are my offspring or not, could as well.

Any other form of relationship construct would make us ineligible to share my employee benefits. So if I were simultaneously in a intimate and polyamorous relationship with a woman who had a child that was not my offspring and an intimate and polyamorous relationship with a man who also had a child that was not my offspring, each of us living in different spaces, my ability to share the benefits of health insurance and educational access/funding with them would be blocked by the fact that the relationship was structured outside of the confines designated for relationships. Add to the descriptions of those relationships the possibility that the role of sex in them was fluid, dynamic, and unresolved and the issue becomes more controversial. "What do you mean you don't have sex with him? You only have sex with her once a year? Then what makes those relationships relationships?" "And you want your employer to subsidize their health care and their children's education? What's to stop you from asking your employer to provide health care and educational benefits to any person you just randomly pick off the street?" The quoted statements reflect particular axiological frameworks that position value in human relationships based upon a capitalist, sexist, and heterosexist understanding of what human relationships can be. The five of us should have health care insurance and other employee benefits through my employer regardless of whether we live together, or the three adults are having sex, or the nature of the genders/sexes involved.

Relationships that transgress heteronormative, monogamous, and coupled constructions of legitimate and legitimizing relationships can function to really problematize and destabilize the current construct of marriage in the US as well as highlight the big-money interests that stand quietly off to the side in the current debate about marriage. But those relationships aren't solely and aren't necessarily same-sex relationships. Those relationships may be same-sex relationships but they may also be polyamorous relationships (polyandry and polygamy),

BDSM/leather relationships, kink relationships, transgender relationships, etc. Rather than forming a coalition of the socially queer and transgressive to radically confront the entrenched political and economic interests that benefit from the social organization of love, lust, and relationships, mainstream same-sex marriage, i.e., gay marriage, and lesbian marriage, advocates have sought to paint themselves as "normal" or at least just as "normal" as those individuals who currently enjoy the political and economic benefits of marriage in the US. Their actions, whether deliberate or not, maintain the status quo and reinforce hegemonic values, norms, and standards. They don't call into question a social order that denies people unalienable human rights to health care, education, economic wellbeing, etc.

Because of the inability and incapacity of same-sex marriage advocacy to envision these larger questions, it, same-sex marriage advocacy, becomes a reformist, assimilationist/conformist movement to accommodate the social, political, and economic interests/agenda of a few while maintaining/reinforcing a hegemonic, exploitative, and restrictive structure of social control and social organization of love, life, lust, and relationships. Current marriage equality advocacy is devoid of a critical and radical definition of equity and equality. All of this leads me to offer this advice to the thought-leaders of that movement: try again.

REFERENCES

Cott, N. F. (2002). Public vows: A history of marriage and the nation. Cambridge, MA: Harvard University Press.

Goody, J. (1983). The development of the family and marriage in Europe. Cambridge: Cambridge University Press.

Howell, D. R., Madrick, J., & Mahoney, M. (2005). New labor market indicators underscore a weak economic expansion. Center for American Progress. Retrieved August 28, 2006, from http://www.americanprogress.org/site/pp.asp?c = biJRJ8OVF&b = 1144751

National Coalition on Health Care. (2006a). Health insurance cost. Retrieved August 28, 2006, from http://www.nchc.org/facts/cost.shtml

National Coalition on Health Care. (2006b). Health insurance coverage. Retrieved August 28, 2006, from http://www.nchc.org/facts/coverage.shtml

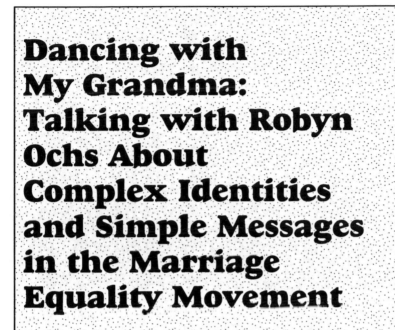

Dancing with My Grandma: Talking with Robyn Ochs About Complex Identities and Simple Messages in the Marriage Equality Movement

Laurie J. Kendall

In the early 1990s, when Robyn Ochs was in her 30s, a national magazine named her the "grandmother" of the bisexual movement. In 2001,
Heidi Randen, who wrote a detailed article on Robyn's life, suggested
that the nickname was "surely a testament to the newness of the bisexual movement, as well as the magnitude of Robyn's work" (p. 11).
Robyn Ochs was raised in the 1960s by parents and grandparents,
and relatives, some of whom were active in the Civil Rights, antiwar,
and feminist movements. She grew up in the oceanside community of
Far Rockaway, on the southern edge of New York City. The diversity of
this community, as well as the political activism of her "pink diaper"
family helped Robyn recognize "economic injustice, racism, sexism
and anti-Semitism from a very early age" (p. 9). However, it was not until she moved to Boston in 1982 that she found the courage and opportunity to become an activist and educator around issues of sexuality.

After attending a "Women's Rap" for bisexual women at the
Women's Center in Cambridge, Robyn began meeting once a month
with seven other women. They named their group the "BiVocals."
Shortly thereafter, Robyn helped form other bisexual support groups in
the Boston area. By September of 1983, these groups joined to form the
Boston Bisexual Women's Network. That same year, a contingent from
Boston attended a conference at the University of Connecticut. This
conference may have been the first conference held in the United States
on bisexuality. Then in 1984, this contingent hosted the second East
Cost Conference on Bisexuality. Over the next few years, the Boston
Bisexual Women's Network helped activists in other east coast states
form groups and host conferences. By 1985, this loose-knit network of

east coast groups named itself the East Coast Bisexual Network, which later became the Bisexual Resource Center.

Since then, the Bisexual Resource Center has published four editions of *The Bisexual Resource Guide*, and Robyn has become a nationally known bisexual activist and educator. She has published several articles and essays, taught courses at MIT and Tufts University on bisexuality, and acted as a bisexual community spokesperson in articles that have appeared in *Newsweek*, *Playgirl*, and various other national newspapers and magazines. She has been interviewed by Phil Donohue and Maury Povich, and she has co-hosted a cable television show called *PRIDETIME*. In 2005 she co-edited, with Sarah E. Rowley, a book titled *Getting Bi: Voices of Bisexuals Around the World*, an anthology of personal writings by authors from 32 different countries. In addition, Robyn keeps a full speaking schedule, lecturing and giving workshops at colleges and universities around the country. But one of the greatest testaments to her life of activism came on May 17th, 2004 when she and her partner, Peg Preble, were legally married in their home state of Massachusetts.

MY INTERVIEW WITH ROBYN

I went to Boston to talk with Robyn about her activism in the bisexual movement, but more specifically about her role in the "marriage equality" movement. As I entered the picturesque neighborhood of the Bourne area of Jamaica Plain, a community on the south side of Boston with a village atmosphere, I noticed the plethora of Pride flags and equality signs scattered along its winding narrow roads. Clearly, LGBT folks and allies occupied a number of the single-family homes in the Bourne neighborhood. On that sunny and warm July morning in 2006, Robyn greeted me at the door with an invitation of join her for breakfast. As she stood in her kitchen flipping apple pancakes, she told me about her three cats (including one who had been rescued from New Orleans after hurricane Katrina), and about her neighborhood and the close relationships she has developed with the folks in her community. After we ate, Robyn gave me a tour of her home, during which she stopped often to share stories about the pictures hanging on her walls. She spoke with love and tenderness, and a modicum of pride, as she told me about each of her friends and family members, and her feline companions.

When we sat down for our formal discussion, I asked Robyn how being a bisexual activist in the same-sex marriage debate shifted the discussion or politics of the movement? She replied:

> I care very, very, very much about marriage equality. The marriage equality movement is about so much more than marriage–at its core it's about *equality,* about our right to full, 100 percent citizenship.

> A major challenge for me is that arguments and strategies that may help people understand bisexual identity are sometimes different from–or even at odds–with strategies that will help us achieve marriage equality. I struggle to find ways to talk about each that do justice to both and harm neither. Here's an example: when I speak about marriage equality, the thing that moves people is the simple story of my relationship with Peg: "Here I am, and here is my life partner, the woman I love. We intend to spend the rest of our lives together. We want to have the ability and resources to care for one another in sickness and in health. Love is a beautiful and precious things. See, look at the video of our marriage, look at our wedding pictures. Look at how happy we are!" At some level, this discussion is most powerful when it is kept simple. When I'm speaking with an audience, is there an added benefit to discussing my bisexual identity, or to discussing previous relationships? Usually, there is not.

> But when the topic is bisexual identity the opposite is true: I find it most effective to present a reality that is as *complicated* as I can possibly make it. For example, one of the exercises I developed uses the Kinsey scale. I have people situate themselves on this scale, either anonymously by way of a questionnaire that is completed and then randomly redistributed so that each person represents *someone* in the room, using a number of different measurements. Some of the questions include: "Put yourself on the Kinsey scale." "In terms of your actual crushes on actual people during the past 3 months, put yourself on the Kinsey scale." "In terms of your actual crushes before you graduated from high school, put yourself on the scale." "In terms of your actual sexual experiences, including kissing, during the past three months, put yourself on the scale." "How about the average of your entire life?" "Now, in terms of your fantasies, put yourself on the scale." "If you could choose your own

sexual orientation, where would you want to be?" I ask all these different questions and while there are usually a few people who stay fixed, more or less in one spot during the entire exercise, most people move quite a bit. Then I ask folks a question that forces them to choose: "Now choose just one. Which one are you, gay or straight?" And people choose. Most people go to one end or the other of the scale. Finally, I ask folks to tell us which word they use to describe themselves. The power of this exercise is that it demonstrates visually how any one person, and sometimes the entire room, will move to different places on the scale depending on what question you are asking. It also demonstrates that "straight" does not necessarily mean "zero" on the Kinsey Scale, and "gay" often does not mean "6." And "bisexual" does not necessarily mean "3."

One of the challenges of speaking about bisexuality is that it has so many different meanings. In any given conversation, we may be employing numerous definitions of bisexuality. Are we talking about behavior? Are we talking about identity? Are we talking about attraction? Fantasy? Now? Recently? Ever? And for some people there may be little correlation between those things. Behavior may not correspond to identity. We may fantasize about things that we have no interest in actually doing. And some people base their self-identity upon current behavior or feelings, others upon recent behavior or feelings. And so on . . . So I just try to make it as *complicated*, messy, and as unclear as I possibly can.

After doing–and discussing–this exercise, I ask people to think more about the multiple and varied definitions of all sexual orientation identities: "You people here in this room are now on the Committee in Charge of the World. You get to decide where on the spectrum bisexuality begins and ends. At what point does heterosexual become bisexual, and at what point does bisexual become lesbian or gay? Where would you draw the lines?" And then I have everyone silently think of their answers. Then ask them to share what they came up with. Everybody says something different. "Oh, bisexuality is 3," or "It's 2 to 4." Or "it's point 1 to 5.999 or it's everything." One of my favorites was "Straight is 0 through 3; bisexual is 1 through 5; gay is 4 through 6." Sometimes they say, "oh, I wouldn't use a scale at all." People have so many different answers. And then I ask, "Well who's right?" And the answer is clearly all of us, none of us. There is no one right answer. So when

I teach about bisexuality it's all about *complication*. I think it makes things clearer to make things less clear. By making things less simple, less solid, less clear, less over simplistic, you gain a better sense of reality. You start to see the world more clearly in all of its permutations, in all of its lack of clarity and simplicity.

One reason I do my "Labels and Identity workshop" is because I often hear comments like "I hate labels" or "Why should you have to call yourself *anything*?" I believe labels can do a lot of damage and harm, but they can also do a lot of good. They're not real–they're social constructs that have multiple and varying meanings. But there's a real political power in treating them as though they were more simple, more real than they actually are. It's reasonable and productive to utilize labels as the tools they can be. But at the same time, you must constantly hold out a more *complex* reality. You have to always understand that these labels are working tools but they are not reality. Use them, but you can't get locked inside of them as though they were real things or concrete boxes. So that's the challenge of teaching about bisexuality, or teaching about labels and identity in general. The challenge is to make it as *complicated* as I can. I also teach about the value, about the good things that labels do for us, because I believe they help us find each other. They help us organize politically. They provide a shorthand to help us communicate.

So when you talk about marriage equality to people who are not part of LGBTQQIA lesbian, gay, bisexual, transgender, queer, questioning, intersex, and allies communities, you are most likely talking to people who have not thought about this stuff a lot. And what is useful is *not* to make things complicated, but to make things *simple*. Because in terms of messaging, people need *simplicity*. They need little, simple, sweet sound bites, slogans, ideas, concepts. And I don't want to be dismissive when I say that people need something as simple as, "when two people love each other, they should be able to marry." "Love is love." "Love makes a family." "It's all about equality." "It's all about families." "It's all about protecting all families." You know, wishful thinking won't make families headed by same-sex couples disappear. It just leaves us vulnerable, unprotected, and without the same social support that other families have. That's bad for children because all children deserve social support and protection. A marriage is two people making a commitment to take care of each other in sickness and in health, for better or for worse, and if you deny people legal protection you are putting them at great risk. All we want to do is be able to take care of each other. These are very *simple* messages. When talking about marriage, pick something and explain it as *simply* and in as straightforward a manner as is possible. Complicating things does *not* help.

So my challenge, as someone who not only identifies as bisexual but as someone who is a public poster-child for bisexual identity, is to talk about marriage equality in ways that *simplify* it while at the same time *complicating* labels and identities. I often feel like I have to choose my message. What can I, as a bisexual person, add to the discussion? I think about this a lot. One of the things that I can add to the discussion is that I have been there and I've done that. I have been in serious relationships with men. I have been is serious relationships with women. And honestly, my experience tells me that love is love. A relationship is a relationship, and people are people. When I look at the differences in the various relationships I've been in over the course of my life, I didn't experience men as this way and women as that way. It's about individual people, and their specific personalities. You know, if I could make a list sorting people by personal characteristics, it wouldn't much matter if they were male or female. That's my experience. Relationships are relationships.

For me, it's not love, desire, or attraction that feel complicated. To me, identity and labels are complicated. All identities are more *complicated* than they first appear, especially as the questions become more complicated. Lots of people who are straight have had same-sex desires, fantasies, and sometimes experiences. The same is true for people who identify as lesbian. And the other thing I try to do in my workshops is to introduce a more *complex*, and to include the complexity of gender identity, the realities of transgender folks. Ultimately, linear scales have serious limitations. Think about the exercise I described earlier. If you are transgender or gender queer, how do you answer these kinds of questions? What is your opposite? What is your same? Sex? Gender? Sex/gender? So I try *not* only to *complicate* the obvious, but I also try to point out the ways in which the tools we are using are limited in their actual usefulness, and how the tools, used uncritically, leave some people out. But yet they are still useful as tools, as long as we understand the limitations.

In my workshops, I try to make people really dizzy. I tell people that if they walk out of the room feeling very confused and with their head spinning, then I have done a good job. I will feel like I have succeeded in my mission. Anyone who walks out feeling that they now understand everything clearly, missed the point. So in those kinds of workshops it's really about *complicating, complicating*, and *complicating*, and arriving at a more nuanced, subtle, and *complicated* understanding of everything.

But then, when I talk about marriage equality–it's like here I am, I'm 47 years old, I'm in love with a woman, I want to spend the rest of my life with her, and I want to be able to have the same rights and protections as anybody else. And my next-door neighbors are two women with two beautiful little children, and I want their family to be protected too. The message is that *simple*. That's what works for people. We are real people with real stories. We feel the same pain that everybody else feels, the same love and the same joy, and we deserve the same protections. And so that's the contradiction sometimes, when I'm talking about this stuff: which message am I on?

And on some level, it's really that *simple*. On some level, all of this stuff I'm talking about is just so *simple* when you relax your preconceptions. We are so locked up in the ways we were taught. When you talk to someone who has never thought about this stuff before, there's a lot at stake because you are destabilizing their platform. When selecting a strategy, I focus on what I am trying to accomplish. Who is my audience, what is their starting point, and what will it help them to learn? If I start deconstructing gender to an audience of people who still aren't quite certain that bisexuality–or even homosexuality–exists, I will be wasting both their time and my own.

I cover a wide range of topics. I do homophobia workshops. I do workshops on labels and identity. I do workshops on bisexuality, and bisexuality and feminism, and marriage equality workshops. And each of those is really *complex*. I could sit down and talk to you for hours about each of those. So I think about my audience

and I think about my message, and I try to stay on message. And
sometimes I feel like I'm leaving a piece of myself out.

My passion varies from moment to moment. Sometimes I really,
really want to talk about marriage equality. And sometimes I really, really want to talk about identity and labels. And sometimes I
can't do both, so I have to decide where the need–and interest–is
greatest.

I asked Robyn if she had faced any obstacles or resistance from
within the marriage equality movement because of her bisexual identity. She pondered the question a few seconds and then replied:

I'm not one hundred percent sure. I do know that I often get turned
into a lesbian. Even when we were on the cover of the Washington
Post, on the day after marriage equality started in Massachusetts.
The title of the Washington Post article was "A Long Considered
Rush to the Altar," and it said, "a lesbian couple" right underneath
the headline. And when I read that I thought "uh huh." I know it
wasn't our journalist, that it was the headline writers, but that kind
of thing–ok so you get turned into a lesbian and then so? So then
what? Does that matter? How much does that matter? Who does
that matter to?

And here are some of my answers. It matters to me as a bisexual
activist that people in the LGBT community understand that bisexually identified people are activists for equality, that transgendered people are activists for equality, that we are here. That
we are here, that we are active, that we are doing our part, that we
are fighting the good fight, and that we are part of the struggle.
And so when we get erased it makes me frustrated because it
would be easy for people to think that we're not here. For example,
there was a march in New York a couple of nights ago, after the
New York City court ruled against the marriage law. And there
was a big demonstration that night in New York. There was one in
Manhattan. There was one in Albany, and several others all over
the state. And I found out about them from a bi-activist who had
been there, and who wrote on the bi-activist email list. Then when
I read the headlines the next day on 365gay.com, it said that, "lesbians and gays come out in large numbers to protest." And that
same old feeling of "lesbians and gays and who else? Hello, who

else was here? Hello, we are here." I felt frustrated because we are here. We are always here. And so part of me, in that context, wants to say "huhum, huhum! You are missing part of reality." So on that level it really matters.

In terms of messaging to a straight world, I don't think it matters that much. It matters that people know that bisexuality is a legitimate option or identity, and that it exists. But in this particular moment, in this particular discussion, is it gonna matter personally to a lot of people? Less. Less. So in that discussion it matters less. But it still bothers me. And one of the questions around marriage equality is, "what are you going to call it?" Is it lesbian and gay marriage? You know, when you are messaging, when you are a marriage equality organization and you are messaging, do you talk about lesbians and gay men being able to marry? Or, do you talk about same-sex marriage? Personally, I like same-sex marriage because that includes everyone.

I often see people (even people who get it), they still talk about lesbian and gay marriage, and lesbian and gay couples. I mean, I am a woman in a marriage with another woman. Therefore, we could be considered a lesbian couple–small "l" I guess. But not lesbian with a capital "L" because only one of us identifies as lesbian. But then when you try to separate us out, when I try to say that this is not a lesbian marriage because one of us identifies as bisexual, I don't want that to feel to anyone that I am trying to distance myself from lesbians. Because, (I like to joke that some of my best friends are lesbians, and I'm married to a lesbian) I have been part of this community for almost 25 years. So it's not about separating from lesbians. It's about being seen clearly as someone with a different identity from lesbians, as someone with my own identity.

But in terms of resistance from within the lesbian and gay community, that's something that I really can't answer with a definitive statement. I'm sure that if I identified as lesbian, it would make it easier to make me a poster-child. But then again, if I had children, it would be easier to make me a poster-child. Or if Peg and I had long hair, and looked like the lesbians on *The L Word*, it would be easier to make us the poster-children. There are lots of different reasons we're not the perfect poster-children. When you're organizing a statewide marriage equality thing, and you're looking for your plaintiff couples or your public voices, we're not really what you're looking for. But I have not felt resistance in a direct way. I just know it's true. And this is actually an issue that all communities face.

So when you are thinking about a community and you need a public voice, and you need three people to represent our community on a panel or we need three people to go meet with the mayor or the governor, how do you choose those people? Do you choose people who those people you are talking to will feel most comfortable relating to? Might not be a bad idea. Do you choose people who represent the diversity of the community? That might be a really good idea. But sometimes those things are very much at odds. So then what do you do? How do you decide? Are you going for the most realistic cross sample or the one that's going to have the best rapport with the people you're talking to?

And everybody deals with this. When I go out to speak (I've been part of the group "Speak Out" here in Boston for almost 25 years, and I used to do the annual training every year) this was a big question. Like when you go out to speak, how do you represent yourself? How do you dress? What if you have someone with purple hair or a Mohawk and 900 piercings, and you're going into a place where this is the only gay person they are ever going to talk to? One could make arguments like, "absolutely this is the person who should go because this person is part of the community." And I believe that. One could also make the argument that people are going to come out with a rather skewed perception of what the community is, or what lesbians look like, or whatever it is, based on this one person who might not be too representative. And what the Speakers Bureau said was, "you make your own decision about how to represent yourself, but do understand that you are representing yourself and that every little detail about you will get noticed. And if you want to go out in your Mohawk and 900 piercings that is your choice, but understand or just be aware of what you are doing, how you're doing it, and what your impact is. Just be thoughtful." Which was actually a good resolution.

And that's not to say that a woman with a shaved head should not go out and speak. It's just to say that people have their prejudices. But there are also people in our community who say, "those people should never be allowed to go out there. Those drag queens give us all a bad name. Those 'Dykes on Bikes,' all those people are giving us a bad name. We should only be showing them our lipstick lesbians." I do believe everybody has the right to be seen and heard, but I also understand that sometimes it can have its costs, and that who you put out there can make a difference in terms of accomplishing what you want to accomplish. And it's the same thing in the bisexual community. Which bisexuals do you put out there, and who gets to decide?

When Robyn mentioned "the bisexual community," I asked her if she had a sense that there is a real, tangible, or physical bisexual "community?" She answered in the affirmative, but suggested that where to begin finding the bisexual community is on the internet. However, she also said:

But some cities have real, physical, live communities. There's the Bisexual Women's Network in Boston, and there's a group called "Biversity," which is a social group that meets twice a month. Boston is hopping! San Francisco is hopping! Minneapolis is hopping! New York is hopping! Some other strange places, that you wouldn't expect, are hopping because there were people who were doing some really amazing work. But overall, if you're in most places, you're not likely to have a support group or organization.

You know, one of the things that I see changing is that the success of the bi-movement (such as it is) is having a profound cost to the bi-movement because many student groups are much more welcoming than they were 20 years ago. Most students who identify as bi don't have the need to go off and make their own groups. They can be part of the larger alphabet soup community. And, even though it might be uncomfortable at times, overall it is much more comfortable, and that means that people aren't feeling such a need to go off and create separate bi groups. In the old-days, we were so profoundly unwelcome that creating our own group was the only option. We formed our own groups because we had to. So in a way, our success is costing us in that direct way, in that people aren't feeling the need. And that is great because I don't want people to feel that they have to go create their own planet out there.

And I think that's even happening with the bigger LGBT community. The straight world is getting less hostile overall. It used to be that gay people hung out with gay people. Now I see a lot more mixing. With college students it doesn't matter. The really cool kids are hanging out with the really cool gay kids, and lesbian kids, and bi kids, and transgender kids, and queer-don't-identity kids. And I love that because it makes me feel like we've done our job, or like we've evolved.

There's so much that's changed though. I love it. I love it. I mean, the fact is that when I remember back to when I was a teenager, I didn't know that "gay" existed until my junior year in high school. And then I only knew because a friend told me that a couple of our male friends were gay. That was it. I knew there were two or three gay men in the whole world. There were three in my high school, that I knew were gay, and that was it. So that was my idea of "gay," just these three people.

There was no other place to get information. And then, I went to college and there was a lesbian and gay group on campus, so there was more information. But it was still really scary. And I remember there were twins in my women's studies class, and their parents were trying to get my lesbian professor fired because "lesbians shouldn't be teaching children." I mean this was the times, the early 70s. And by the way, my lesbian teacher was Esther Newton, the anthropologist. She was my advisor. When I came to college I randomly got assigned to her. She was pretty scary. I think she was under so much attack that she was pretty defensive. I think it was really hard to be an out lesbian professor in the 70s.

So think about the times. There was nothing on television. Nothing. Nothing. Nothing. So anyway, we have all this. We have the situation now where kids have *Will and Grace*, and *The L Word*, and *Queer is Folk*, and tons of stuff in films and movies–newspapers–there's something in the newspapers everyday now about marriage. It's a huge public discourse. And there's the internet. I mean there's only so much information you can get by looking up words like "lesbian" in the dictionary.

So I feel like the knowledge base is so different now. But the fact is that people feel like they are protecting their kids from this whole discourse, but the kids are hearing it everywhere. And what I think the parents need to do is help the children filter it. Help the children make sense of it, make it something they can talk about or ask questions about. Cause you can't avoid it these days. It's everywhere. Kids are getting the information and what they need is a way to process it. They need a system to process it in whatever way parents think is sensible. But what they can't do is block it out. Cause it's there. It's everywhere. So that's the difference in the times.

But it also depends on where they are, because one of the things I've seen is there are huge regional differences. I mean, there are some states that GSAs [gay/straight alliances] are in every high school. Massachusetts for instance, Connecticut, Minnesota, I mean there are some schools that have so much support for LGBT youth. There's GSAs in schools. There's after school groups, and there's all kinds of stuff out in the community. And then there's other states where there's absolutely nothing. So, I don't want to draw any sweeping conclusions. The realities are so different. But at least people have information now, and that's the difference. People have more information now.

Within the marriage equality movement, I asked Robyn why it is important for her to retain a bisexual identity. She replied thoughtfully:

One of the things that has come up is there are a lot of different voices in the bisexual activist community, and some of the voices very strongly support marriage equality. But there are other people who don't, or who don't think marriage should be the focus. Just like lesbians and gay men, there are some people who are *not* one hundred percent for it, and don't think it is really important. And I struggle with that. I often feel really frustrated because I didn't wake up one morning and think "oh this should be the central organizing topic for our community." But right now it is. It's up there, and we have to respond to it. It's really important.

But it's really about equality. It's not about marriage. It's about equality. And I'm not one of those people who thinks that everyone should get married, or want to get married. I'm not one of those people who think everyone should be monogamous, or everyone should be in the same kind of relationship I'm in. I don't believe that. I think everybody should be in the kind of relationship they want to be in. People who want to be single, more power to them. People who want to be in more complex relationships involving more than two people, more power to them as long as everybody's ok with it. And people who want to be in monogamous relationships, more power to us. So for me, it's not about saying everyone should or shouldn't get married. But I struggle sometimes with the hostility that some people feel toward marriage. Because I'm not saying everyone should get married. I'm saying that everyone should have the right to choose. Everyone should have the choice to embrace or reject that institution, and it should be no one's choice but their own.

And some of the rhetoric of the marriage equality movement has been a little bit disturbing, a little bit scary. Some feel it's like we're saying "oh, we're just like everybody else." Well actually, we are just like everybody else. But everybody else isn't that *simple* either. Everybody else is really *complicated* as well. Straight people are not all monogamous people who want to be married. A majority are, but there are a lot of other people out there who are straight and who have chosen different kinds of relationships. Or straight people who don't want to be in relationships at all. I mean there are so many different ways that straight people are, and the LGBT community has the same complexity. We are complicated just like they are. And any kind of rhetoric that pretends we're not disturbs me because I think we need to embrace all of us. And I think we need to use rhetoric that dose *not* cut people out.

This happens sometimes with the argument that "if we let gay people get married then the next thing you know we'll have polygamy." But the fact is, some people are already practicing it. And then people say "oh no, we don't support that." My response is, "that's not what we are talking about right now. That's a different discussion." And it is a different discussion. But I think we can separate the discussions out without trashing other people's choices. That's not the discussion on the table right now. And to attempt to join them is, I believe, an attempt to distract. "Oh the next thing you know they'll want to marry their goats and their sheep, their dogs and their cats." But that's not what we are talking about either. That's a way of distracting and dividing.

So people who do *not* want to get married, I want to see them support marriage equality, because it really is about equality and our right to choose. And people who *do* want to get married, I want to see them make their arguments without putting down anyone else or belittling other relationship choices. Because I may be monogamous, and I may be a person who wants to spend the rest of my life with one person, but that does not mean that everyone else needs to want that too. That's what works for me. So we need to have a conversation based on respect.

With so many important issues in the world, I asked Robyn why is it so important for the whole LGBT community to support marriage equality. She said:

Teaching has made me so much more aware of how other issues connect to issues of marriage equality. I taught a course called Family Values, as in "family values," "family" being the euphemism for our community. We did a whole bunch of topics including marriage equality. We also did "aging" as a topic, and that scared me!

Reading stuff about the lack of protections, and also about the amount of dependency on external caretakers, and if you don't have the right to live with your partner when you get old, if you don't have the right to visit them or make decisions about their care, or the right to keep your home. There are things protecting married couples, federally protected married couples. I mean when you think about how much you have to spend of your assets in order to get Medicare, you know, what counts as an asset? And the home that heterosexual couples share is not counted in that calculation, but if you are not legally related to your partner then you could be forced to sell the home you've lived in for fifty years. And then where do you go? You still have to live somewhere. And so it's things like that, just realizing what that could mean to same-sex couples.

I show my students *If These Walls Could Talk 2*. In the first episode, when the woman falls off the ladder and dies, what happens to her surviving partner? And I also give them a bunch of short stories by Becky Bertha. I also give them *Dirty Old Men*, which is about a guy in a nursing home. He's a gay man with Alzheimer's, and he can't be himself. He's just trapped. It's just these amazing, moving, things about what can happen to us. And so for me, that's what marriage equality is all about. It's much more about equality than it is about marriage. And I think once we have marriage equality we can't be denied any other kind of equality. It's the big ring. It's the big ring on the marry-go-round. And I want it. And we are going to keep it here in Massachusetts.

I wrote an article that just came out this week in the local paper. I did a whole series on marriage equality (having people tell their stories) and I talked about Massachusetts. I said, "a very strange thing happened to me this year. I sat down to pay my taxes." This year I owed a lot of money, more than I ever owed before. So I sat down and wrote the federal check, and I felt sick to my stomach knowing what was going to happen with that money. Knowing that a big chunk of that money was going to be used to pay the interest on the national debt. It's just that feeling of paying my federal taxes and feeling sick knowing that my taxes were going for war and all these horrible things. And then going to pay my state taxes and actually thinking "yeah!" I feel like I got my green card, my citizenship. Two years ago when I got legally married, I got my full citizenship. It's really cool. And then I wrote about the "welcome to Massachusetts" sign, and how when I drive across the border in my car and I read "welcome to Massachusetts," I take it personally. And I do feel welcome here. I think I ended that article by saying that we should change the license plates and we should call Massachusetts the "equality state." That's how I feel living here. I feel so lucky.

And it wasn't like I moved to Massachusetts to be in the first state that got marriage equality. I was fortunate enough to be living here already. It's great. It's an unbelievably good feeling. I'm tired of fighting to keep it! I'm looking forward to the day when that's done because there are so many other things that demand our attention.

And they keep talking about Massachusetts as the only place with marriage equality, but we have other places too. We have Canada. We have Belgium. We have the Netherlands. We have Spain. And we're gonna have South Africa this year, before the end of 2006.

And just the fact that almost all of the western European countries have some sort of civil union. And then there's New Zealand.

When I went to the Netherlands it changed me. I went to the Netherlands in 1998, just after marriage had become equal there. And it was an amazing feeling. It was truly an amazing feeling because I had never imagined that possibility. I've written about this. I went home and I though, "wow." I met these guys who were married, and I just wanted to keep pinching them. Like, are you real? I get that a lot now when I travel around. But for me, that was an amazing thing. As I had dinner with them, I just kept looking from one to the other and thinking "these guys are married to each other. Really married! And its legal." It was so amazing.

And then when I went home and we were waiting for the Massachusetts supreme court to rule, I remember thinking "I hope we get civil unions like Vermont. I hope we win this." And then when we didn't, when they came out with their decision that gave us equality, that's when I started to change inside. Because when I read the Supreme Court decision, it was very powerful. It said something about–separate is rarely, it ever equal–and it talked about the fact that we deserved full equality. And it changed me. I thought, "actually, you know, we do *deserve* equality." We do. We *deserve* equality. We *deserve* it just like anybody else. We pay taxes. We are citizens. We *deserve* the same rights to all civil benefits and protections. And now, I believe it even more strongly. There's no doubt in my mind. We *deserve* to be treated just like anybody else.

Now, when I travel around, people respond to me like I did to those guys in the Netherlands. One young man from the mid-west said to me, "I feel like you are a space traveler from the future and you're here from the future I hope to have some day." It gave me the shivers. It made me want to cry because I think he should have it now. When I look at the stuff that's happening around the country I feel sick. I do understand that change takes a really long time and that it's a long process. And you really have to be in it for the long haul.

I also realize that in the last five to ten years we have made changes that were unimaginable. We've come so far in so short a time, so when I start to feel frustrated I try to remember that. I try to remember that in the 1960s and even the 1970s, people were getting kicked out of college for being gay. Yeah, and then by the 1980s I'm actually getting paid by colleges to come talk to their kids about LGBT issues. That is huge! You know, most colleges that are not based in some religion that doesn't support LGBT people, most colleges have some type of institutional support. So just looking at that, that's huge! Things are different. It's huge! Now, with the concept of equality, we are having conversations that would not have been possible ten years ago. People are changing and support is going up. Unfortunately, it's still definitely very low in some places, but in every single place it's much higher than it was ten years ago. Every place.

Even the worst places, the most hostile places, support is going to go up. And every place that has marriage equality or civil unions, every state, every country in the world that has protections in the law, support goes up after the law is passed. So for instance, after Vermont's civil union, support for gay people and equality is rising. Massachusetts, since we've had marriage. All these different places, California, Canada, Spain, support is going up. I feel that the future is going to be good. Better than the present. The future is going to be a whole lot better than the present and we just have to keep our eyes on the big picture and keep on fighting. Not keep on fighting, but keep on persevering. You know, we have to keep on pushing for equality and we can't loose perspective."

I asked Robyn what it was like to be married. "Now that you and Peg are legally married, what does it feel like inside the relationship? Outside the activism, outside the speaking, what does it feel like for the couple? Does it change anything? Does it feel different? What does it do inside the relationship?" Robyn grinned broadly and said:

It was magic. And it's funny; cause what's changed is the external validation. We were committed to each other before, but what changed is having that kind of excitement and enthusiasm from the people around us. That kind of public manifestation of support. As LGBT people, we're just not used to it at all. It was just really amazing. It was just this thing that filled up the whole world. It just made the whole world sunny and happy and warm and beautiful and welcoming. We felt a sense of welcome for our relationship. And that was the most giddy, ecstatic, happy feeling. It was beautiful, and that affected our relationship, because I do believe that one of the reasons traditional marriages have so much pomp and circumstance is that there's real value in those things. There is something substantial about having witnesses, having support, being embraced by your community in a way that I never expected to know.

I had decided that I would never get married until such a time as I could marry anybody. If I couldn't marry anybody, I wasn't going to marry anyone. So even if I ended up with a male partner, I had already made the commitment that I wasn't going to get legally married. And who would have expected this! So I never though I was going to get married. I never though I would be able to marry anyone. You know, I've been to 17 weddings in Massachusetts since May 17th, 2004, including our own. And almost all of them had their parents there. And that was really amazing just watching, one after the other, watching sisters and moms. For me, the absolute highlight was (we got legally married on May 17th) our celebration on September 4th.

We had 128 people at our celebration. It was a big event with a swing band and the whole bit, and for me, one of the absolute highlights was dancing with my grandma (who at the time was 92) at my wedding. I was 45 years old. I finally got to do that. The last of all my siblings. The oldest and the last. Yeah, that was just amazing, dancing with my grandma. Yeah, it was, dancing with my grandma. It just makes me want to cry.

I commented that I was jealous of how supportive Robyn's blood family was of her marriage, and she responded with the idea that family can also be chosen.

Even in this neighborhood, I think we have created a lot of family. Cause I know that some of my neighbors don't have good relationships with their families, or they have uneasy relationships, and some of them don't have any relationship with their families. But I also think that we have created a family of choice here. For instance, my neighbors next door, they have boys who are four and one years old. Those boys are my nephews as much as my blood nephews are, and I see them almost every day. These people are my extended family, and they feed us about once a week. You know, we have dinner with them a lot and we hang out in the yard. In a way, we are creating what most American families don't even have at all anymore. But we have it here, by creating families of choice. Most American families are isolated in the nuclear family thing, without the extended family around. And I feel like here, we have rebuilt that. We have it.

Hanging in Robyn's living room is a framed plot-map of her Bourne area neighborhood. Each plot where an LBGTQ person lives is shaded in pink. In bold letters, the title reads "The BAGAL MAP." I asked Robyn what the map meant, and what it was like living in the Bourne neighborhood. She smiled and said:

I just have such a strong sense of community here. One of our neighbors made up the plot-map of the neighborhood on his computer. All of the houses where LBGT people live are colored pink. So that's the BAGAL MAP of our neighborhood. Our neighborhood is called "Bourne Area Gays and Lesbians," but I actually made up another name for our area. "BAGAL Bits," for the "Bourne Area Gays and Lesbian, and bi, intersexed, and trans folks." So there are over one hundred families on the map of our little neighborhood. The thing about this neighborhood, I guess because its modest single-family houses mostly, it's heavily, heavily, heavily coupled, and there are lots and lots of families with kids. There are so many gay people in this neighborhood, and there are so many kids, so many spawn of gay people.

And some people have been here for thirty years. Yeah, we have parents with grown kids now. But for some reason the "under six crowd" has just taken off. Yeah, and now the oldest of the kids is actually applying to college. But what is actually amazing is that one of my friends grew up in this neighborhood, diagonally behind us, and he's gay. And when he grew up here, it was really a straight place. He didn't know any gay people. And when he comes home now, he loves it because there are three women-couples all adjacent to his parents' house. And he just loves that fact because it makes him feel like he is coming home in a way that he didn't when he was growing up. And it makes him feel all bubbly just watching his dad talk to the women-couples over the fence. And he loves how much his parents love all the neighbors.

It's a great place to live. But we did something to create it though. We've been doing some recruiting. We recruited our close friends next door. And not just because we knew they would cook for us, but because we wanted to have good friends next door. We have so many good friends right here, and so much of our socializing is done within a block. You can't walk in this neighborhood without stopping to chat. It's really funny. Sometimes it can take a really long time to walk down to the subway. There are more women, but it's pretty even. It's about sixty/forty.

The other thing that's really special about this neighborhood is the straight people. It really does feel like a comfortable place for everybody. It's funny though. There is no neighborhood-wide group for everybody, and sometimes some of the straight neighbors are a little bit jealous about BAGAL, and they say things like, "I wish we had a BAGAL too. I wish we had a list." Because BAGAL has an email list. And that's often how information about the community spreads, if there's been a crime or something. We inform each other, and then we tell our other neighbors. But, in a way, I would love to have a BAGAL for the entire community, because that's still missing. We have a block party every year for everybody. But I really would like to have a group for everybody because that's one of those things, it's not just BAGAL that makes this neighborhood special. It's the other neighbors too. So there it is. It takes extra work to cross certain boundaries, but once you've crossed them it's wonderful.

CONCLUSION

Queer scholars like Valerie Lehr, argue that the traditional concept of "family" is founded on the oppressive patriarchal model of marriage, an institution that excludes people on the basis of race, gender, social class, and sexuality. "The 'family' problems that gays and lesbians face in the United States," Lehr argued "are much more extensive than what marriage rights can address" (1999, p. 10). Lehr suggested that fighting to enter an oppressive system like marriage limits the truly revolutionary potential of the queer movement. She argued for a radical discourse in which family care is discussed as a function of community, one in which the democratization of family could "keep alive a movement that addresses family and private life even if liberal demands begin to be met" (1999, p. 10).

Robyn & Peg's Wedding - 5/17/04 - photo by

Likewise, Mary Bernstein and Renate Reimann argued that the conservative lesbian and gay movement seeking marriage rights wants acceptance for their "normal" families rather than redefining the entire concept of family itself, which they suggest is a relatively recent and "short-lived phenomenon" that has not worked for many Americans (2001, p. 3). The lesbian and gay movement, they argue, marginalizes those queer (working-class, racial, and transgendered) families who might negatively affect the otherwise "normal" image of conservative lesbian and gay families. Bernstein and Reimann argued that the entire concept of the "traditional family" needs to be redefined, and that "queer families present new challenges to the privatized-nuclear family, contradicting the sexual dimorphism upon which the ideal family is based" (2001, p. 3-4).

Like the "families" on the BAGAL MAP, my research on the families lesbians build in other places and contexts suggests that LGBT folks all over the country are what Chela Sandoval calls "multiply displaced figures" who form families that are not "quite as imperializing in terms of a single figuration of identity" (2000, p. 172). LGBT people may or

Robyn dancing with her Grandma - 9/04/04 - photo by

may not share bloodlines or family structures that resemble the patriarchal model, but they do provide the love and support that is often withheld from people whom the patriarchal legal system refuses to protect. Furthermore, I would also argue that they *do* meet Valerie Lehr's criteria for democratizing the private life of the family, because as Robyn's narrative demonstrates, even after same-sex couples legally marry, family care is still a "function of community" (1999, p. 10). In no way does marriage equality jeopardize the goals of the queer movement, nor does it obscure the ways in which LGBTQ families have redefined the "traditional family."

LGBT families are democratic, and their care is a function of the community because rather than depending solely on a bloodline, they share a similar consciousness which allows them to transcend patriarchal models of family and claim each other as relatives in a web of familial connections that support them in homes, neighborhoods, and community spaces across the country. In other words, LGBT families are structured in a matrix of ideas held together by what Sandoval called the "apparatus of love," (2000). And while this "apparatus of love" is solid in terms of human will and behavior, it is not yet a legally recognized or a federally protected institution in America.

Like queer theorists who seek to blur the boundaries between heterosexuality and homosexuality, Robyn Ochs' work to *complicate* traditional categories of gender and sexuality does not ignore the very real and tangible need to legally protect LGBTQ families. And while her work involves deconstructing hegemonic ideologies by *complicating* identities and sexual categories, her messages about "chosen families" and "marriage equality" are quite *simple*. LGBTQ families of choice need and *deserve* the same rights and protections as heterosexually headed families, and like heterosexuals, they also *deserve* the *simple* right to dance with their grandmothers at their weddings.

REFERENCES

Bernstein, M., & Reimann, R. (Eds). (2001). *Queer Families, Queer Politics: Challenging Culture and State.* New York: Columbia University Press.

Lehr, V. (1999). *Queer Family Values: Debunking the Myth of the Nuclear Family.* Philadelphia: Temple University Press.

Ochs, R., & Rowley, S. E. (Eds). (2005). *GettingBi: Voices of Bisexuals Around the World.* Boston: Bisexual Resource Center.

Ochs, R., (Ed). (2001). *The Bisexual Resource Guide.* Boston, Bisexual Resource Center.

Randen, H. (2001). Bi Signs and Wonders: An Interview with Robyn Ochs. *Journal of Bisexuality, 1*(1), 5-26.

Sandoval, C. (2000). *Methodology of the Oppressed.* Minneapolis: University of Minnesota Press.

Index

activism
  feminists 142
  marriage activists 127, 130, 133-6,
    137, 139-40, 142-3, 183-206
  Ochs, Robyn 183-206
Amatea, ES 37
antimiscegenation law 9-13
  children, attitudes to 23-4
  colonialism 12-13, 20
  constitutionality of law 21-3, 59
  Defense of Marriage Act (DOMA)
    12-14, 18-19
  Englishness as white 13, 20
  God and nature 21-2, 24-5, 27-8
  historical context 12-13
  National Association of Colored
    Persons (NAACP), priorities of 12
  supremacist structure 24, 26-8
  upholding antimiscegenation law
    19-25
  White supremacy, as cornerstone
    of 13, 21, 24-6, 28

Baumeister, RF 60-1
Becker, Gary 61
Bernstein, Mary 204
Bertha, Becky 197-8
biology 64-5
biphobia 82, 104, 116
hisexuality see bisexual-lesbian
  couples, same sex marriage and;
  same sex marriage and bisexuality
bisexual-lesbian couples, same sex
  marriage and 104-22, 191

biphobia 104, 116
commitment 111-12, 119
depoliticizing beliefs 104
explanatory beliefs 104
families of origin, support and
  resistance from 112-15
feminist theory of marriage 110
gay, lesbian, bisexual and
  transgender and questioning
  community
  belonging to 117-18
  reaction from 115-19, 191-2
heteronormative definitions of
  marriage 110
identity, affirming bisexual 108-9,
  111-12, 119
invisibility 117, 118
lesbians and gay men, attitudes of
  115-19, 191-2
public-private dichotomy 113
relationship, effect on 110-13
research 104-20
self-image 108-10
social networks 103, 113-16
wife, thoughts about being a 108,
  109-10
Brown, NM 47
Burgess, Susan 67-8
Bush, George W 58-9
Butler, J 38-9, 133

Calhoun, Cheshire 62
Card, Claudia 68
Carey, Benedict 63

Carlson, Allan C 15
children 15-16, 23-6, 41-2, 44, 131,
    179, 194-5, 202 *see also*
    procreation
class 60
civil rights 18-19, 84, 127, 133, 143
    see also discrimination
colonialism 12-13, 20
commitment 102, 111-12, 119
communal living 137-8
conservatism 156, 157, 160, 204
contract, traditional marriage as a 61,
    171-2
Corbin, J 107
couples *see* dyadic imagery
culture 9-10, 56-7, 68-9, 126, 130,
    136-42

de Lauretis, Teresa 62
Defense of Marriage Act (DOMA)
    10-19, 25-8
    antimiscegenation law 12-14, 18-19
    appellate court decisions 10-11
    children 15-16, 25-6
    Christian evangelists 13-14
    civil rights 18-19
    discriminatory or violates equal
        rights, challenging belief that
        DOMA is 18
    dualism 16-17, 26-7
    Federal Marriage Amendment Act 14
    supremacy of heterosexuals 28
    support, arguments in 15-18, 25-6
    traditional family idea 14, 16-17
Deleuze, G 67
Demetriou, DZ 45-6
Derrida, Jacques 63
discrimination 18, 82, 195-6 *see also*
    civil rights; equal rights
Dobson, James 59
dominance/submissive dichotomy 70

dualistic construction of sexuality,
    bisexuals as threat to 16-17
Dunne, G 38
dyadic imagery 33-51
    bisexuality 37, 46-8
    gender, construction of 42
    gendered institution, marriage as
        40-1
    hegemonic masculine bloc,
        hybridization of 45-6
    heterosexual imagery 35
    historical account of marriage/
        coupling 40-4
    homosexuality and
        heterosexuality, relationship
        between 36
    individualism 41-3
    industrialization, effect of 41-2
    marriage and families,
        conceptualizing 40-1
    non-dyadic relationships 37-9,
        48-9
    polyamory 37-9
    re-conceptualization of love 42-3
    reproduction and heterosexuality,
        sexuality based on 41-2, 44
    romantic love, ideas of 37-45
    social phenomena, love and
        intimacy as 36-8
    women, role of 43

economic issue, marriage as 177-80
Elshtain, Jean 61-2
employee benefits 178, 179
Engels, Friedrich 60, 170
equal rights 18-19, 56-7, 82, 84, 127,
    133, 143, 168, 195-6 *see also*
    discrimination

families *see also* children; traditional
    families

bisexual-lesbian couples, same sex
marriage and 112-15
conceptualization of families 40-1
dyadic imagery 40-1
resistance 112-15
support 112-15, 201-2
World Congress of Families (WCF)
56-7
Fausto-Sterling, Anne 64
federal ban on same sex marriage in
United States 9-31
antimiscegenation law 9-13,
18-28, 59
Defense of Marriage Act (DOMA)
10-19, 25-6, 28
difference, role and understanding
of 11, 16, 25, 27
dualistic construction of sexuality,
bisexuals as threat to 16-17
God 11, 15-17, 25-6
healthy society, promotion of 17
natural law 15
nature 11, 15-17
procreation 15-16, 25-6
religion 11, 13-17, 25-6
support for one man one woman
marriage requirement 14-19
supremacy, structure and discourse
of 24-9
feminism 65-6, 110, 142
Fischer, EF 37-8
Foucault, Michel 67, 133
Fraser, Nancy 66, 68-9
Freire, Paulo 57

Gallagher, Maggie 17
gay, lesbian, bisexual and transgender
and questioning community
(GLBTQ)
attitudes to GLBTQ community
151-2
belonging to GLBTQ community
117-18
bisexual-lesbian couples, same sex
marriage and 115-19, 191-2
conservative gay and lesbian
community 204
identity 142
reaction from GLBTQ community
115-19, 152-61, 191-2
Galupo, MP 156
gender
bisexuality and same sex marriage,
attitudes to 81-2, 92-3
dyadic imagery 42, 43
gendered institution, marriage as a
40-1
same sex marriage, attitudes to
157-8, 160-1
women, role of 9, 43
genital determinism 63
Goldstein, M 38
government, mistrust of 139-40, 141

health insurance 171, 178, 179, 197
hegemonic masculine bloc,
hybridization of 45-6
Heinlein, Robert 137-8
heteronormativity 61-6, 69, 71-2, 110
heterosexuality *see also* traditional
marriage
bisexuality and same sex marriage,
attitudes to 82
complementarity 61-2
dominant cultural assertion of 9
dyadic imagery 35, 36, 41-2, 44
heteronormativity 61-6, 69, 71-2,
110
heterosexism 170-1
heterosexual/homosexual
dichotomy 63-4, 67-8, 72

homosexuality, relationship
   between 36
reproduction 41-2, 44
supremacy 28
Hird, Myra 56
historical account of marriage/
   coupling 12-13, 40-4, 59
Hitler, Adolf 170
HIV and other sexually transmitted
   diseases 82, 84, 87-93
home, losing a 197-8

identity
   affirming bisexual identity 108-9,
      111-12, 119
   bisexual identity 185-8, 190
   equality 195-6
   gay, lesbian, bisexual and
      trangendered people 142
   Kinsey Scale 185-7
   politics 105, 133-6
   representation 192-3
   self-image 108-10
Ingraham, Chrys 35
invisibility 82-4

Jankowiak, W 37-8, 39
Jordan, Winthrop 13

Keller, Evelyn Fox 64
Kinsey, Alfred 65, 170, 185-7

labelling 187, 190
Lannutti, PJ 83, 103-4, 152-4
Lee, John Alan 39
Lehr, Valerie 203, 205
lesbian couples *see* bisexual-lesbian
   couples, same sex marriage and
Lister, Andrew 58
love
   dyadic imagery 42-6

polyamory, marriage and 140-1
re-conceptualization of love 42-3
romantic love 44-6
social phenomena, as 36-8
Luhmann, M 144
male lesbians, body politics of 66
Mann, Patricia 60
Maplethorpe, Robert 13-14
marriage *see* polyamory, marriage
   and; same sex marriage and
   bisexuality; traditional marriage
Martin, Emily 64
Marx, Karl 170
material rights, marriage as vehicle of
   130-1
Mint, Pepper 133
Monahan, Patrick 57
Mormon polygyny 136
multiple relationships *see* polyamory,
   marriage and
Munson, M 37

Naples, Nancy A 45-6
narrow coalitions, concern over 134-6
nature 11, 15-17, 21-2, 24-8, 61-2
Newton, Esther 194
Nicholson, Linda 66

Ochs, Robyn 183-206

Pateman, Carole 60
patriarchy 60-1, 68, 69-70
Pearl, MC 156
Petersen, Alan 64-5
pluralism 134-6
politics
   conservatism 156, 157, 160
   identity 105, 133-6
   male lesbians, body politics of 66
   polyamory, marriage and 126, 133-6
   same sex marriage 105, 177-80

polyamory and marriage
  bisexuality 127
  children 131, 179
  civil rights 127, 133, 143
  communal living 137-8
  cultural aspects of marriage 126,
    130, 136-42
  diversity and solidarity, issues of
    135-6
  dyadic imagery 37-9
  government, mistrust of 139-40,
    141
  health insurance 179
  identity politics 133-6
  instrumental aspects of marriage
    126, 130
  love, emphasis on 140-1
  marriage activism 127, 130, 133-6,
    137, 139-40, 142-3
  material rights, marriage as vehicle
    of 130-1
  mimicking marriage 131-2
  Mormon polygyny 136
  narrow coalitions, concern over
    134-6
  political aspects of marriage 126,
    133-6
  relationship agreements 141
  research 128-45
  science fiction 137-9, 143
  stigma 134-6
  sub-cultures 138-9
  symbolic meaning of marriage
    130, 136-41
postmodernism 66-7
Preble, Peg 184
procreation 15-16, 25-6 *see also*
  children
promiscuity and nonmonogamy 82
property rights 177-80
public-private dichotomy 113

queer theory 67-77
  biology 64-5
  bisexuality 63-6
  civil unions in Canada and United
    States 57, 69, 71
  conscientization 57
  critical theory 56
  culture 56-7, 68-9
  dominance/submissive dichotomy
    70
  equality 56-7
  feminist theories 66
  gender socialization 63
  genital determinism 63
  heteronormativity 62-6, 69, 71-2
  heterosexual/homosexual
    dichotomy 63-4, 67-8, 72
  male lesbians, body politics of 66
  patriarchy 68, 69-70
  postmodernism 66-7
  public policy 56, 71
  same sex marriage 67-77
  social phenomenon, sexuality as 65
  temporal variables, sexuality and 65
  traditional families 56
  two-sex model, repudiation of
    64-5

race-based restrictions on marriage
  see antimiscegenation law
Randen, Heidi 183
Reiman, Renate 204
relationship agreements 141
religion 11, 13-17, 21-2, 24-8,
    58-9, 85, 102-4, 152
reproduction 41-2, 44
Rich, Adrienne 57
romantic friendships 44
romantic love 37-45
Rowley, Sarah E 184
Rust, PC 104, 116

same sex marriage and bisexuality *see also* bisexual-lesbian couples, same sex marriage and; federal ban on same sex marriage in United States
activists 142, 183-206
advocacy 177-80
attitudes 81-97, 151-63
biphobia 82
bisexual attitudes and perceptions 151-63, 167-75
characteristics of stable, long-term healthy marriage 84-5
civil rights 84
commitment, rituals of 102
complication 187-90, 196, 206
conservative gay and lesbian community 204
cross-sex cross-orientation marriages 83-92
defence of marriage 168-9
discrimination 82
dyadic imagery 46-8
economic issue, marriage as 177-80
gender 81-2, 92-3, 157-8, 160-1
health insurance 178
heterosexual attitudes 82
heterosexual marriage, similarities with 102
HIV and other sexually transmitted diseases 82, 84, 87-93
human rights 168
invisibility 82-4
lesbian, gay, bisexual and transgendered community, attitudes of 82, 152-61
marital status 160
marriage-matching research 85-94
political conservatism 156, 157, 160
political issue, marriage as 177-80

promiscuity and nonmonogamy 82
property rights 177-80
religion 85, 156, 160
representatives, choice of 191-2
research 85-94, 102-4
simple messages 187-8, 196, 206
stigmatization 82
transgender people 167-8
workshops 187-90 loki
Sandoval, Chela 204
Sauerbrey, Ellen 55-6
Schiebinger, Londa 64
schools 195
science fiction 137-9, 143
Sedgwick, EK 134-5
self-image 108-10
simple messages 187-8, 196, 206
social networks 103, 115-16
social phenomenon, sexuality as 65
Steele, S 18
Stelboum, JP 37
stigmatization 82, 134-6
Strauss, A 107
Sudakov, M 38
support groups 183-4, 193
supremacist structure 24, 26-9
symbolic meaning of marriage 130, 136-41

temporal variables, sexuality and 65
Thomas, Clarence 13
traditional marriage
children 58-9, 60
Christian right 58
class-based analysis 60
complementarity 61-2
conservative gay and lesbian community 204
contract, as 61, 171-2
Defense of Marriage Act (DOMA) 10-19, 25-8

heteronormativity 61-2
heterosexism 170-2
historical review 59
natural, as 61-2
patriarchy 60-1
queer theory 56
religion 58-9

United States *see* federal ban on same
sex marriage in United States

Voh, KD 60-1

Waite, Linda J 17
Weston, K 38
White supremacy, antimiscegenation
law as cornerstone of 13, 21, 24-5,
28
wife, thoughts about being a 108,
109-10
Wilreker, BC 38
workshops 140-1, 187-90
World Congress of Families (WCF)
56-7